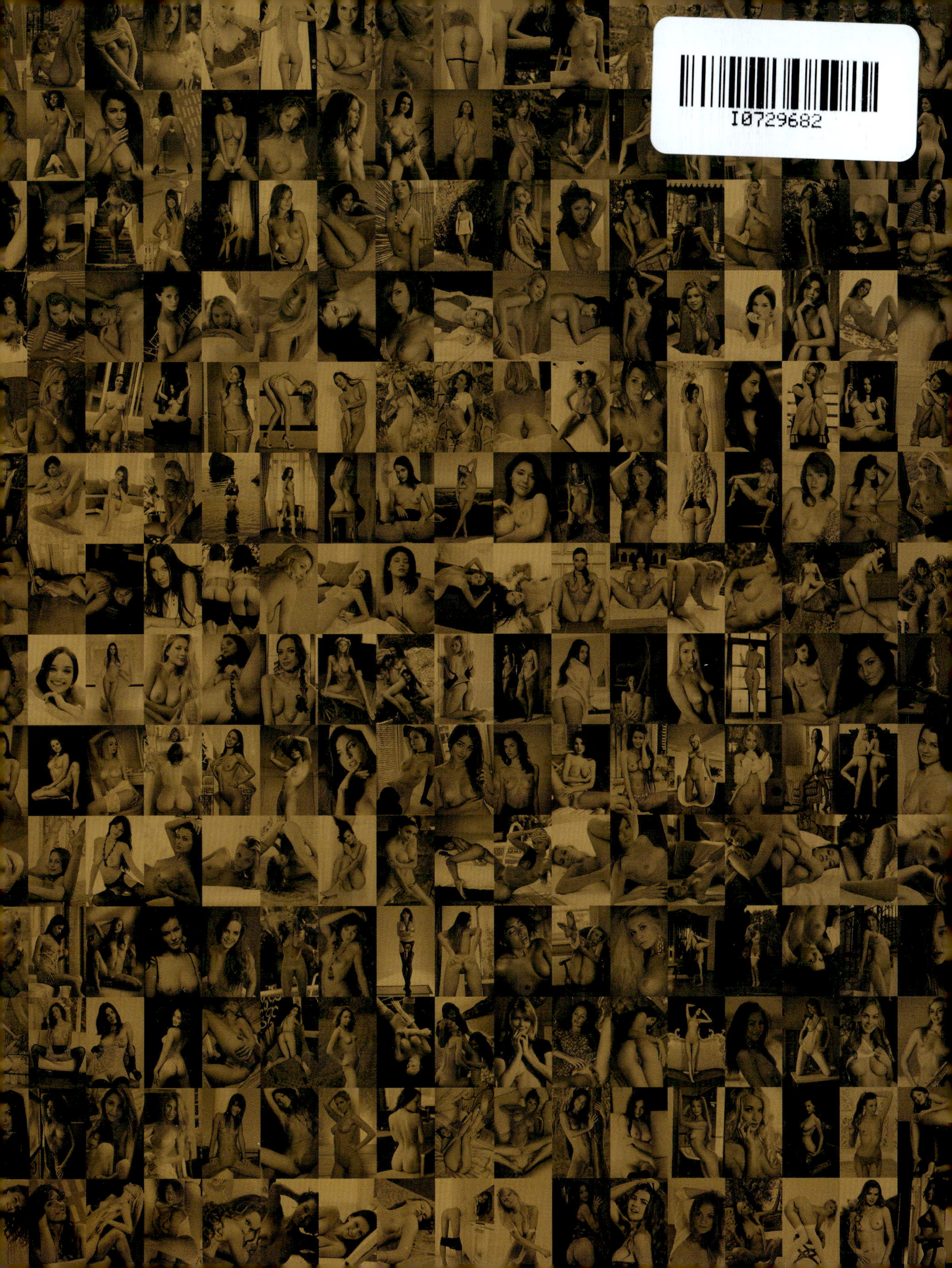
I0729682

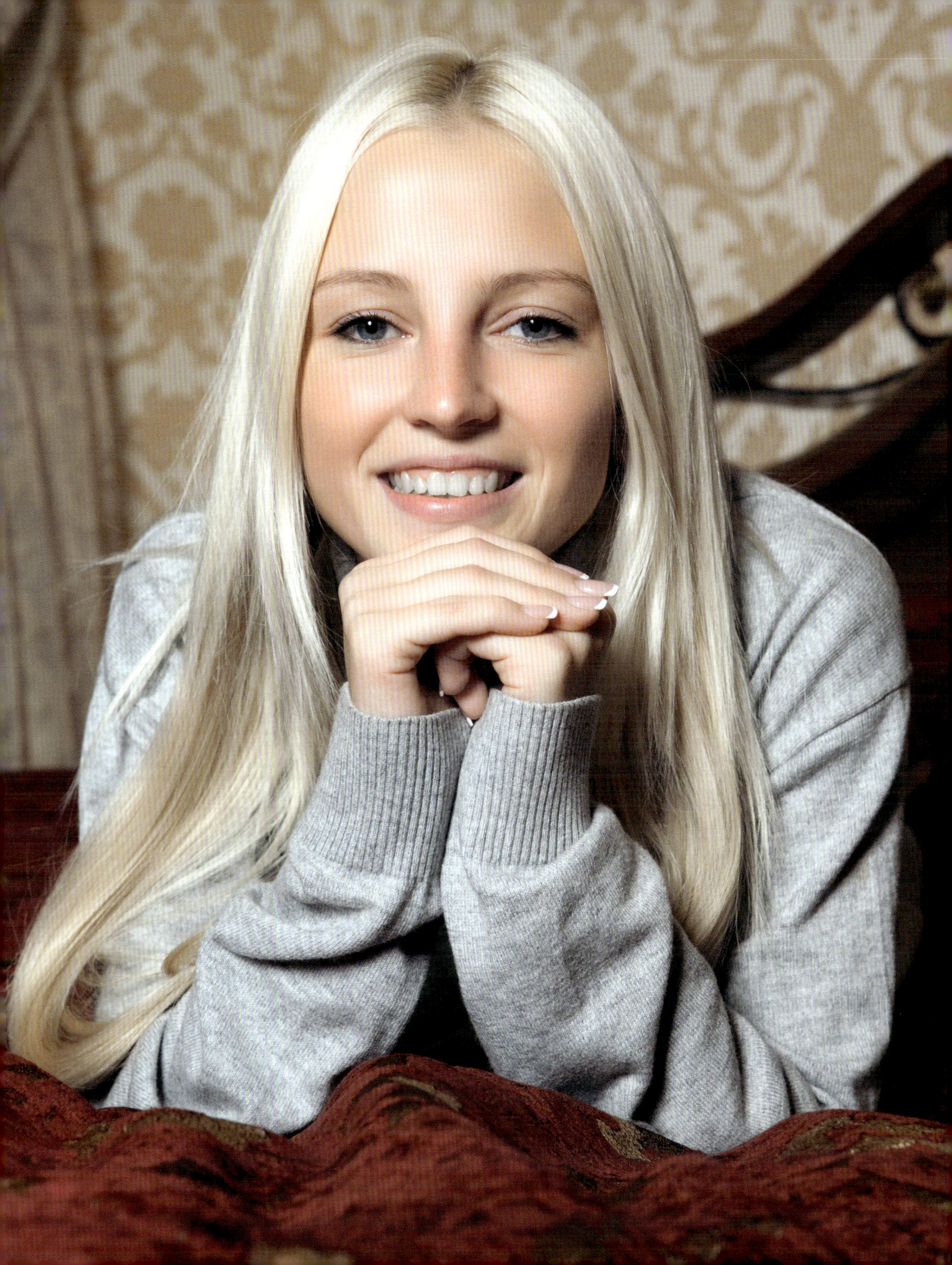

TOP MODELS OF
MetArt.com

WHERE FLAWLESS BEAUTY MEETS ART

ALYSHA A

COLLECTED AND EDITED BY ISABELLA CATALINA

EDITION Skylight

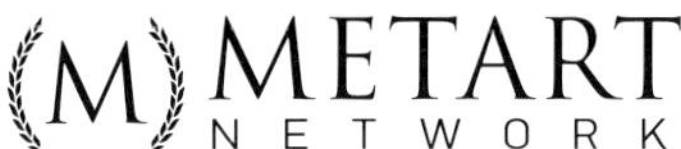

First edition 2023
Copyright © 2023 by Edition Skylight

EDITION SKYLIGHT
Rosengartenstrasse 13B
CH-8608 Bubikon / Zürich
Switzerland
info@edition-skylight.com
www.edition-skylight.com

ISBN 978-3-03766-692-0

Bibliographic information published by Die Deutsche Bibliothek
Die Deutsche Bibliothek lists this publication in the
Deutsche Nationalbibliografie; detailed bibliographic data
are available in the Internet at http://dnb.ddb.de.

Printed in Slowenia

"I LIKE TO DRIVE A CAR AND TO DRIVING MEN WILD!" – ALYSHA A

Alysha A is an Estonian nude model with an exceptionally sweet appearance. She has long blonde hair, lovely firm breasts with slightly puffy nipples and long well-toned legs. Coupled with her angelic features and warm personality, which shines through in her photo galleries, she really is a beautiful artistic nude model, and the dream girl of many admirers all around the globe. Alysha A is a talented, driven erotic model who is currently studying at university to become an expert in pharmaceuticals. Her ultimate goal is to promote health and happiness among all people. She also likes to express her artistic side, believing that the human body is a beautiful work of art that deserves to be appreciated. Her hobbies are modern jazz and disco dancing, and she models a range of styles including erotic, fashion, glamour and fetish; Alysha A loves to explore different forms of expression. In addition to her love of the arts, Alysha A is also a fan of cars, particularly the luxurious, sleek S-class. Her love of driving is matched only by her passion for driving men wild with her irresistible charm and sexuality. Portfolios showing Alysha A can be found on Metart.com, Eroticbeauty.com and Rylskyart.com, where she is described as having a sweet demeanor and stunning features. According to her biography on TheNude.com, Alysha A began her modeling career in 2011, and is still active. At the age of 24, she debuted in the industry with her 33 B boobs and medium areolas, and is featured in 27 galleries on Metart, 1 gallerie on Eroticbeauty and 8 galleries on Rylskyart.

Alysha A ist ein Estnisches Aktmodell und sieht außergewöhnlich süß aus. Sie hat langes blondes Haar, schöne feste Brüste mit leicht hervorstehenden Brustwarzen und lange trainierte Beine. In Verbindung mit ihren engelhaften Gesichtszügen und einer starken Persönlichkeit, die in ihren Fotogalerien zum Ausdruck kommt, ist sie wirklich ein begehrenswertes Model und der Traum vieler Bewunderer auf der ganzen Welt. Alysha A ist ein talentiertes Erotikmodell und studiert zur Zeit Pharmazie. Ihr ultimatives Ziel ist es, Gesundheit und Glück unter den Menschen zu fördern. Sie drückt auch ihre künstlerische Seite aus und glaubt, dass der menschliche Körper ein Kunstwerk ist, das es verdient, gezeigt zu werden. Alysha A liebt ihre Hobbys wie Modern Jazz und Disco-Tanzen sowie Fotoshootings in verschiedenen Stilen, einschließlich Erotik, Mode, Glamour und Fetisch. Neben ihrer Liebe zur Kunst ist Alysha A auch ein Fan von Autos, insbesondere der luxuriösen und eleganten S-Klasse. Ihre Passion für Autos wird nur von ihrer Leidenschaft übertroffen, Männer mit ihrem unwiderstehlichen Charme und ihrer Sexualität verrückt zu machen. Portfolios, die Alysha A zeigen, finden sich auf Metart.com, artnudemodels.com und verschiedenen anderen Websites, auf denen sie enthusiastisch mit ihren beeindruckenden Eigenschaften beschrieben wird. Laut ihrer Biografie auf TheNude.com begann Alysha A im Jahr 2011 ihre Karriere als Aktmodell und ist bis heute aktiv. Im Alter von 24 Jahren debütierte sie in der Branche mit ihrer Körbchengröße 75B und mittelgroßen Brustwarzen und wird in 27 Galerien auf Metart, einer Galerie auf Eroticbeauty and 8 Galerien auf Rylskyart vorgestellt.

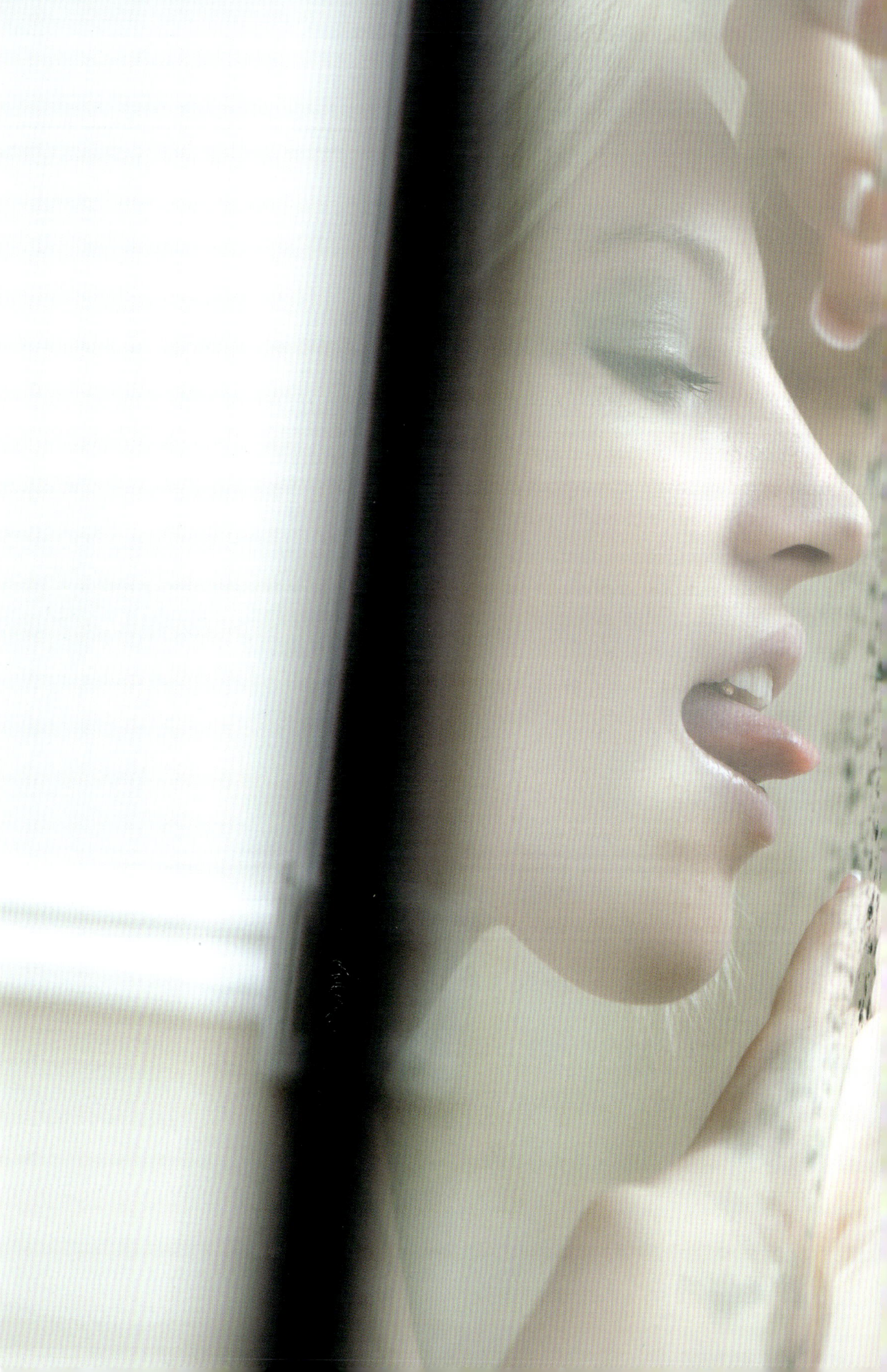

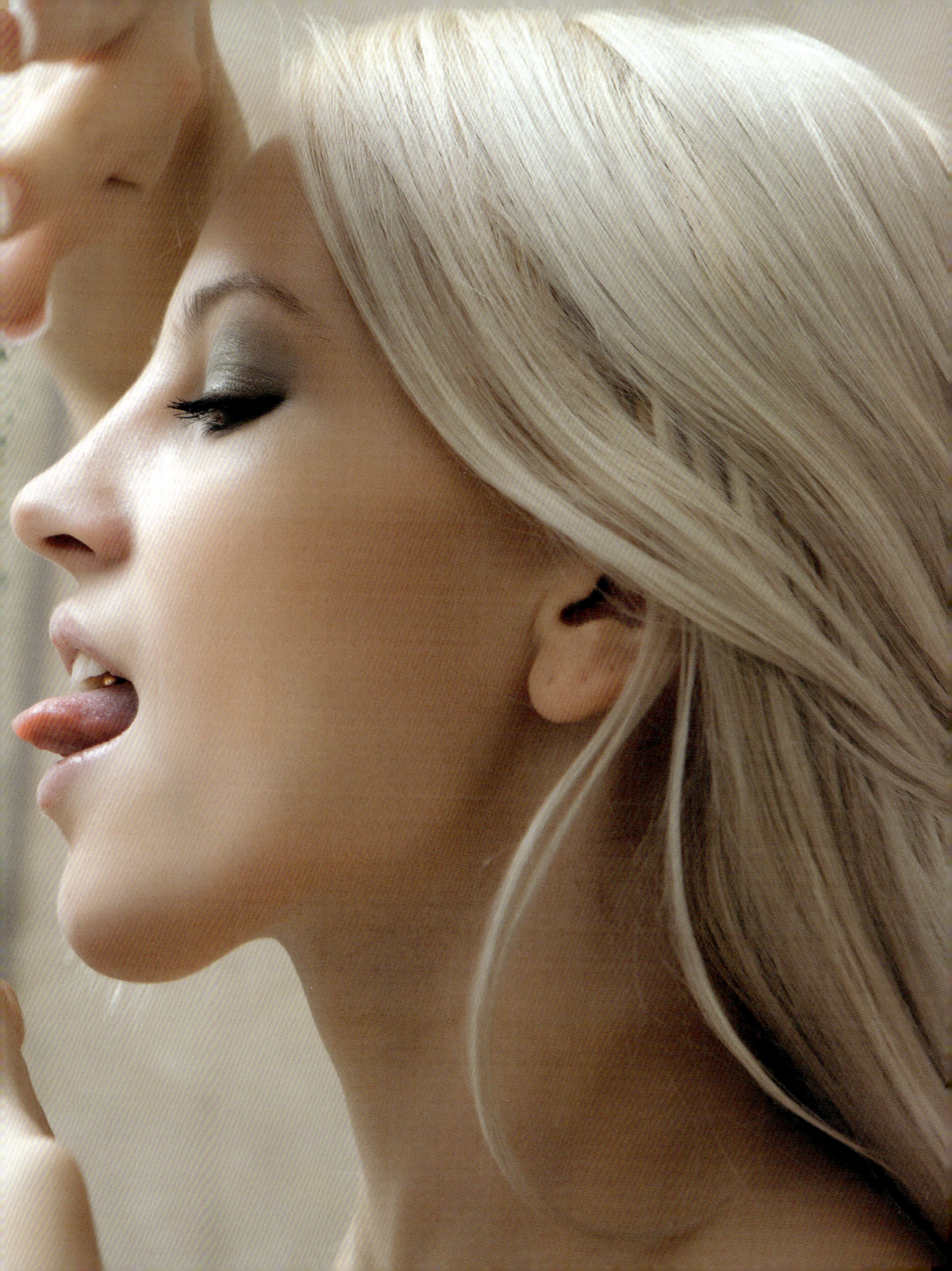

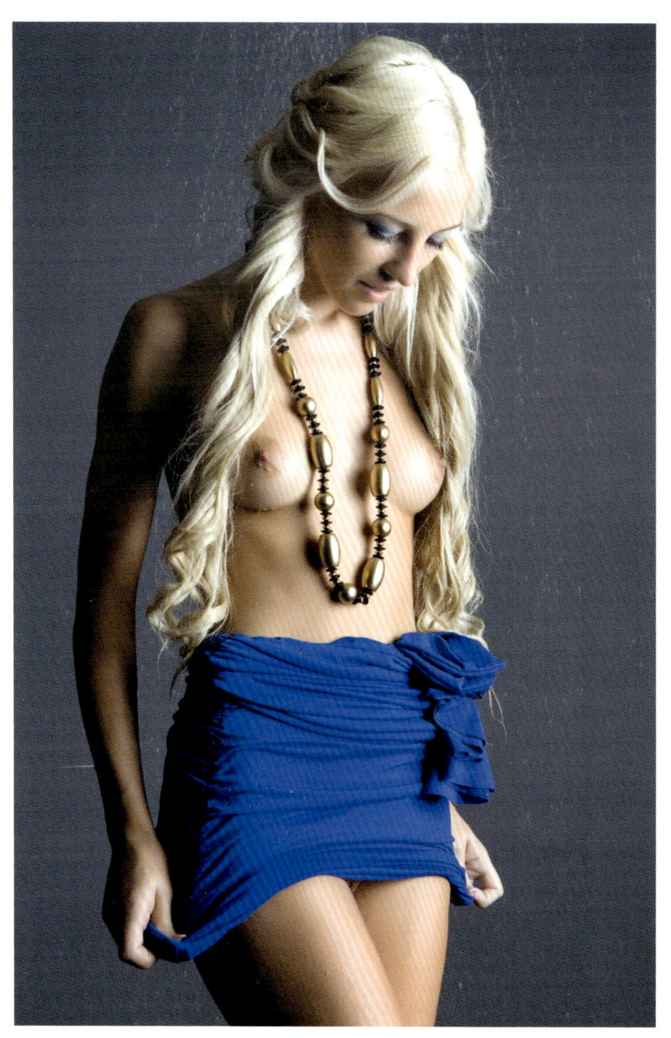

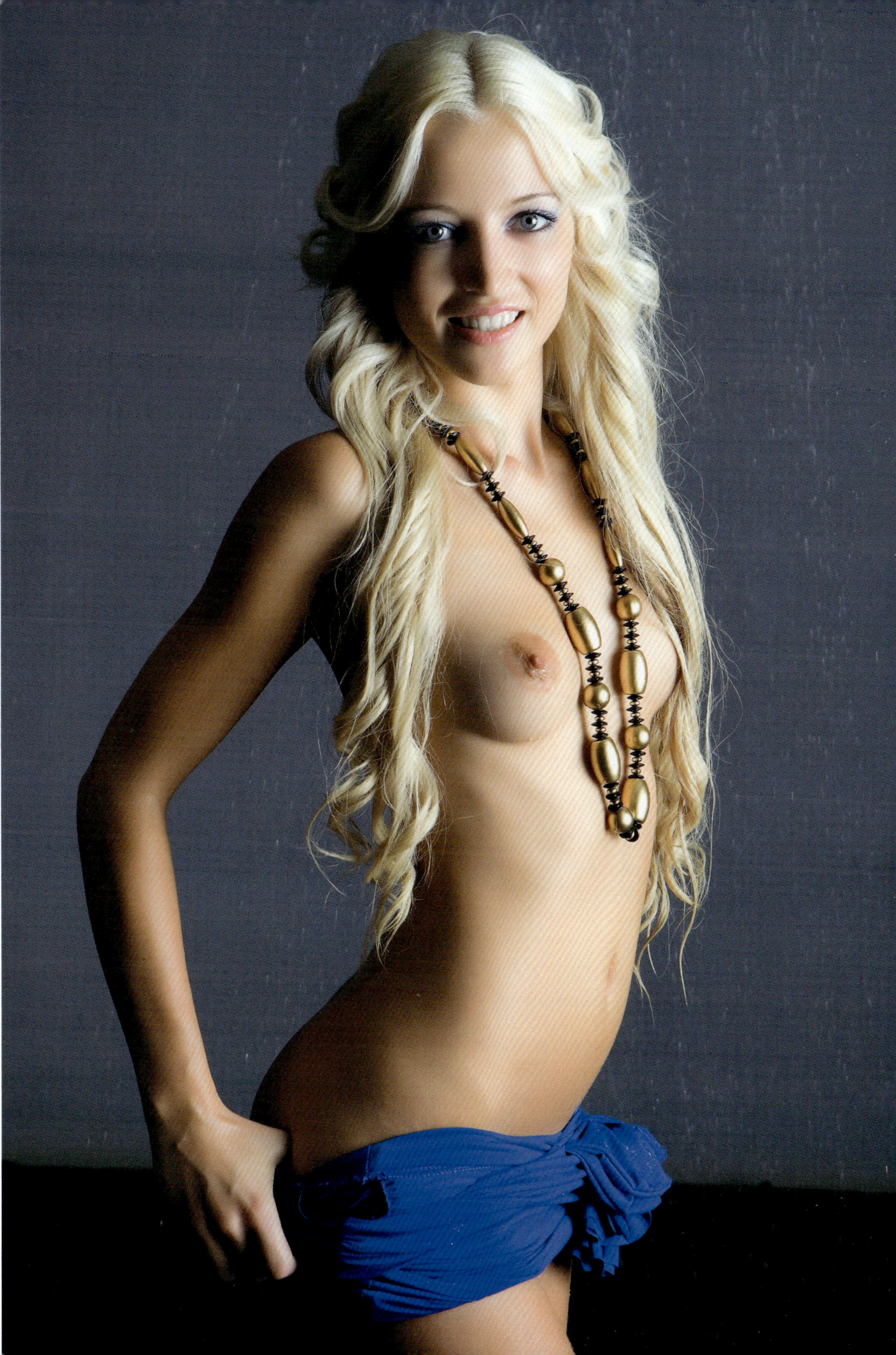

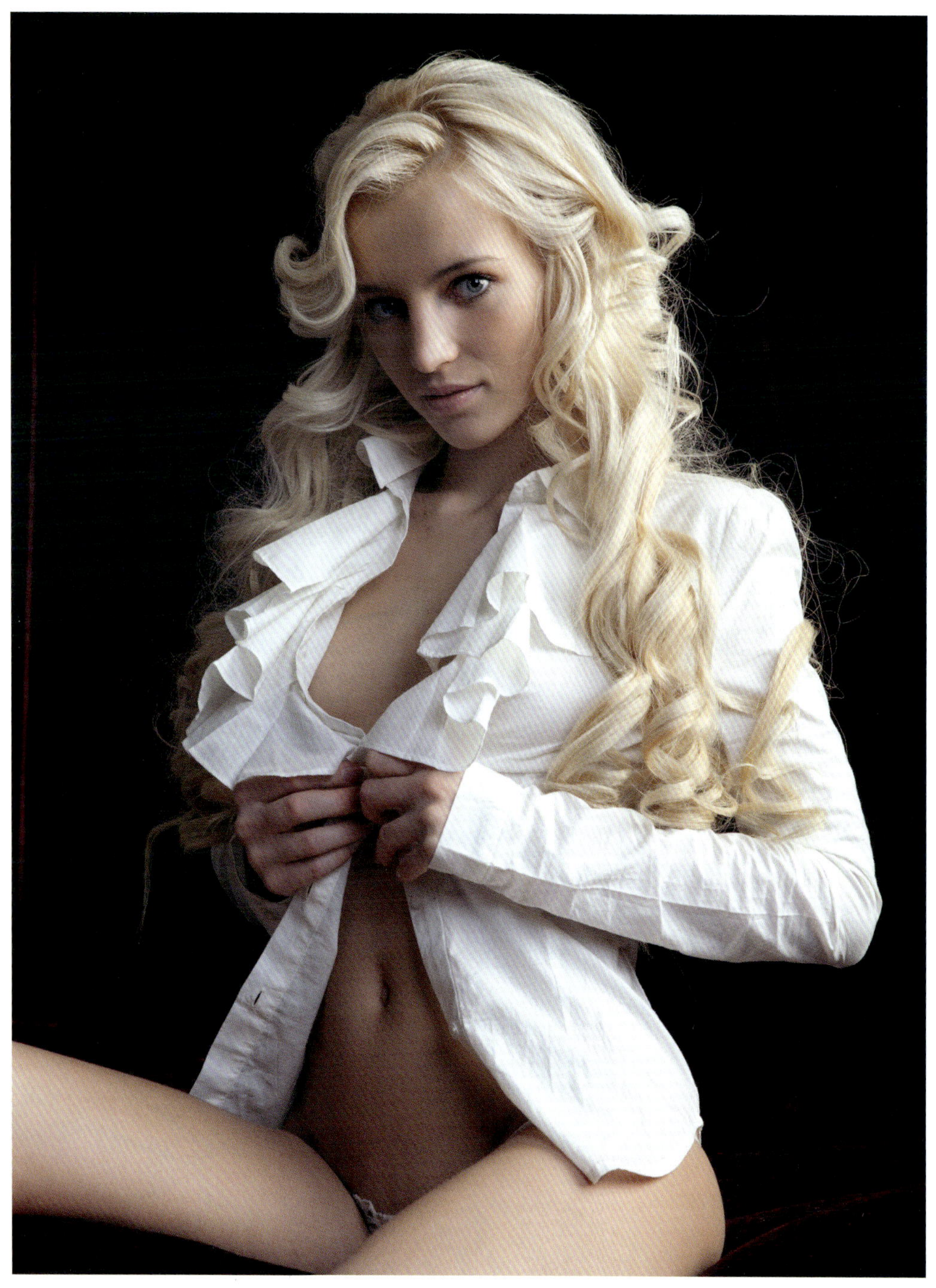

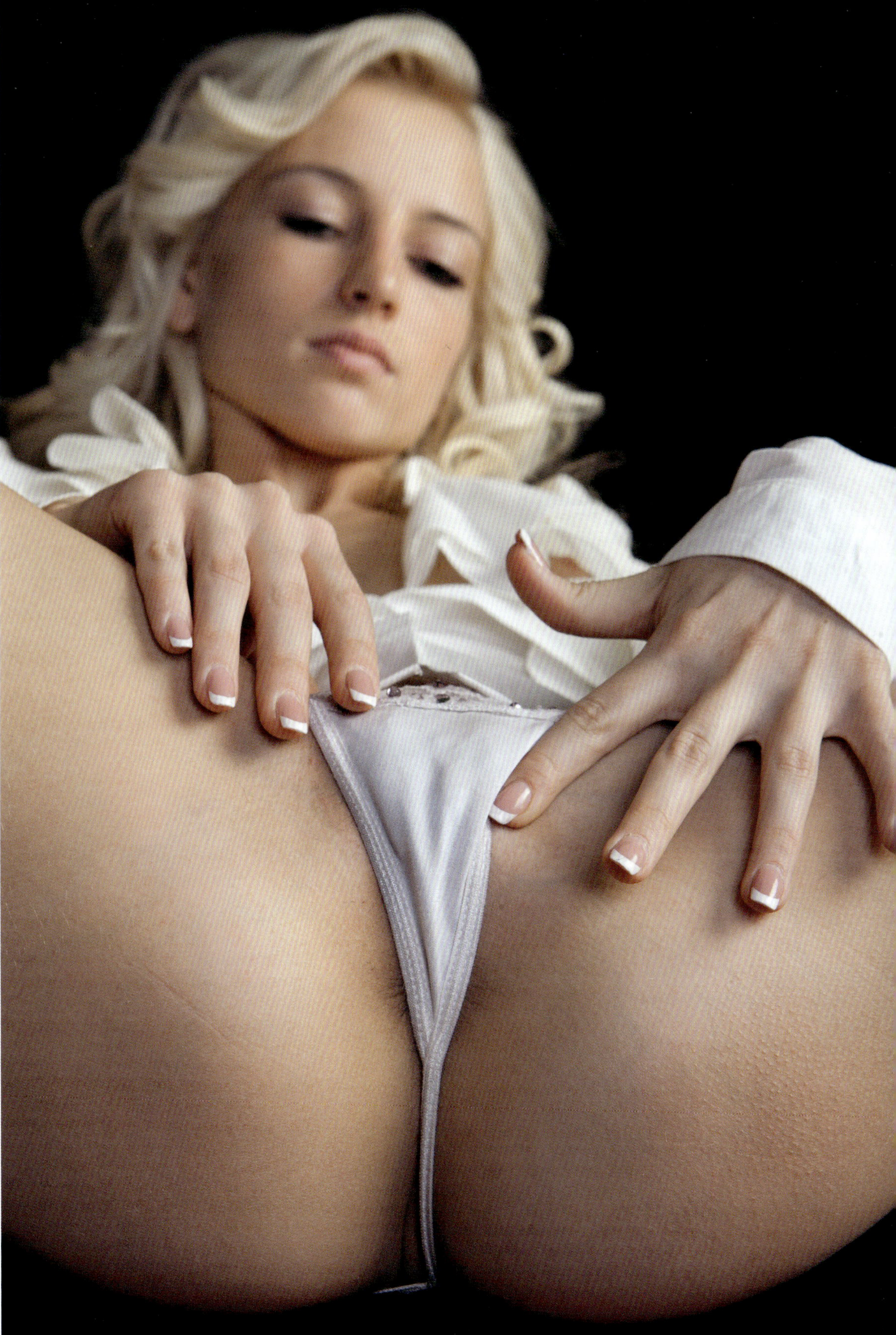

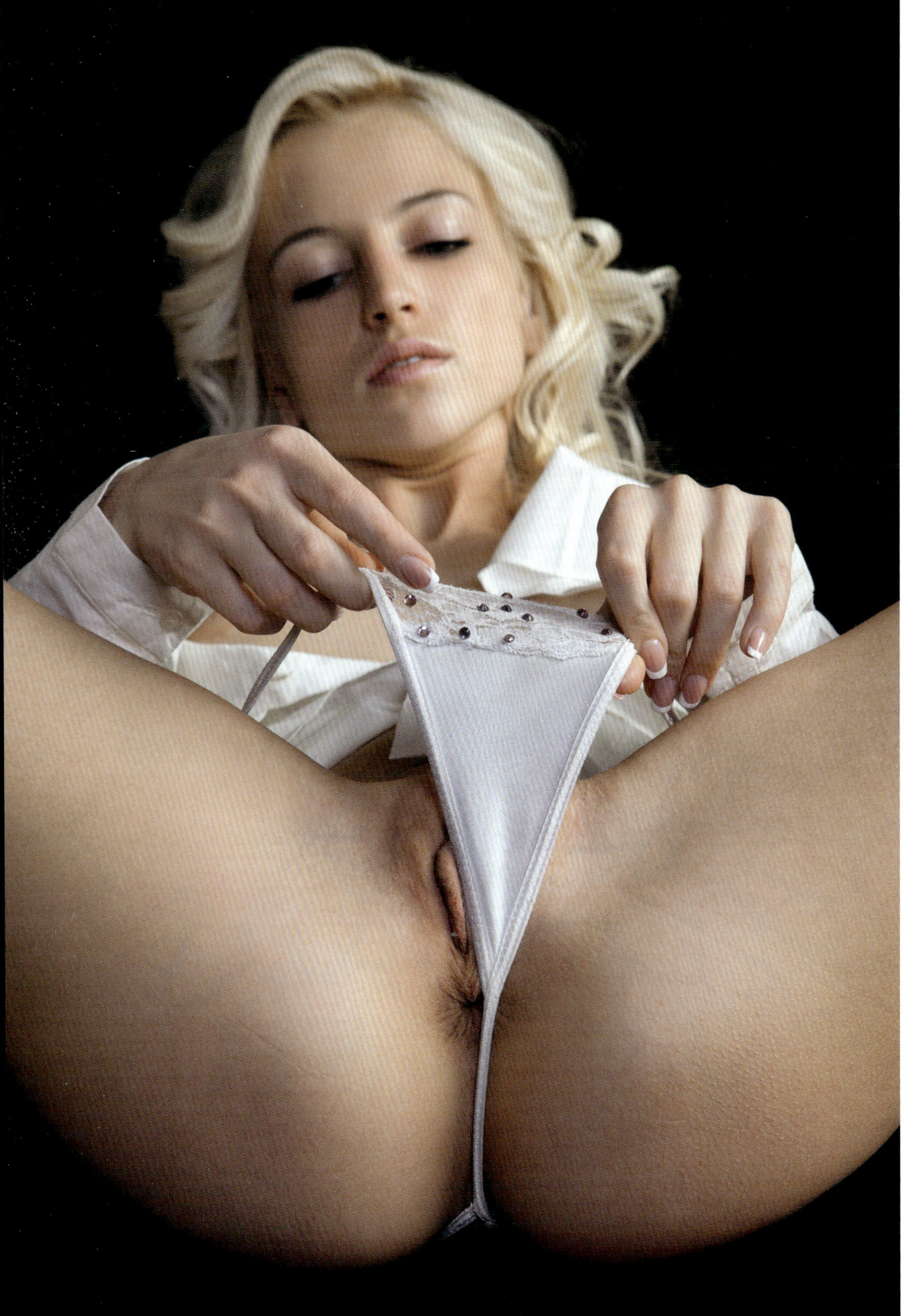

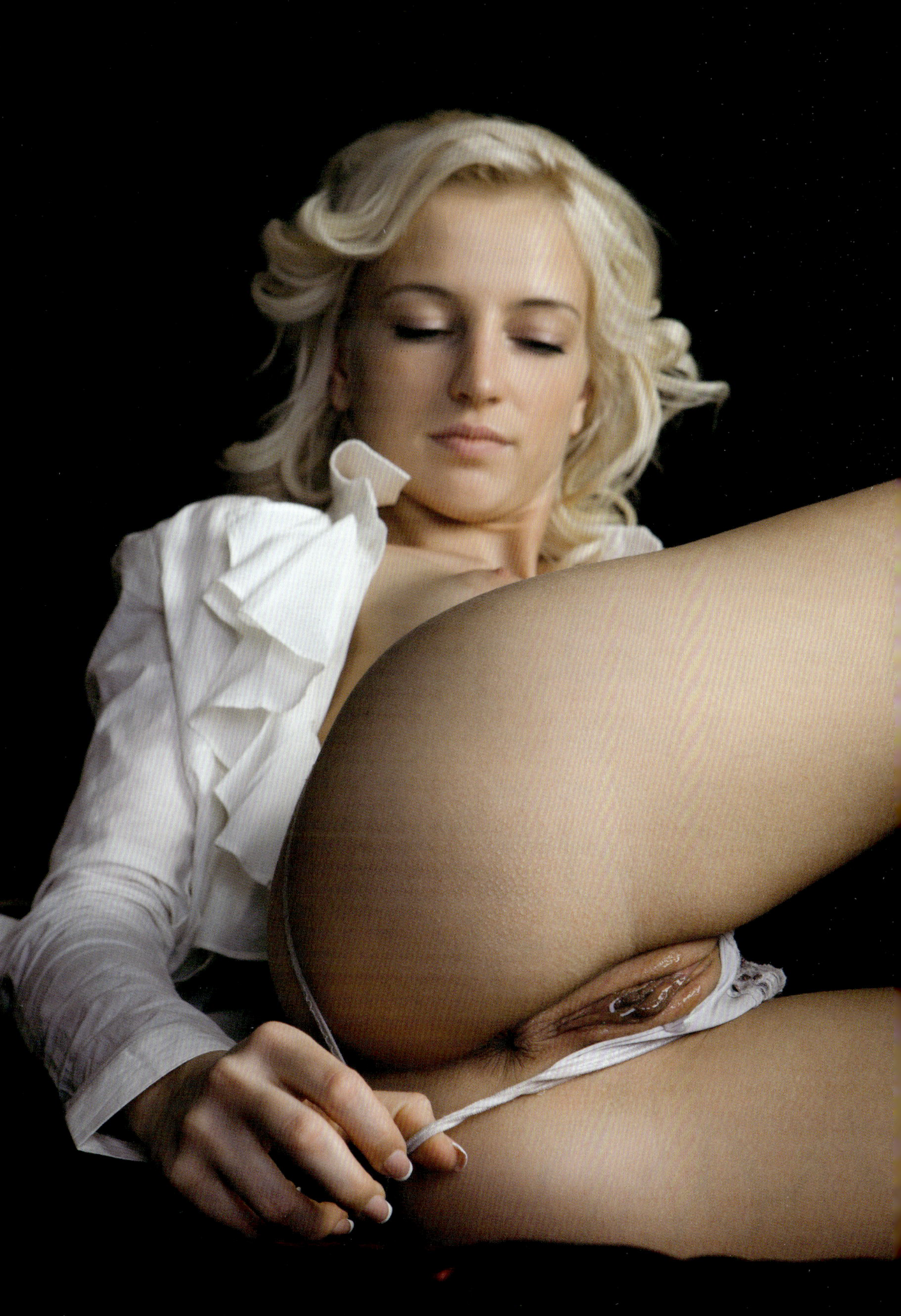

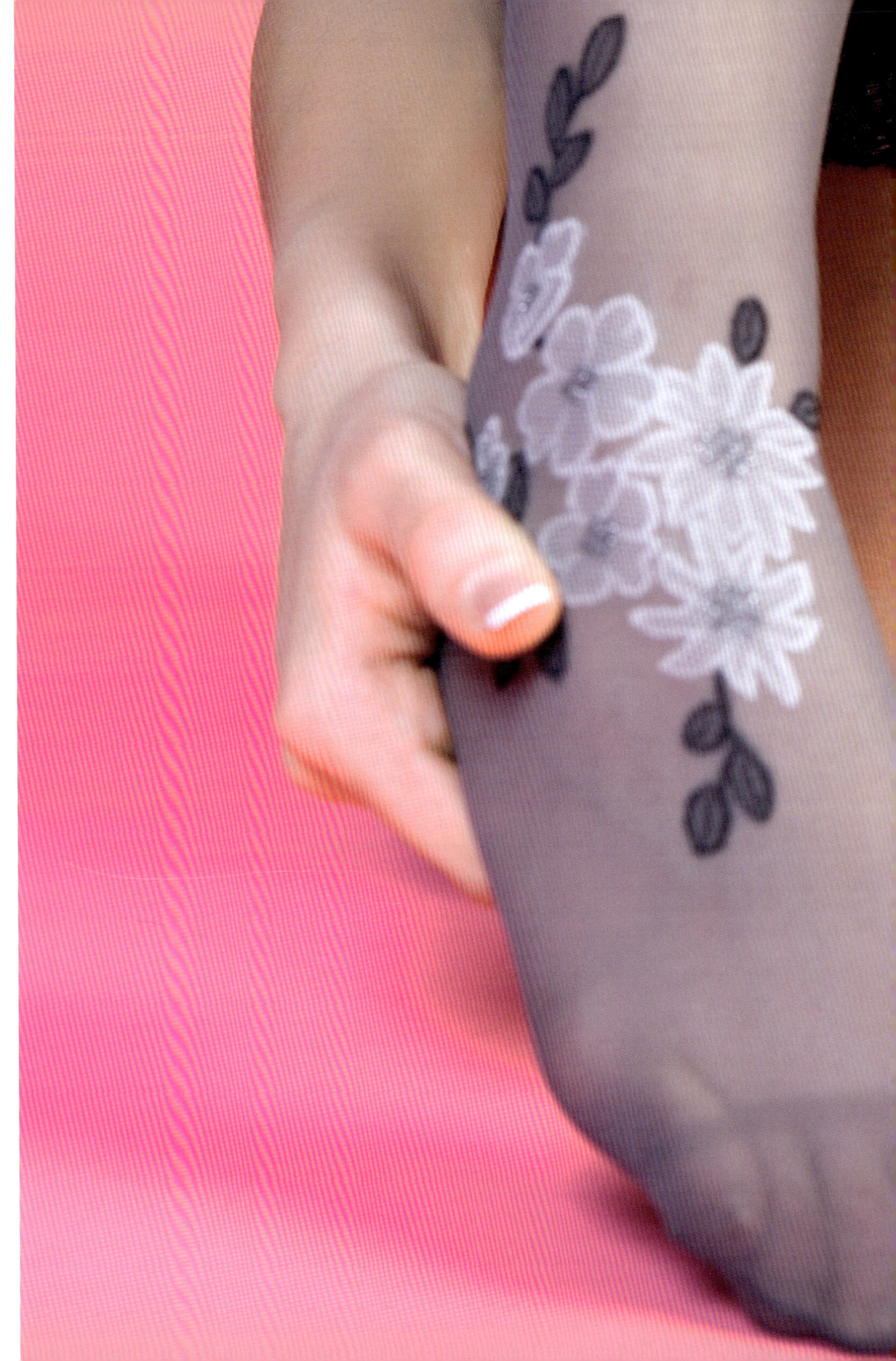

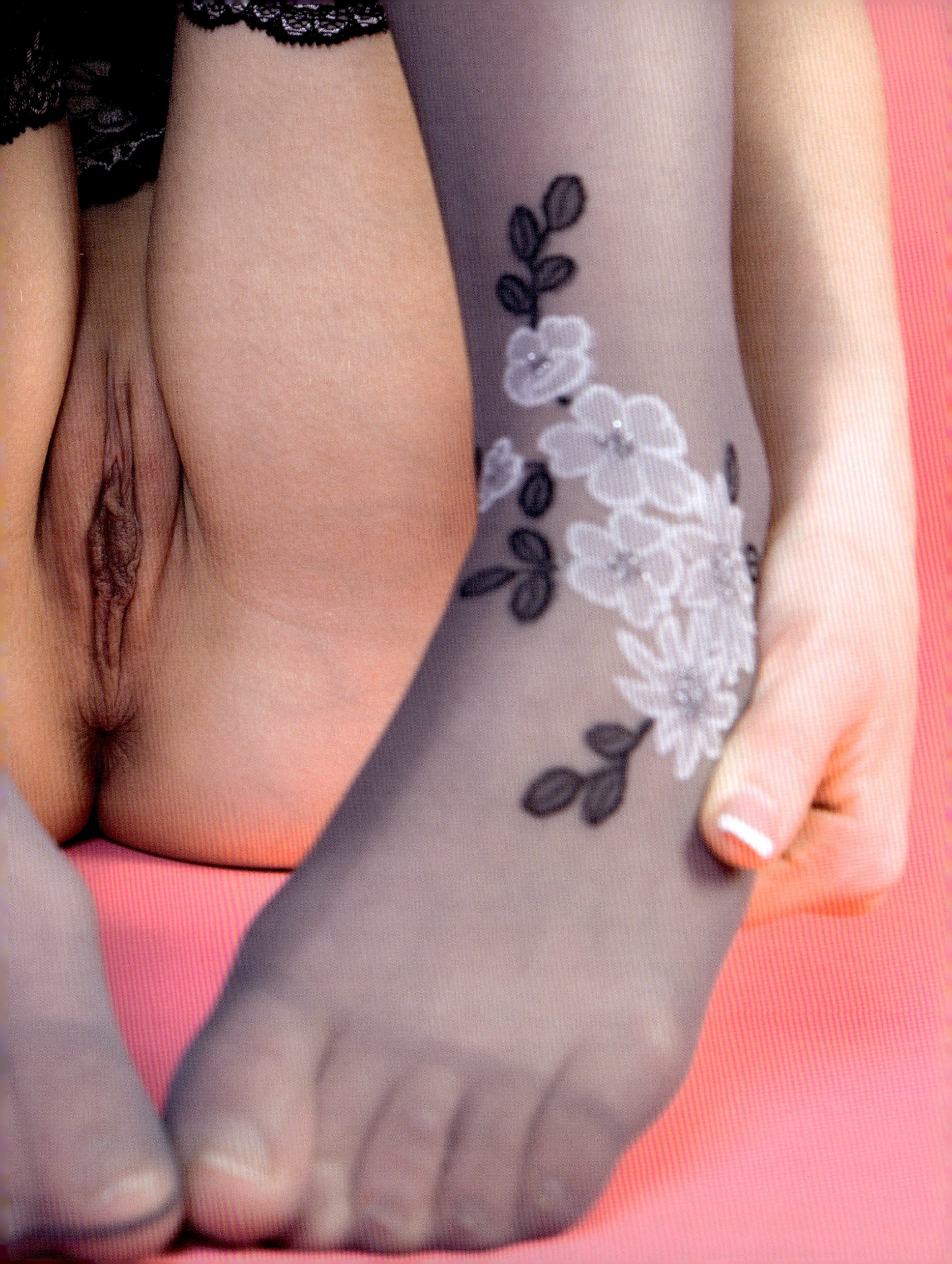

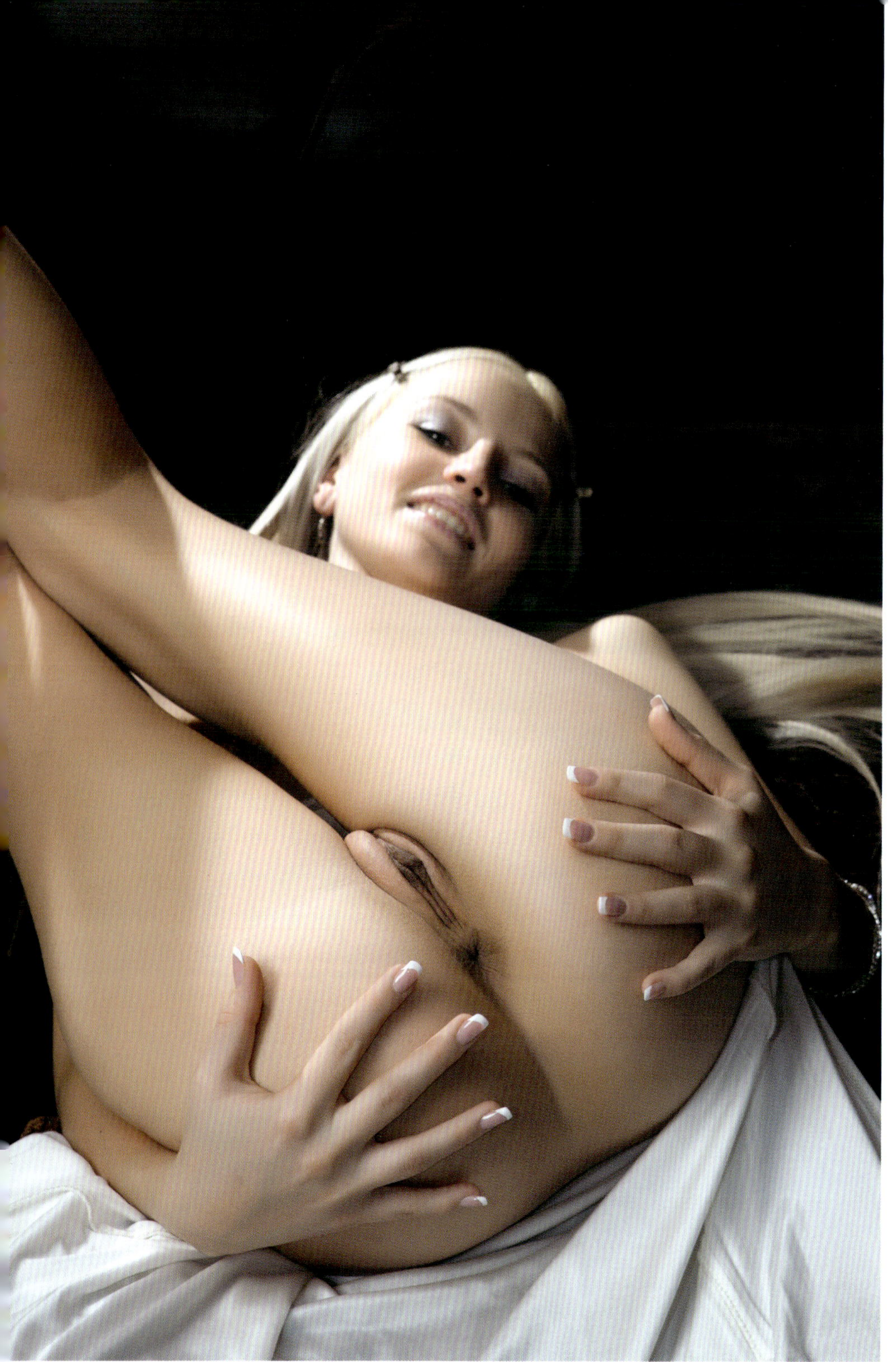

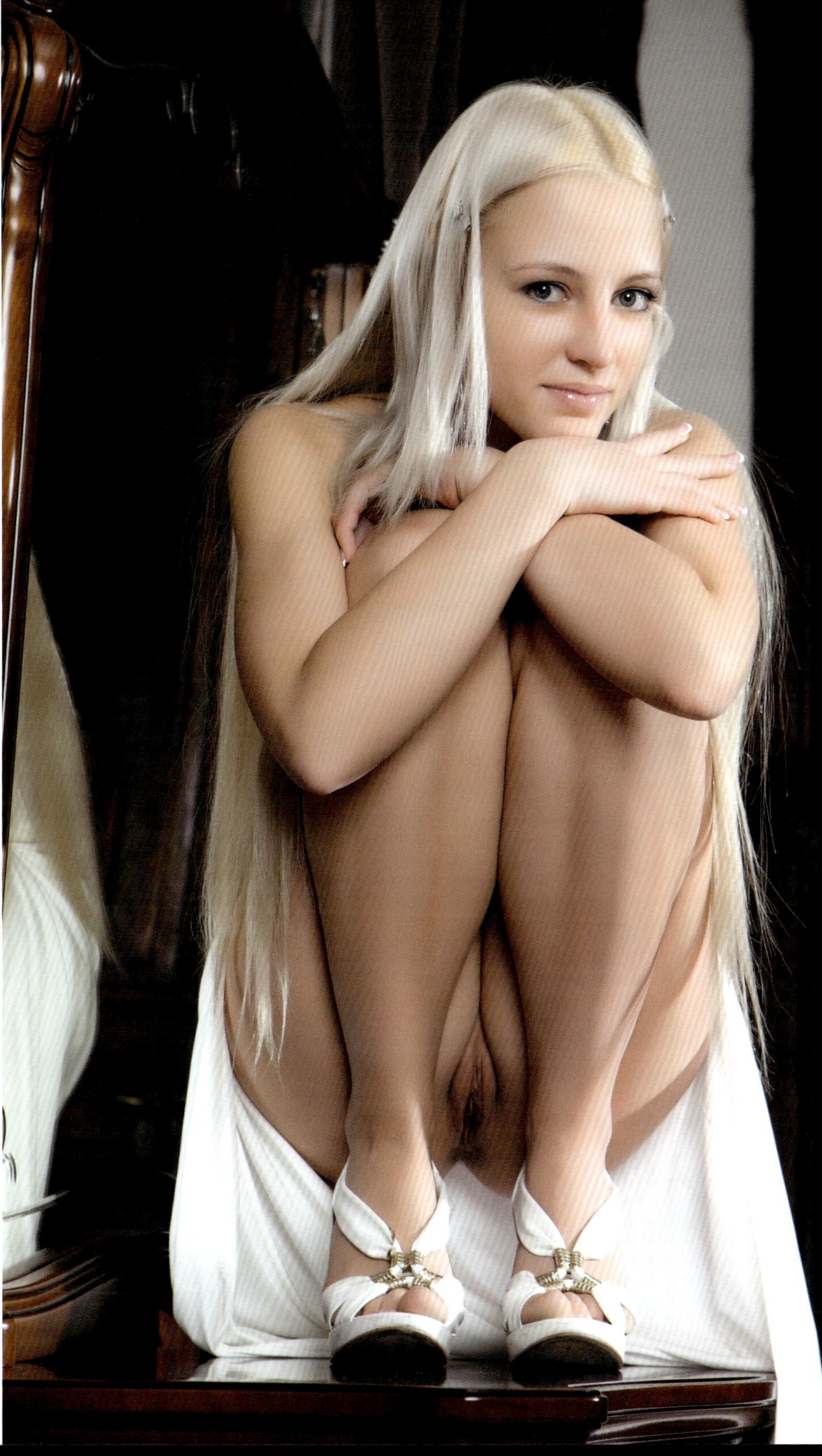

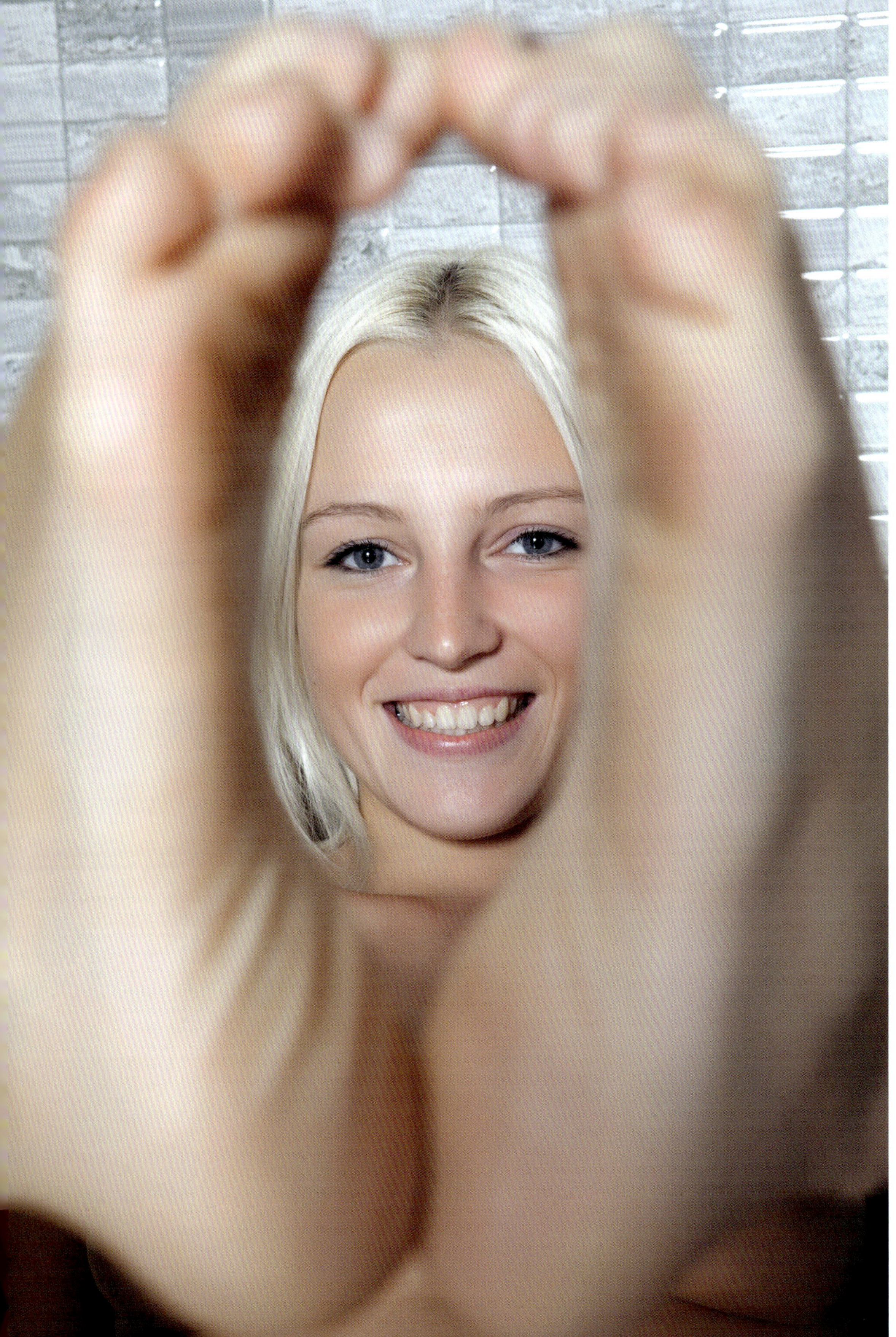

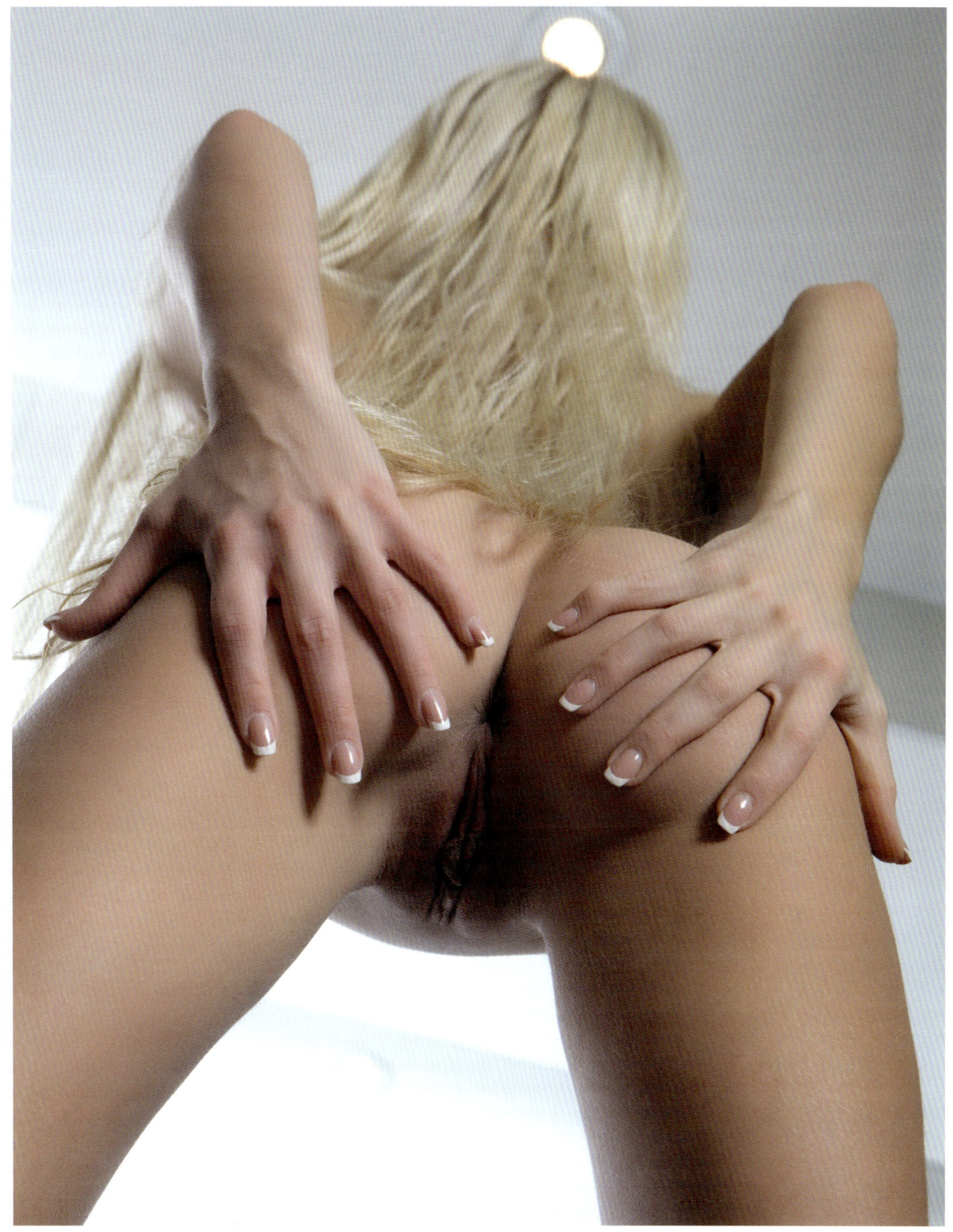

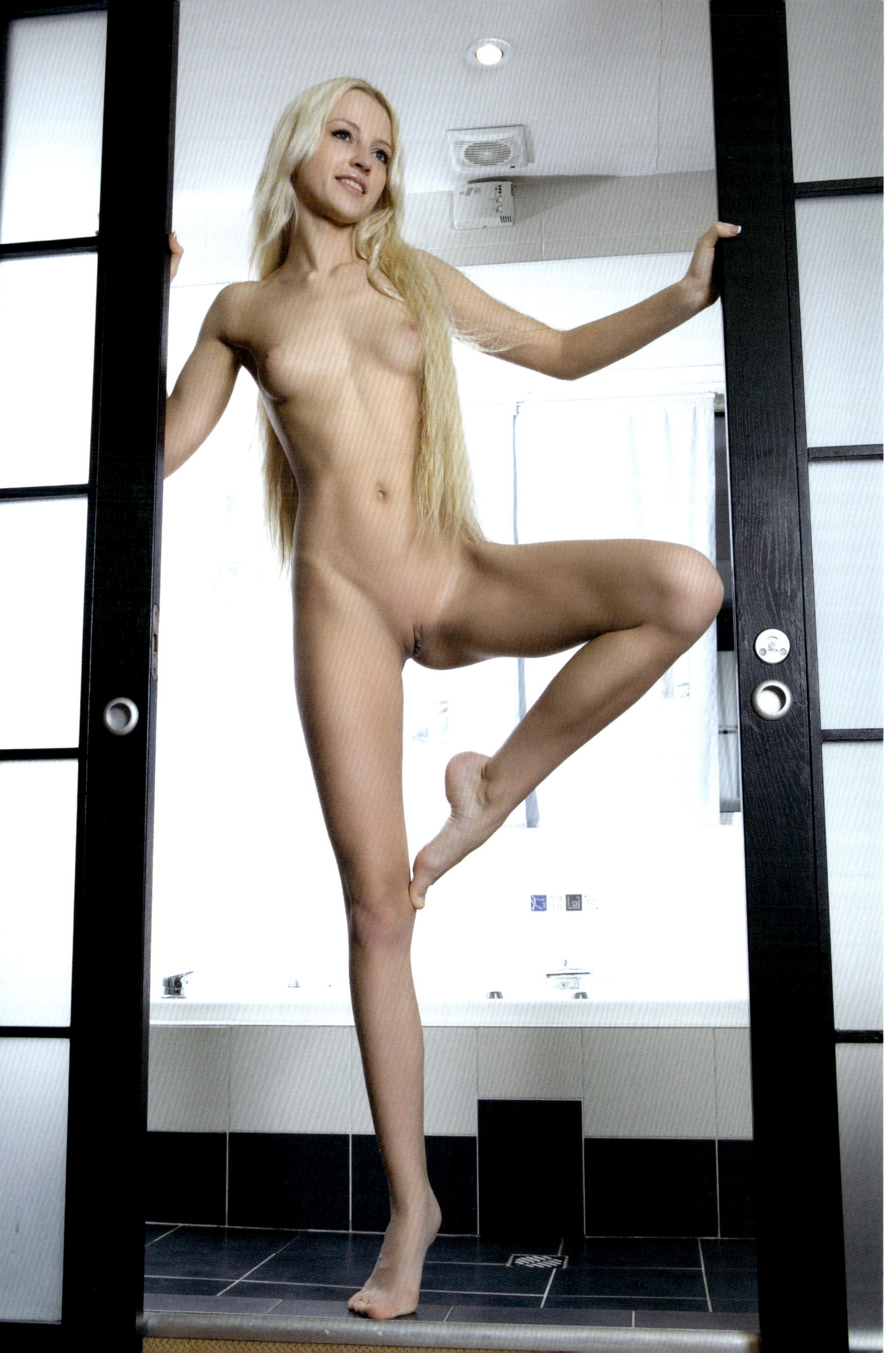

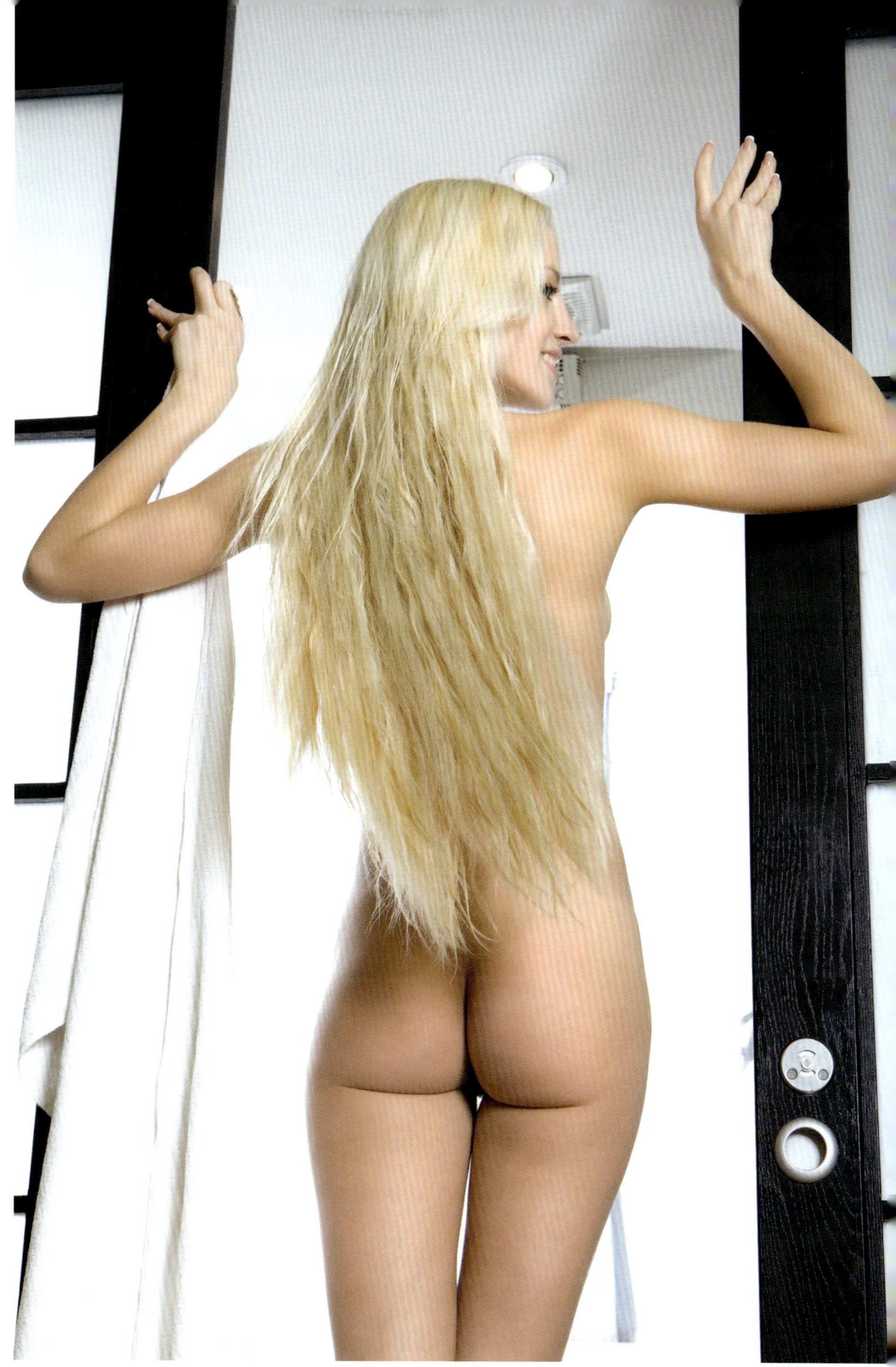

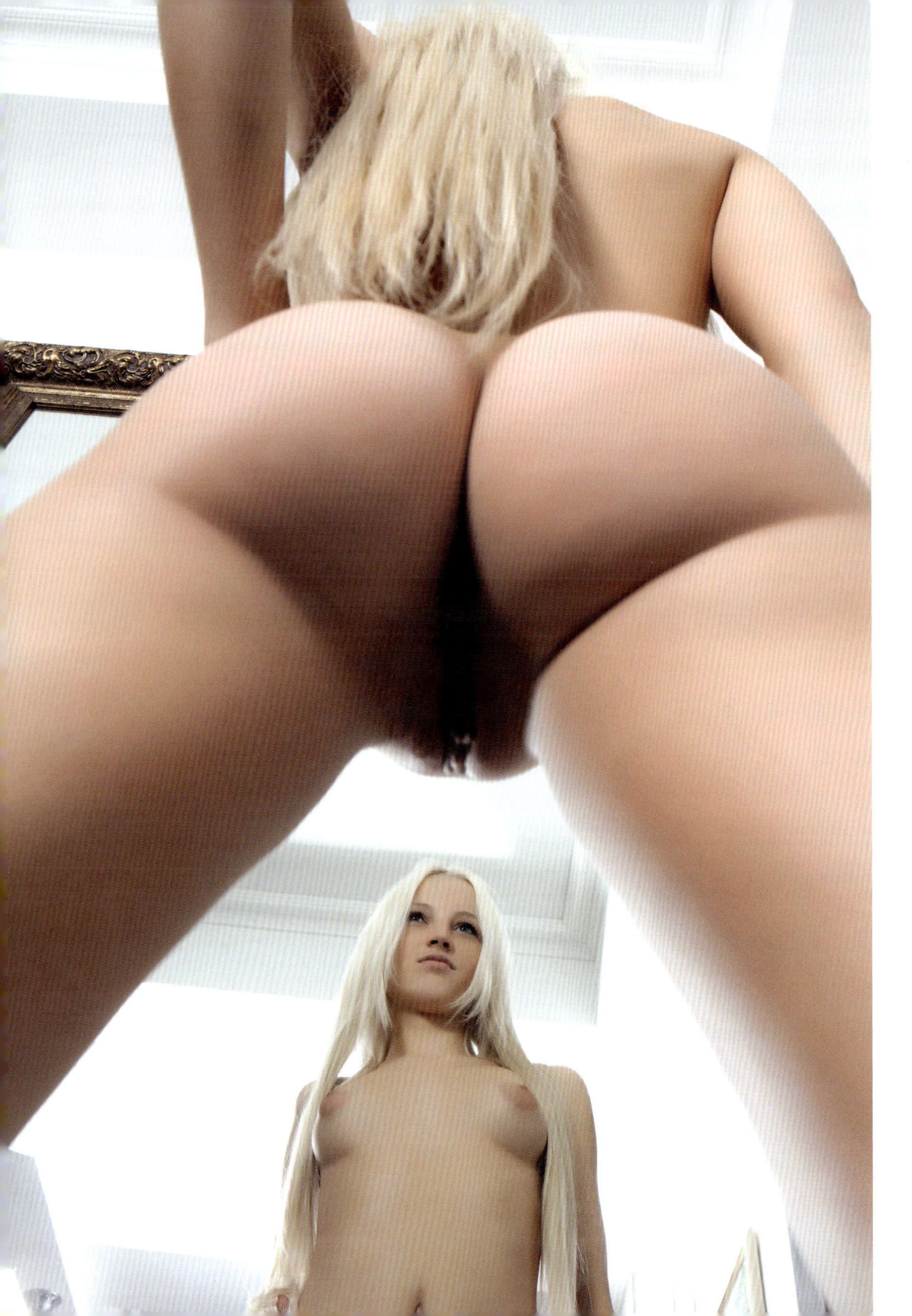

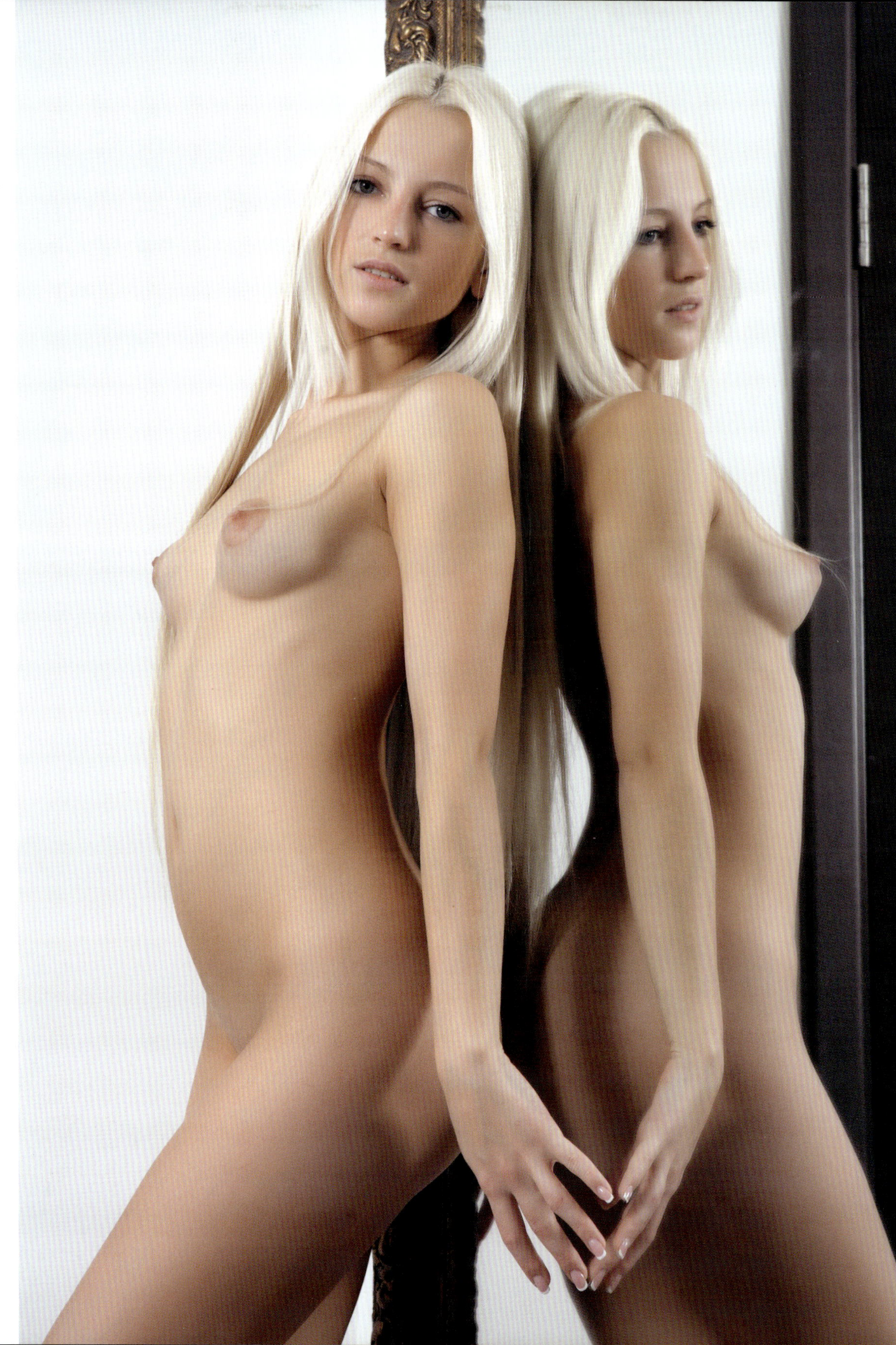

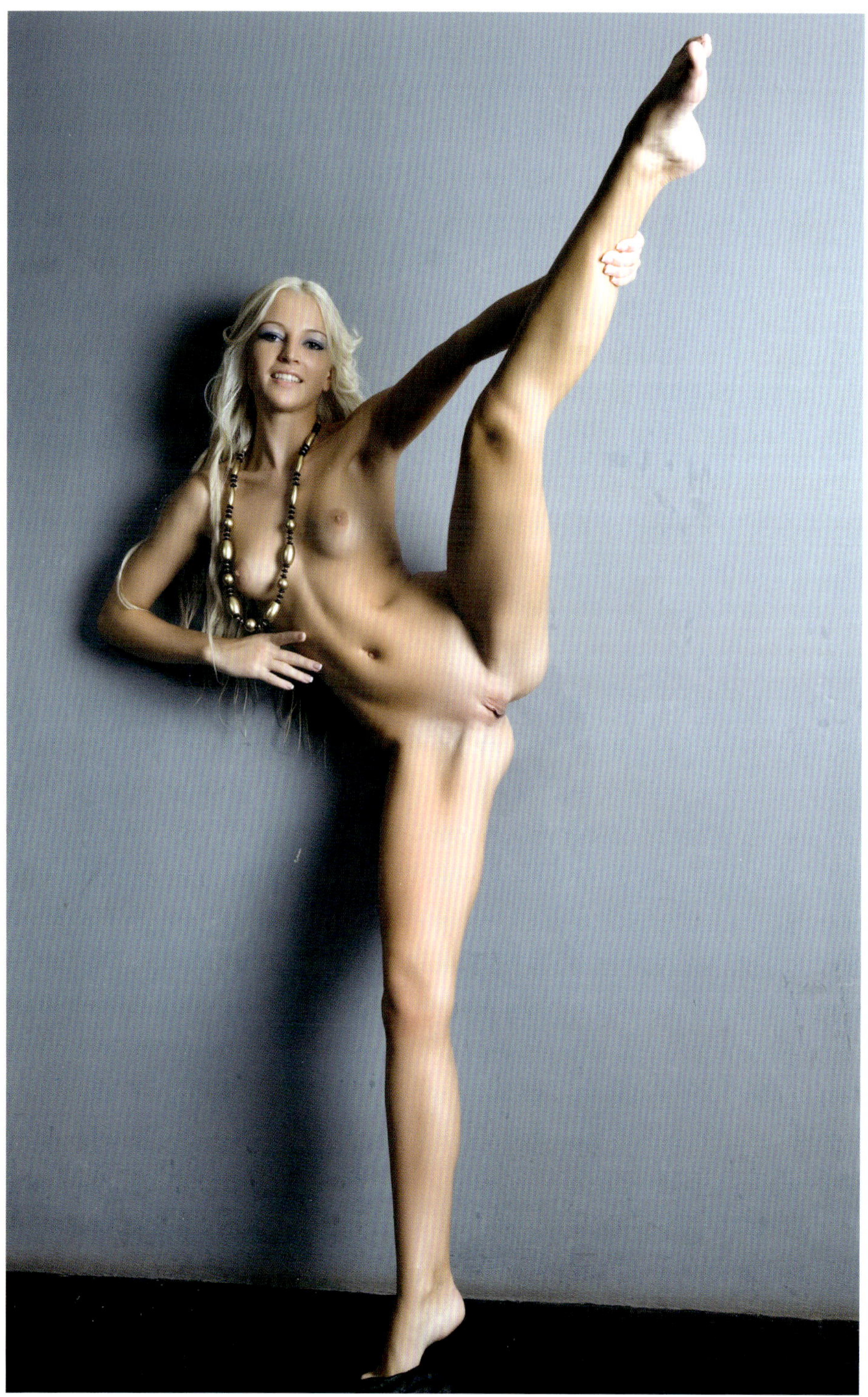

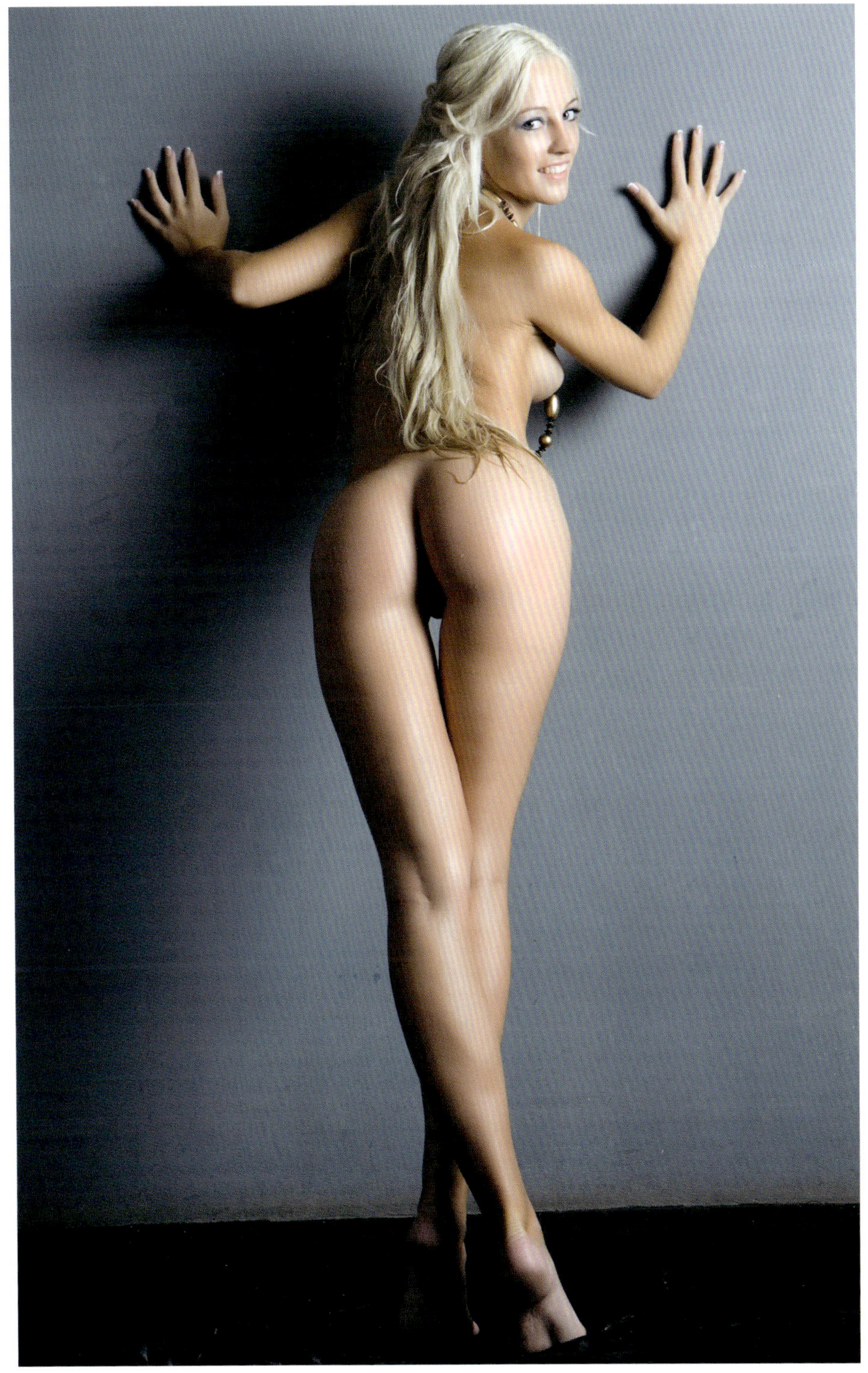

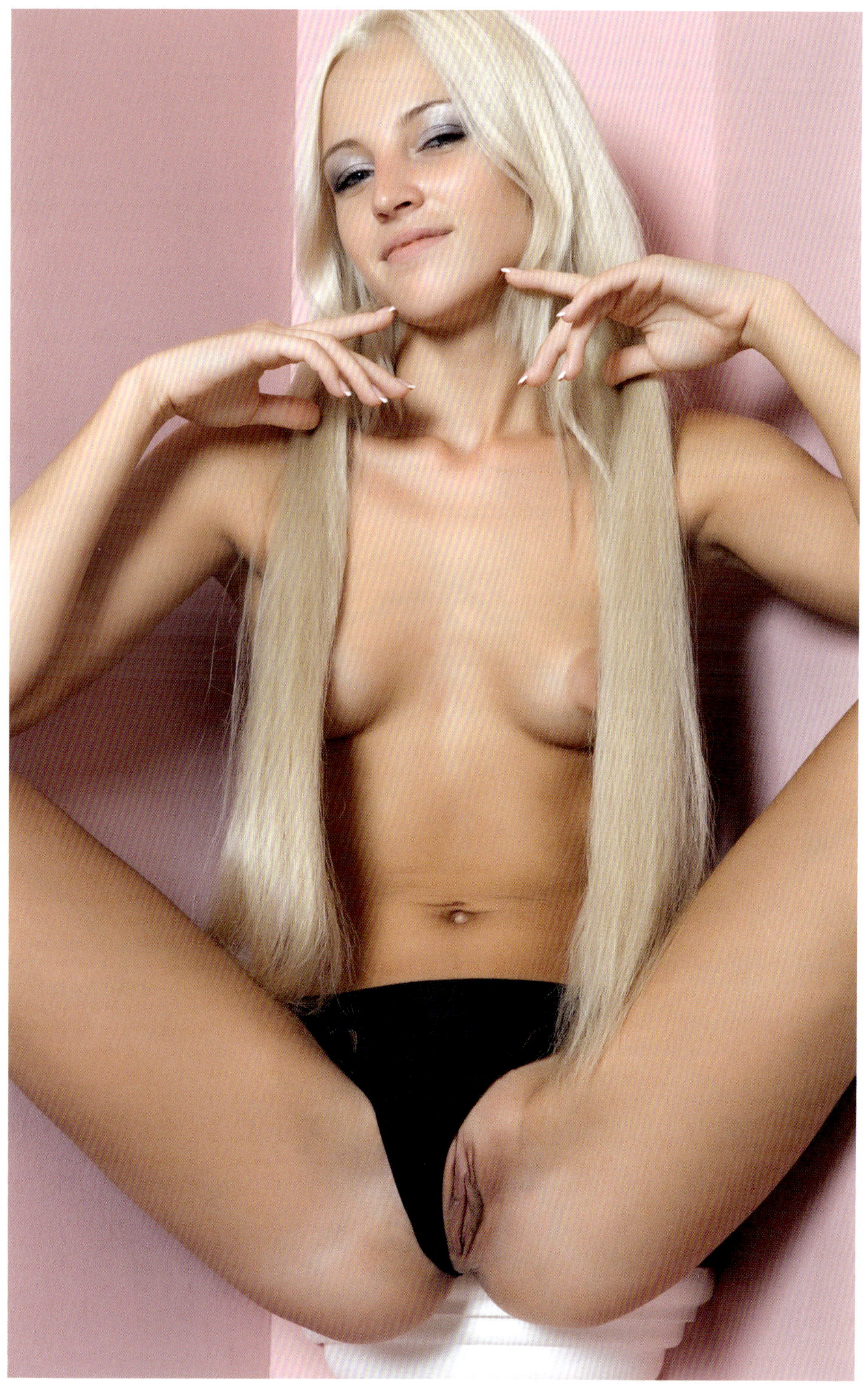

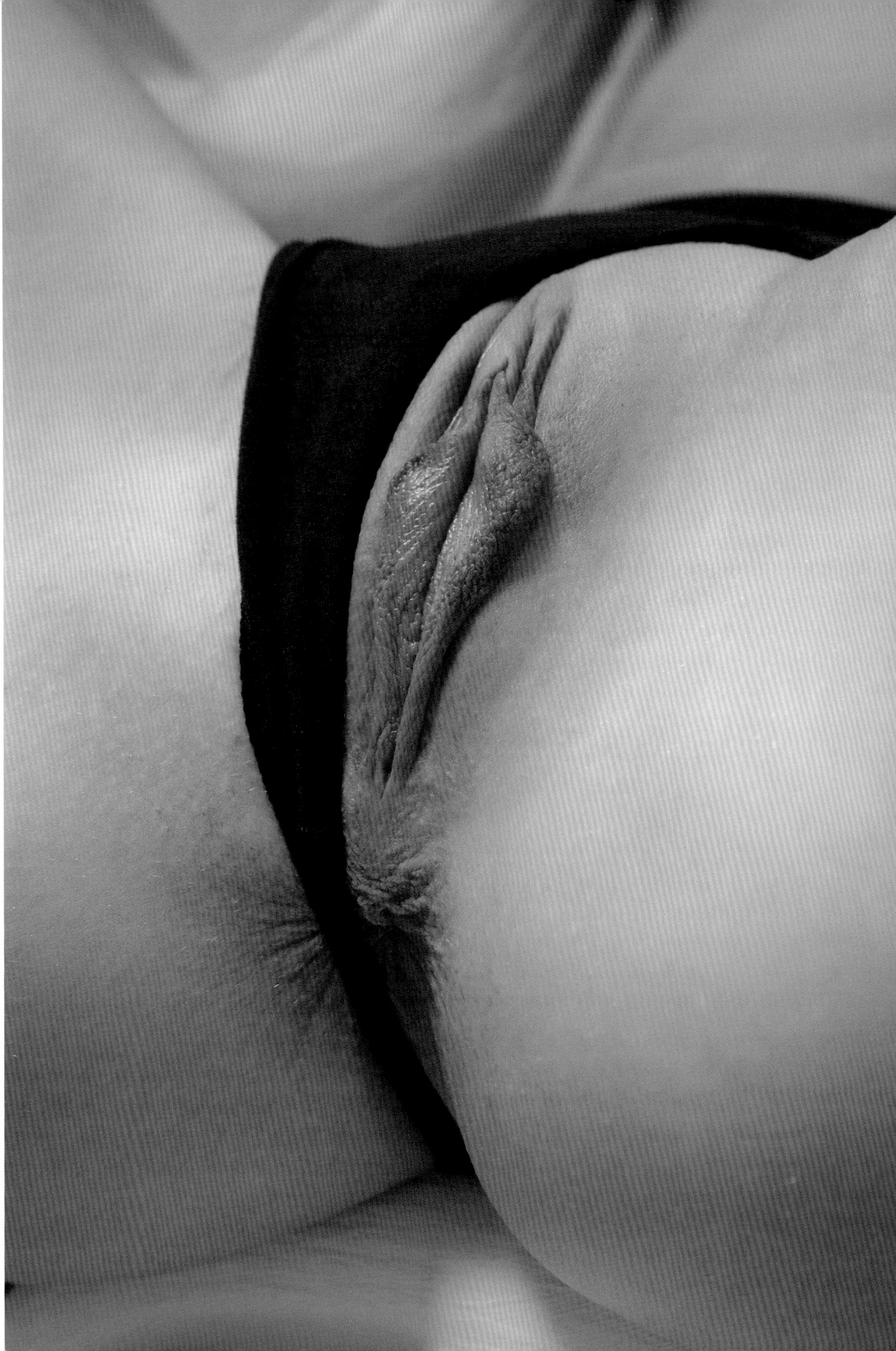

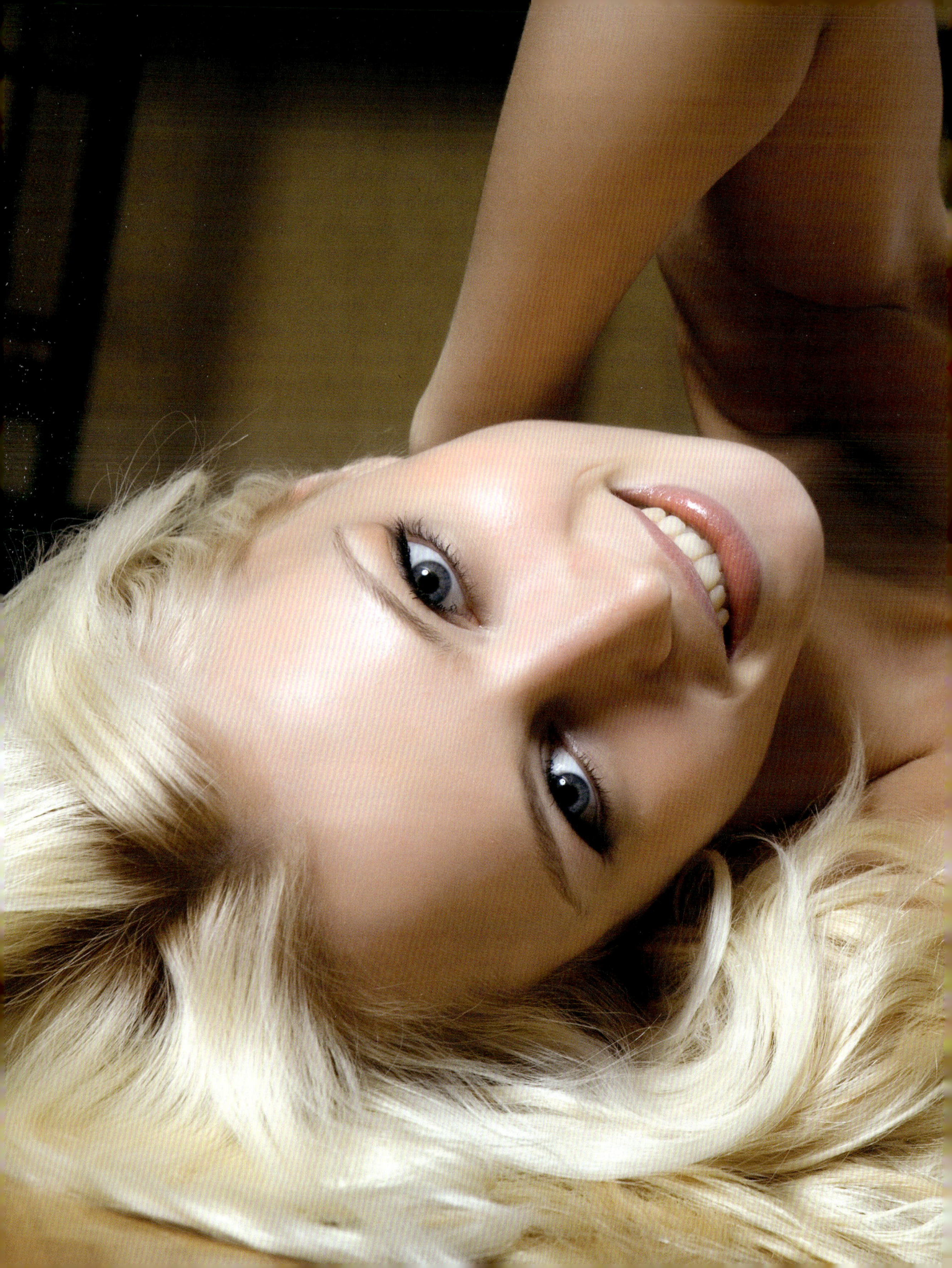

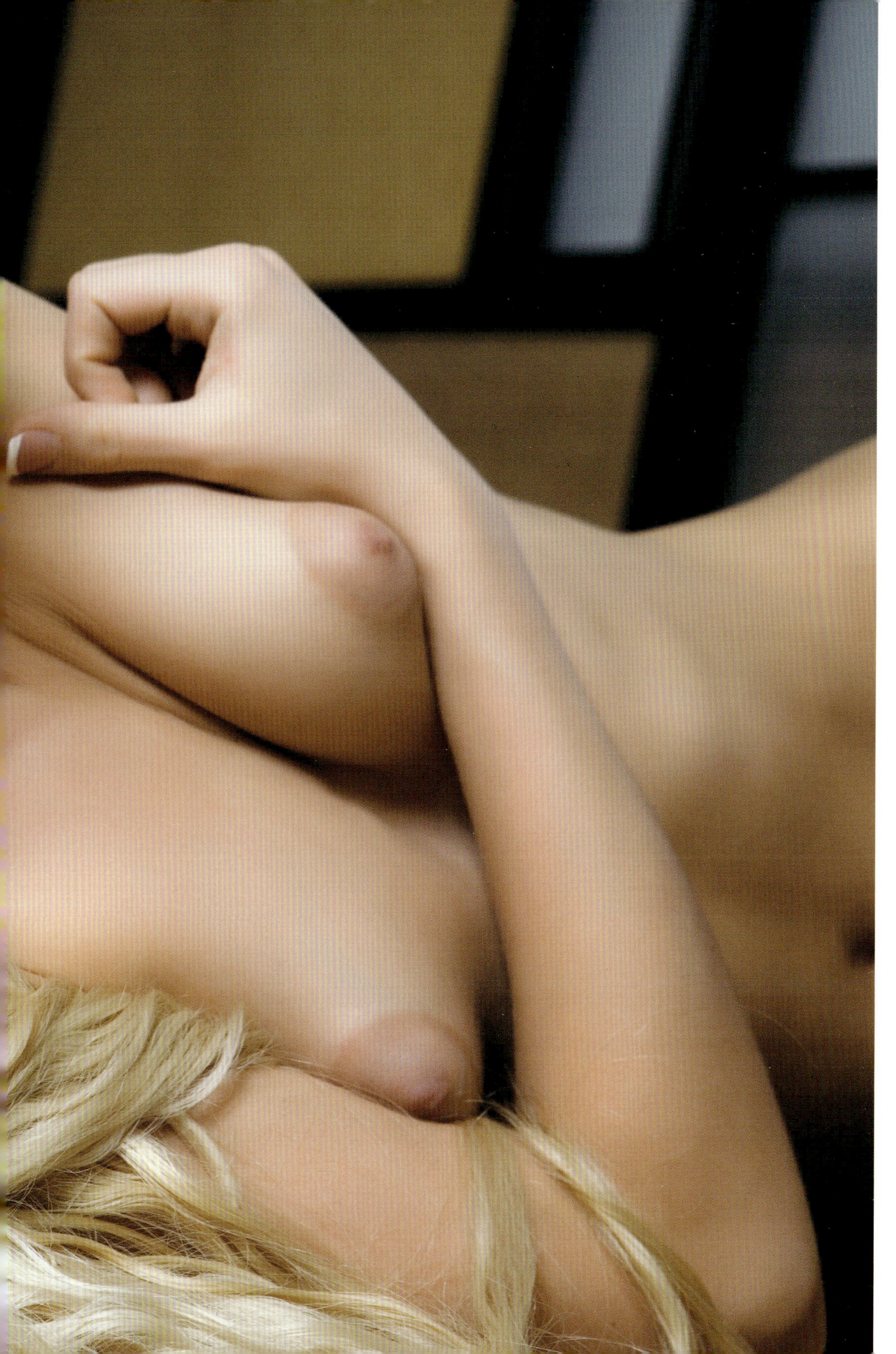

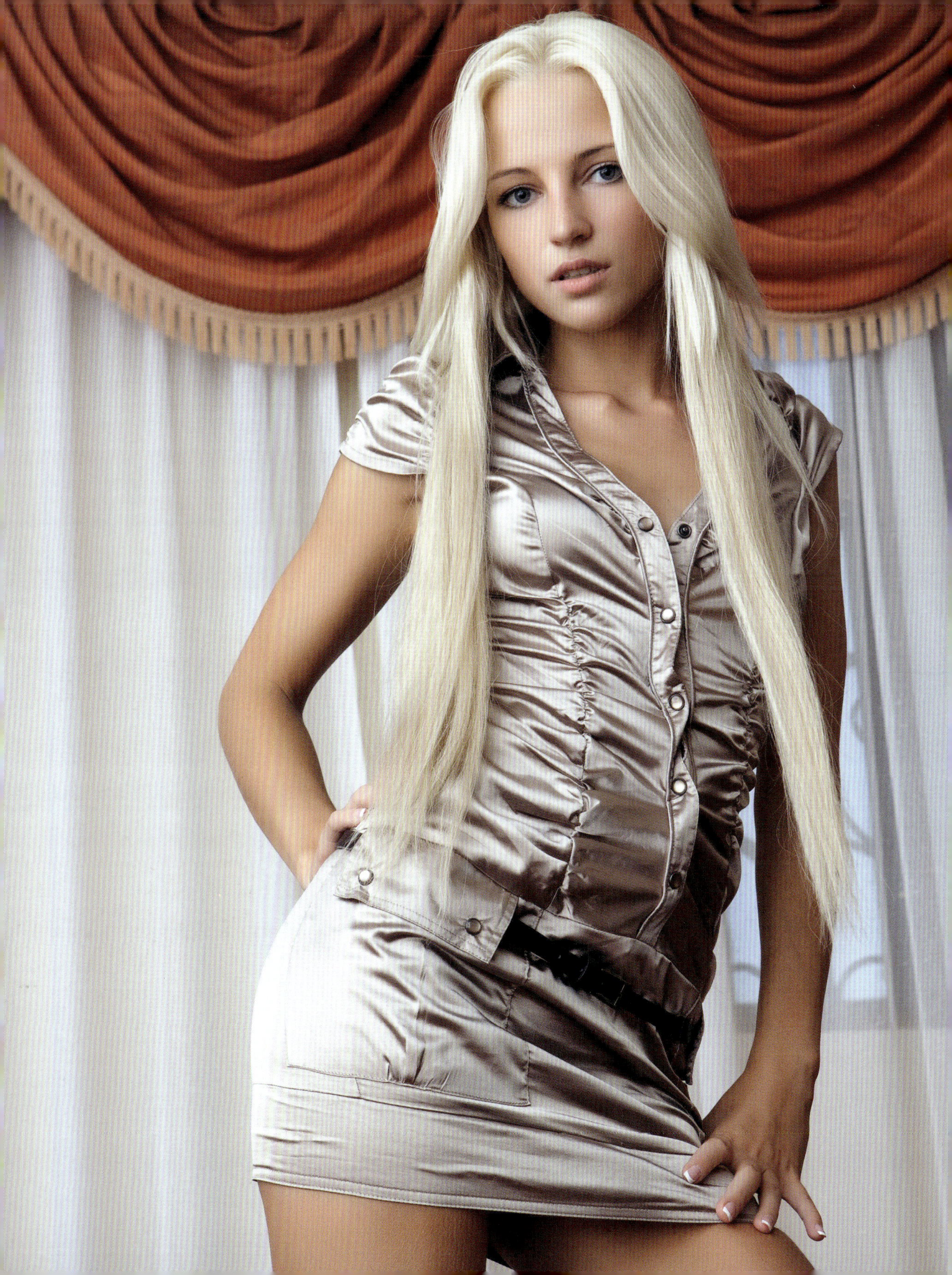

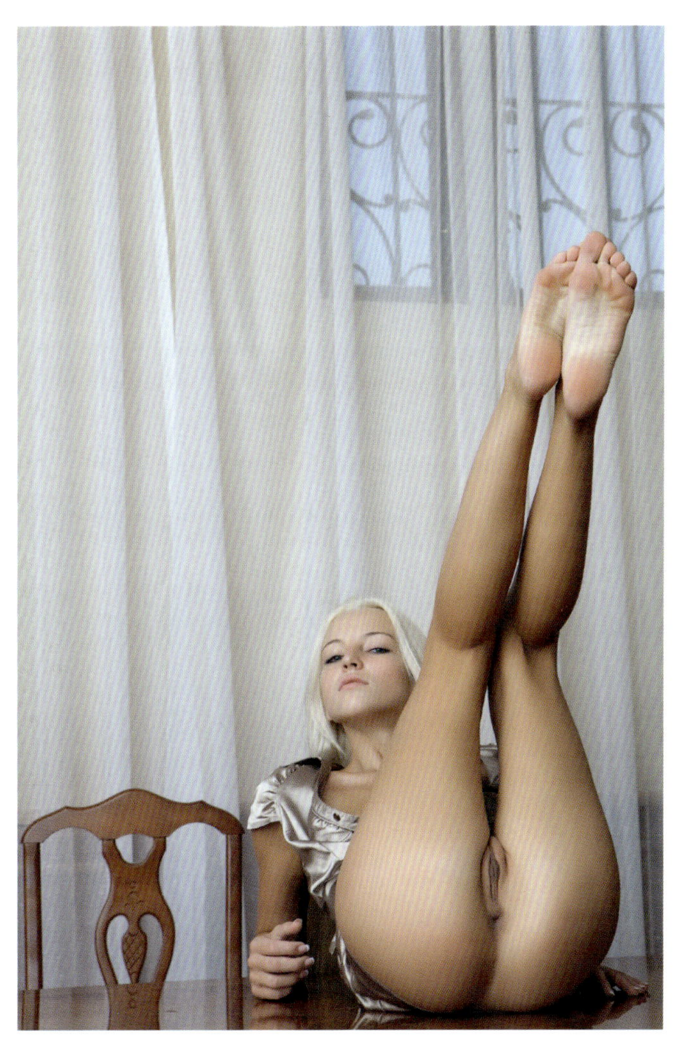

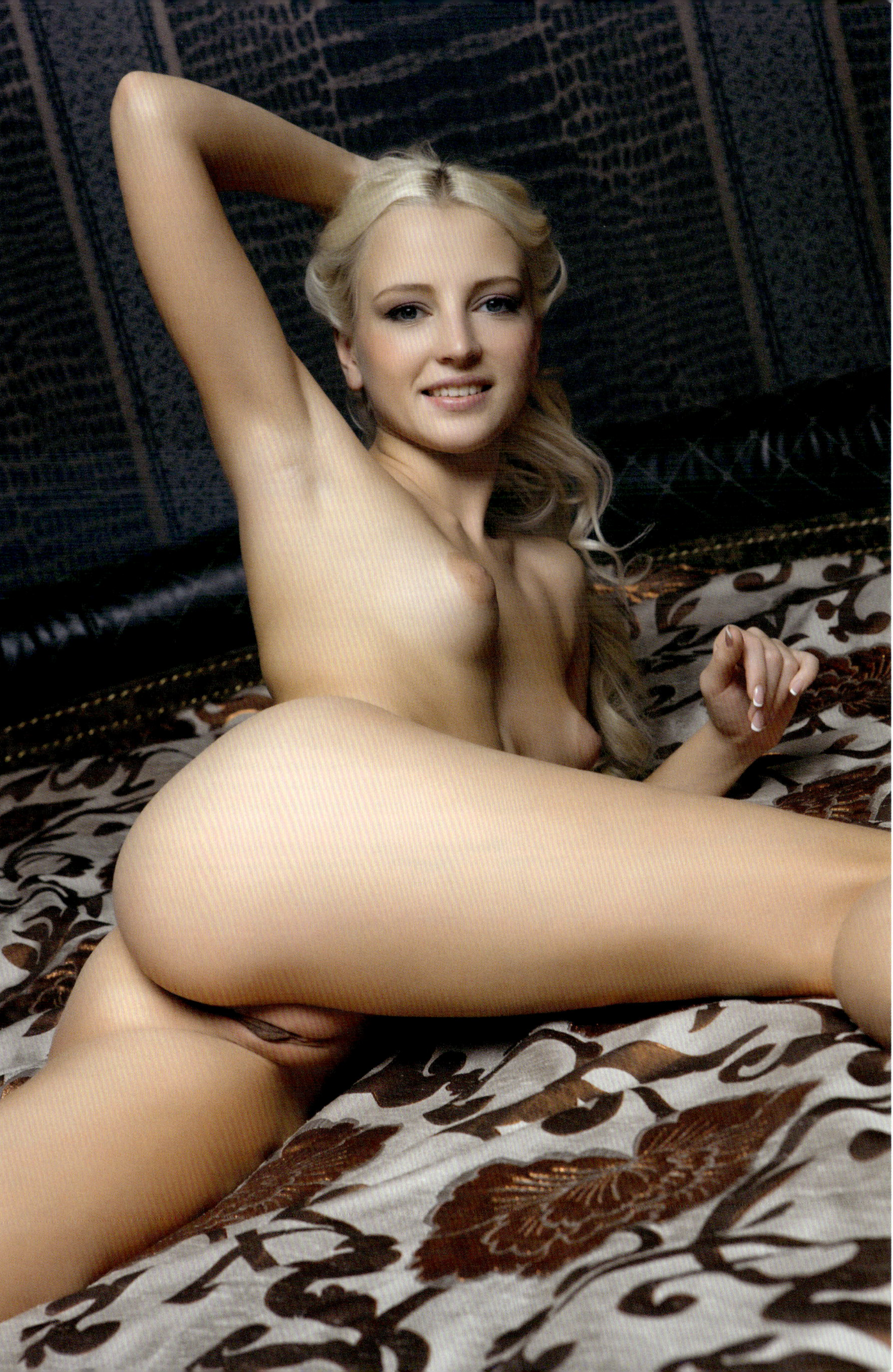

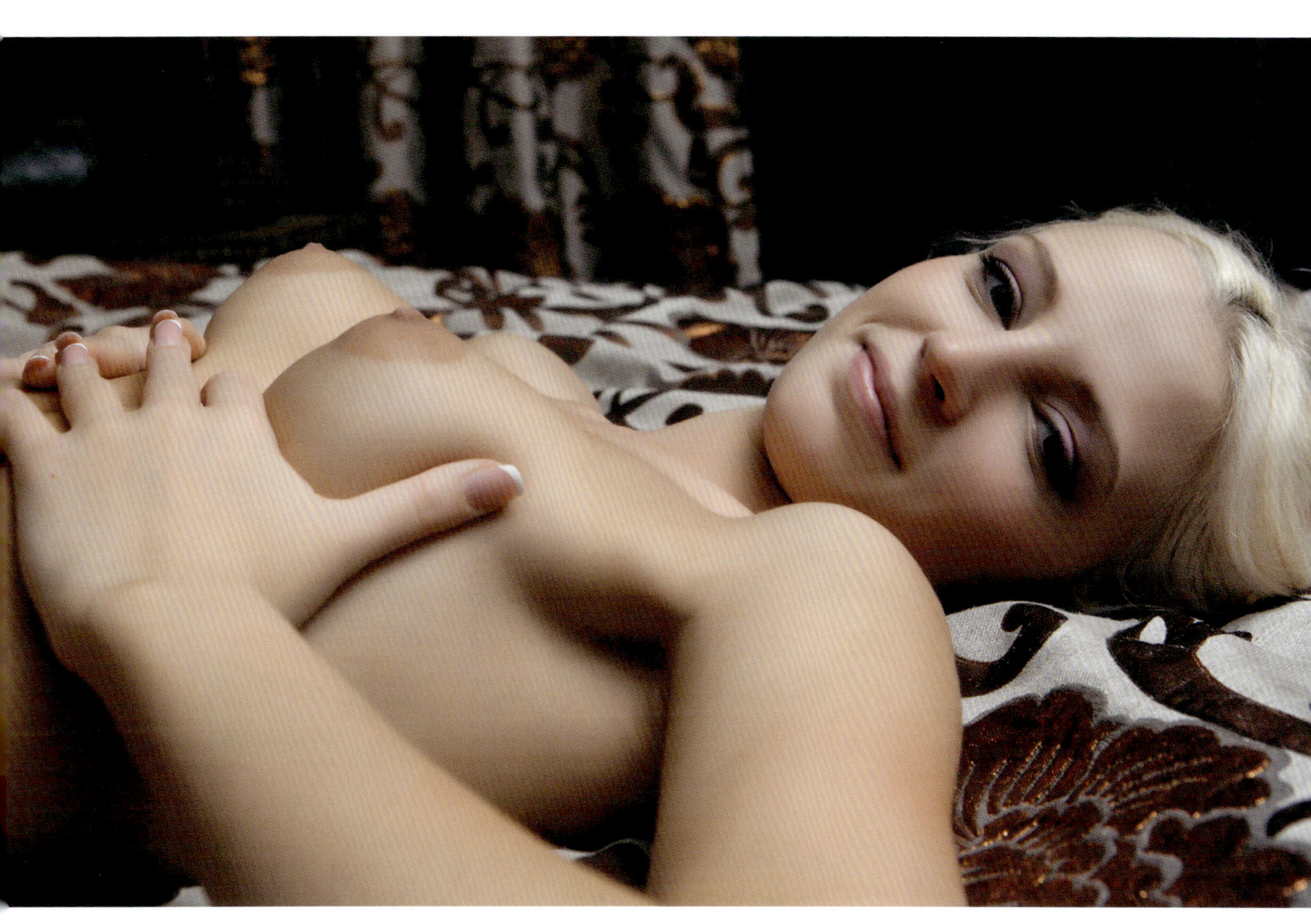

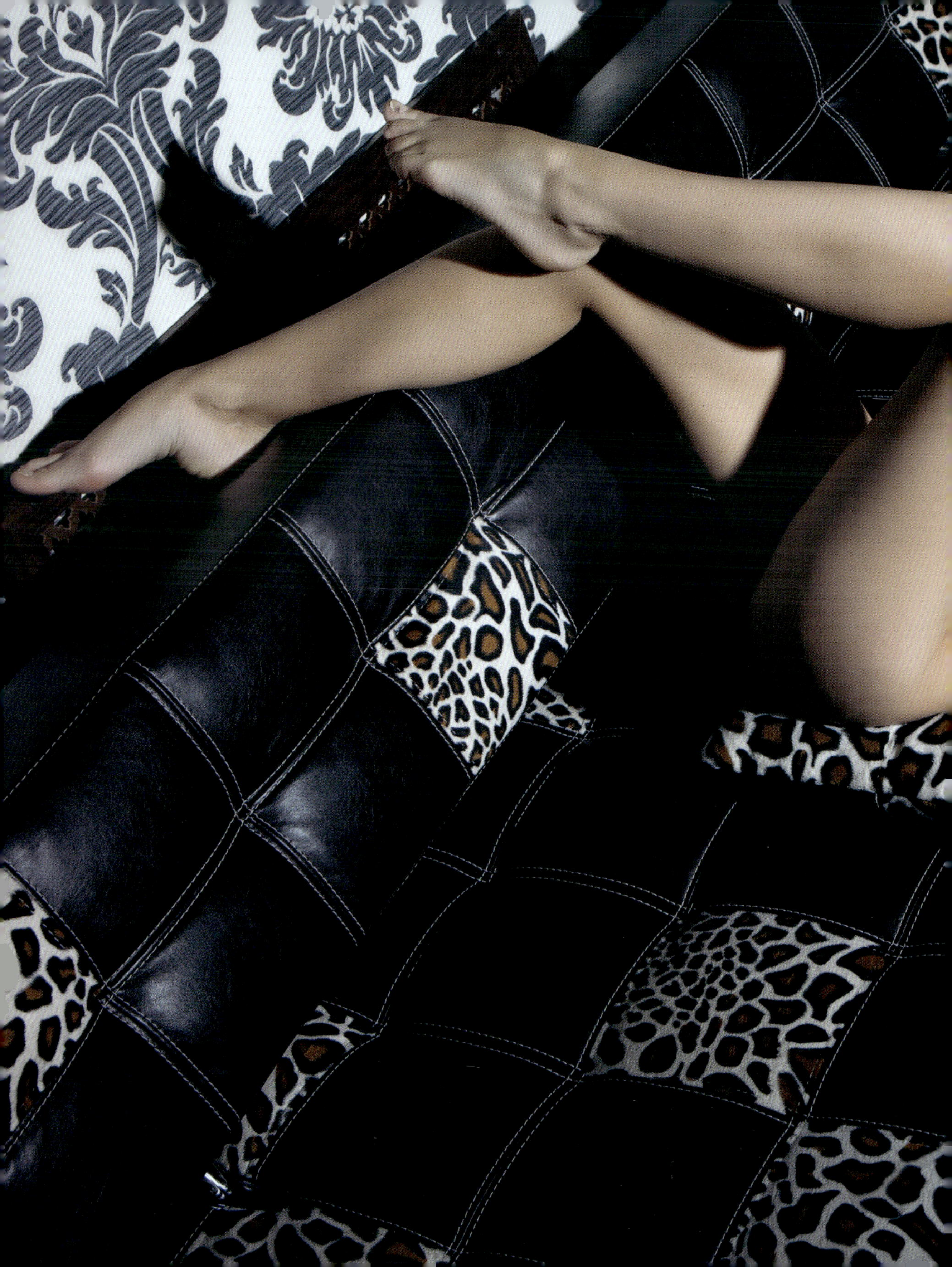

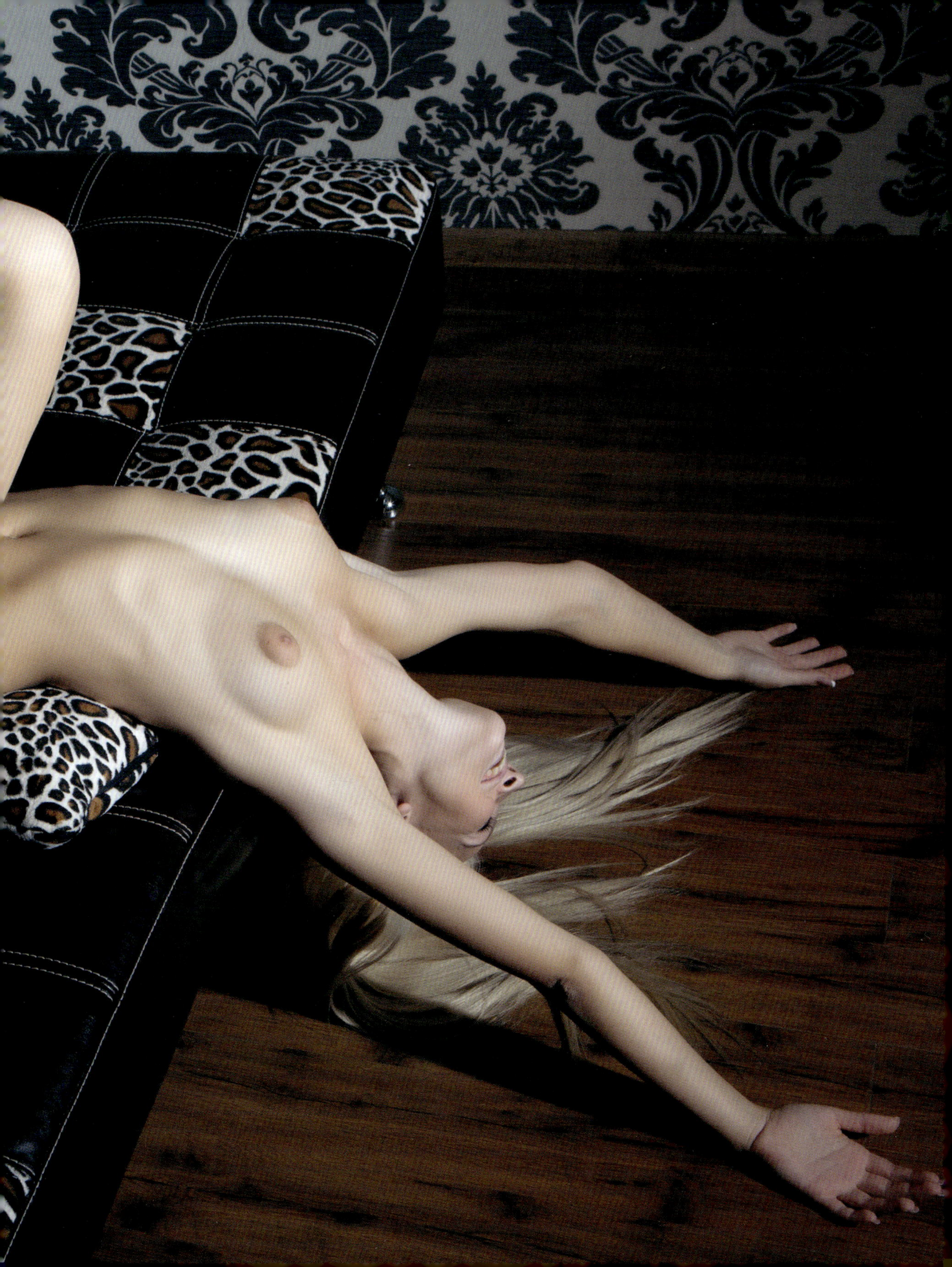

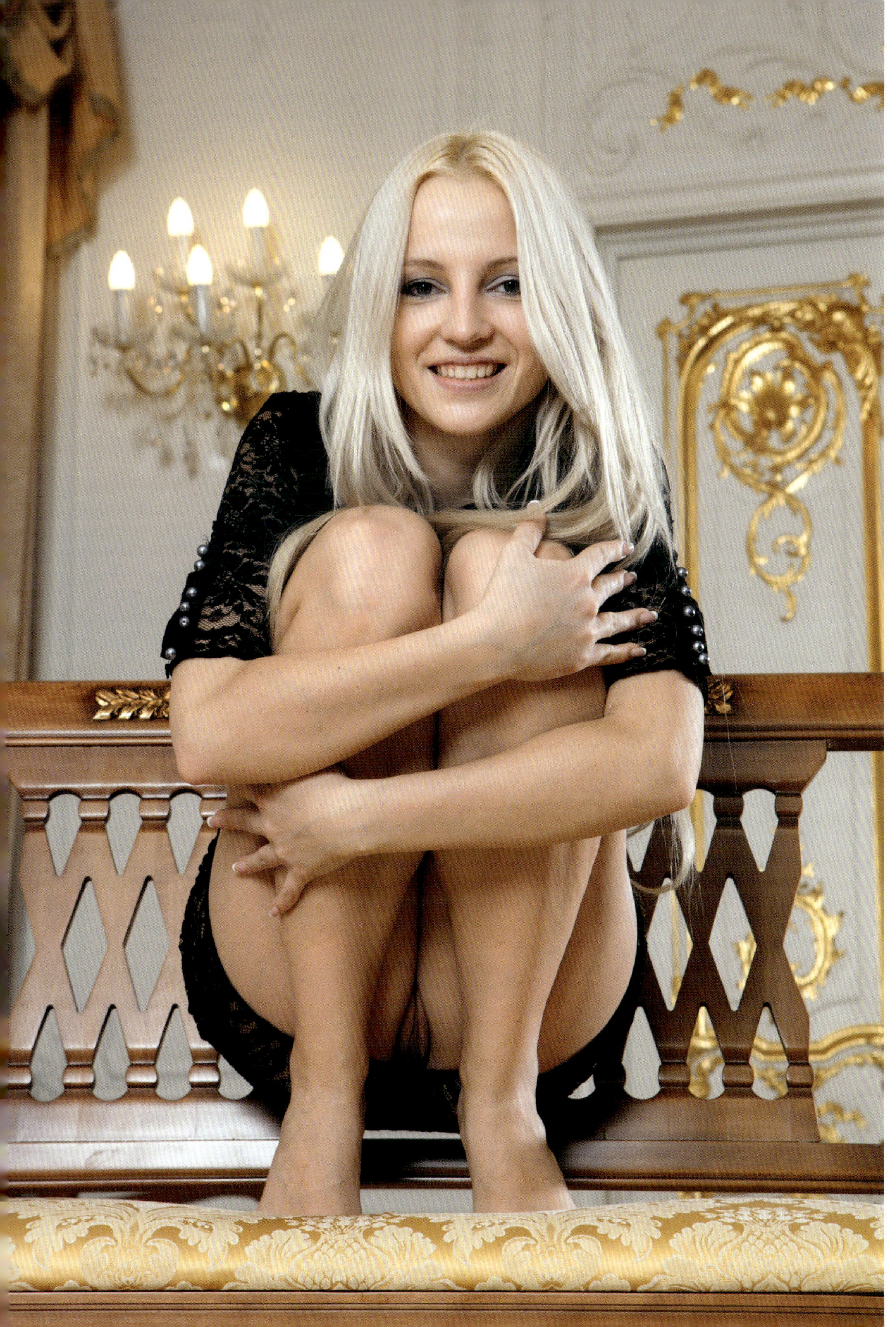

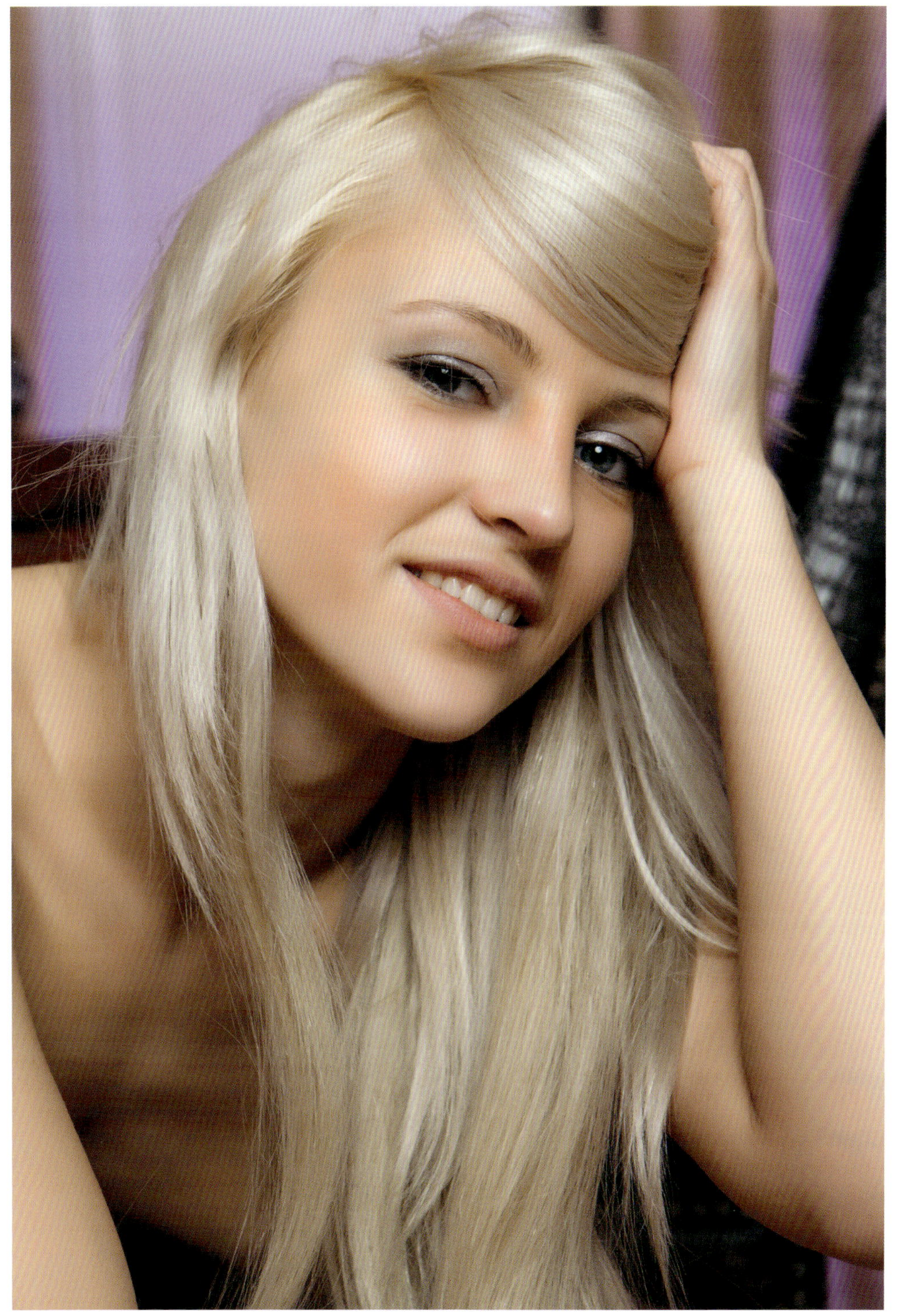

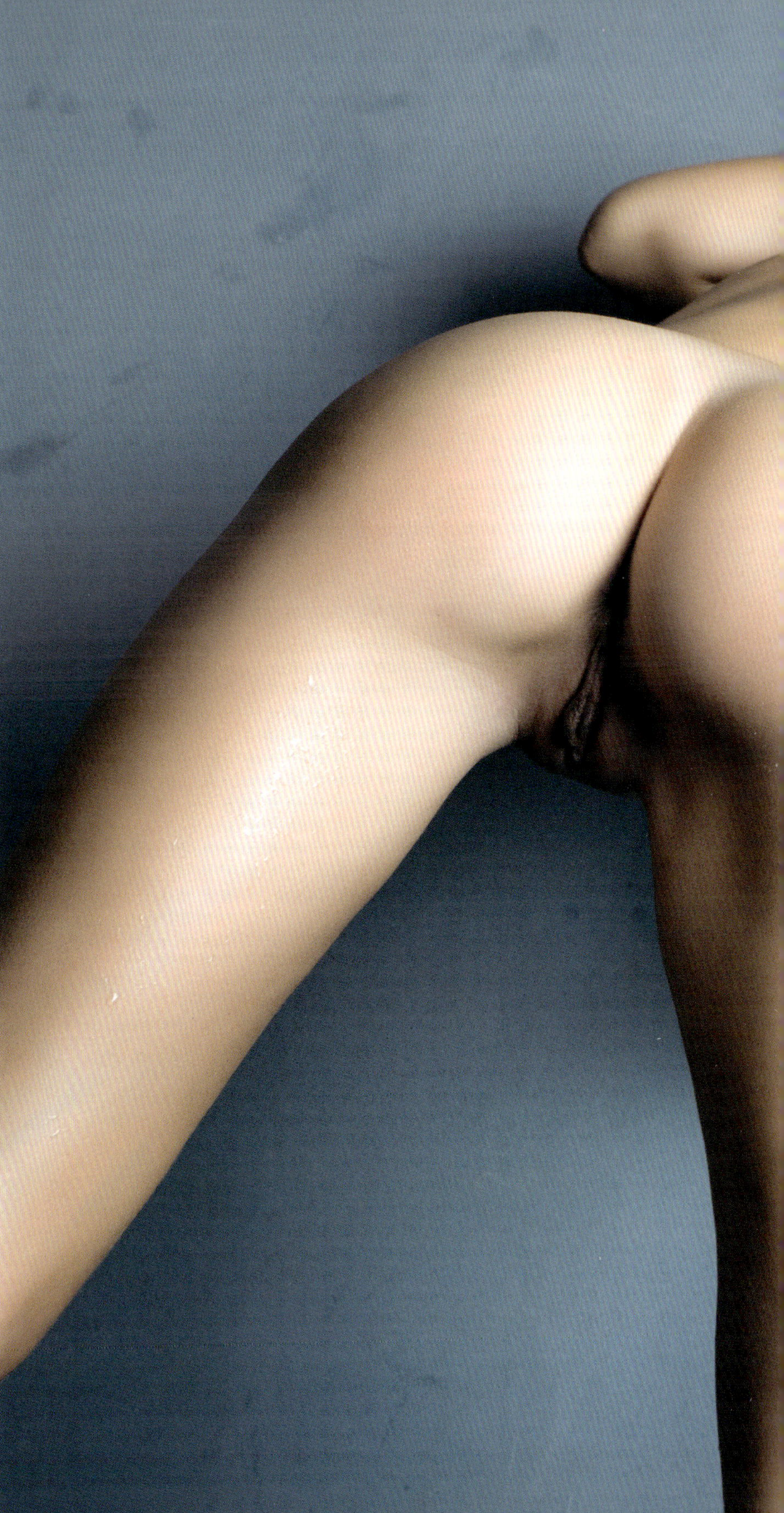

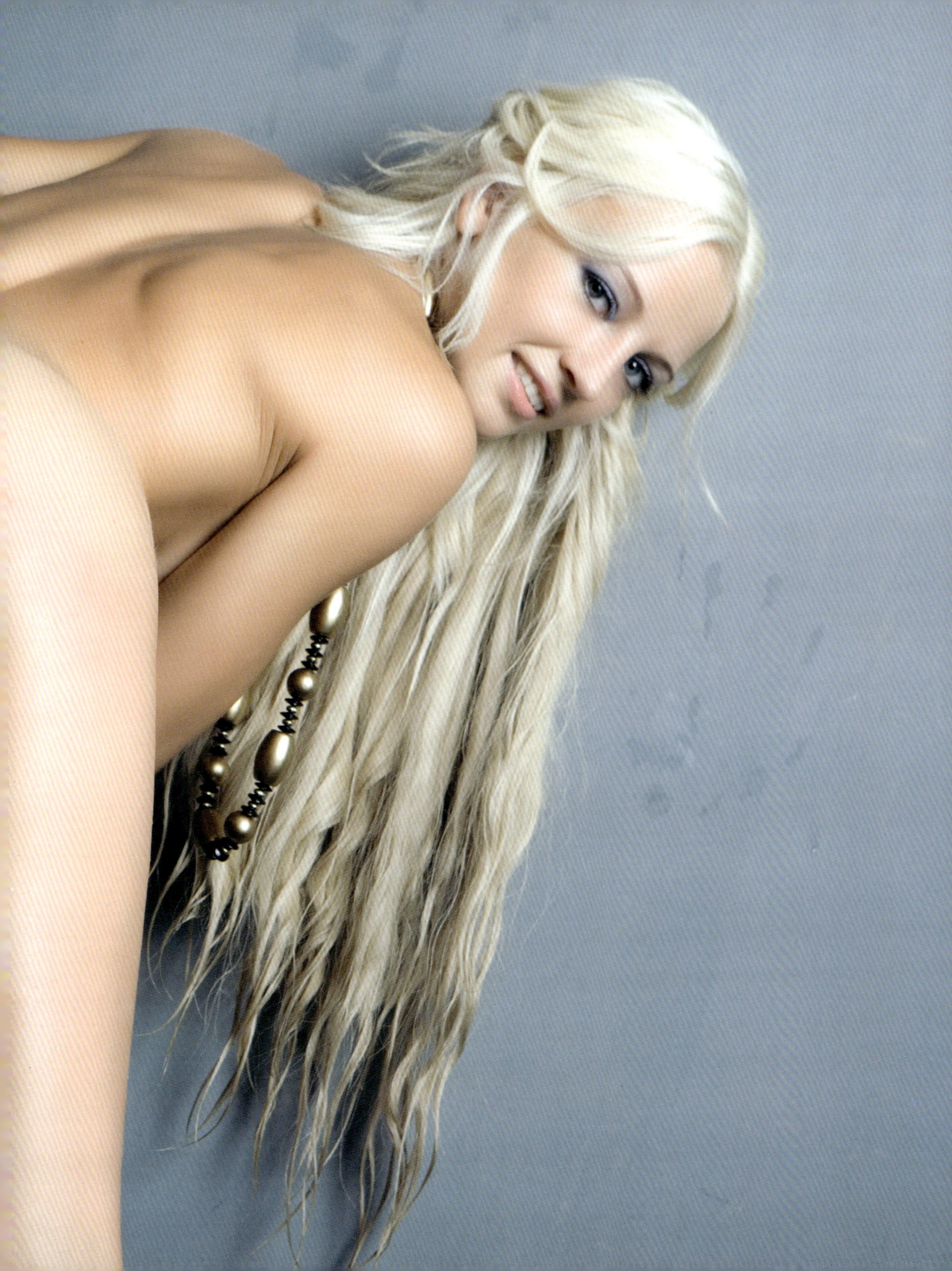

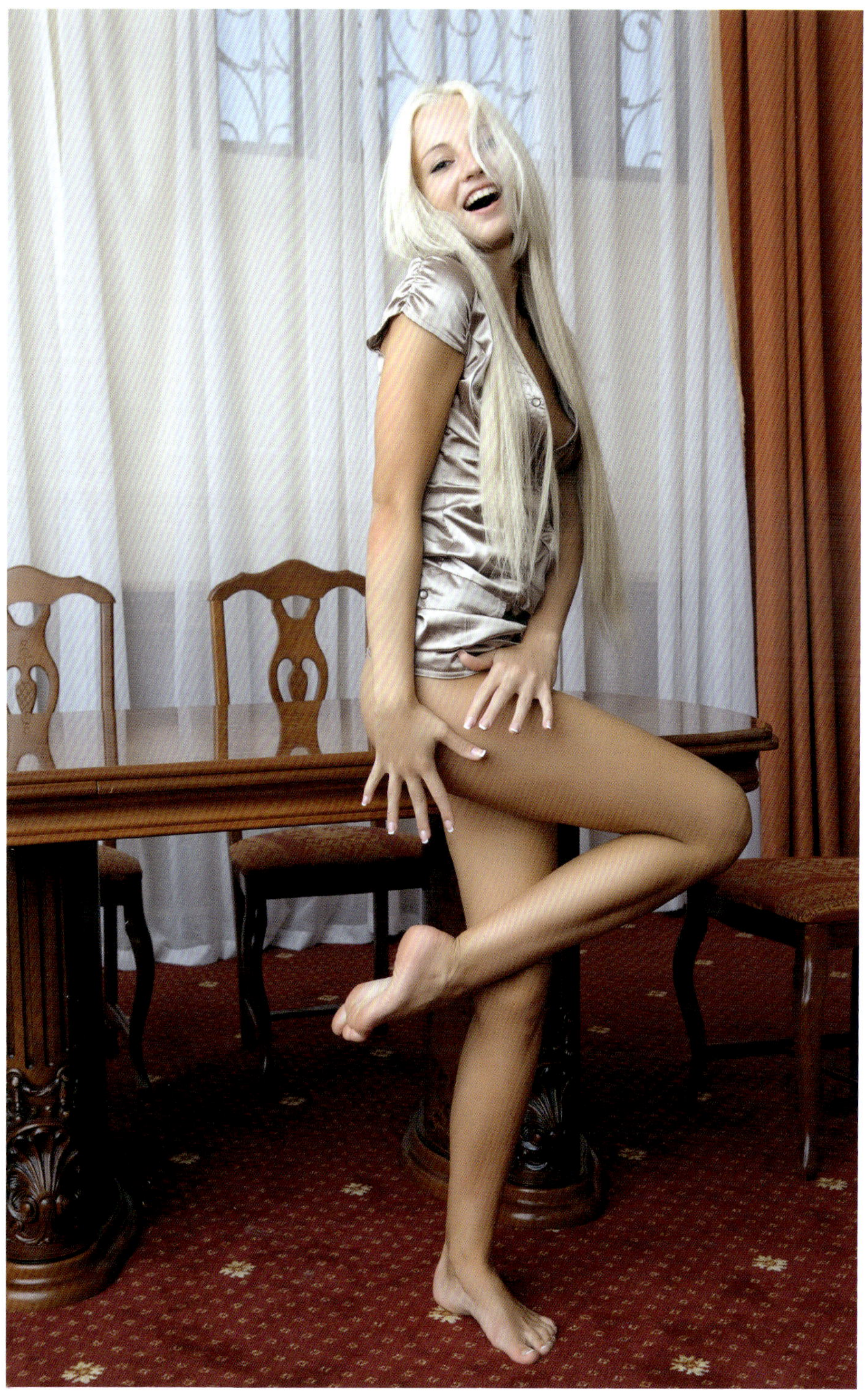

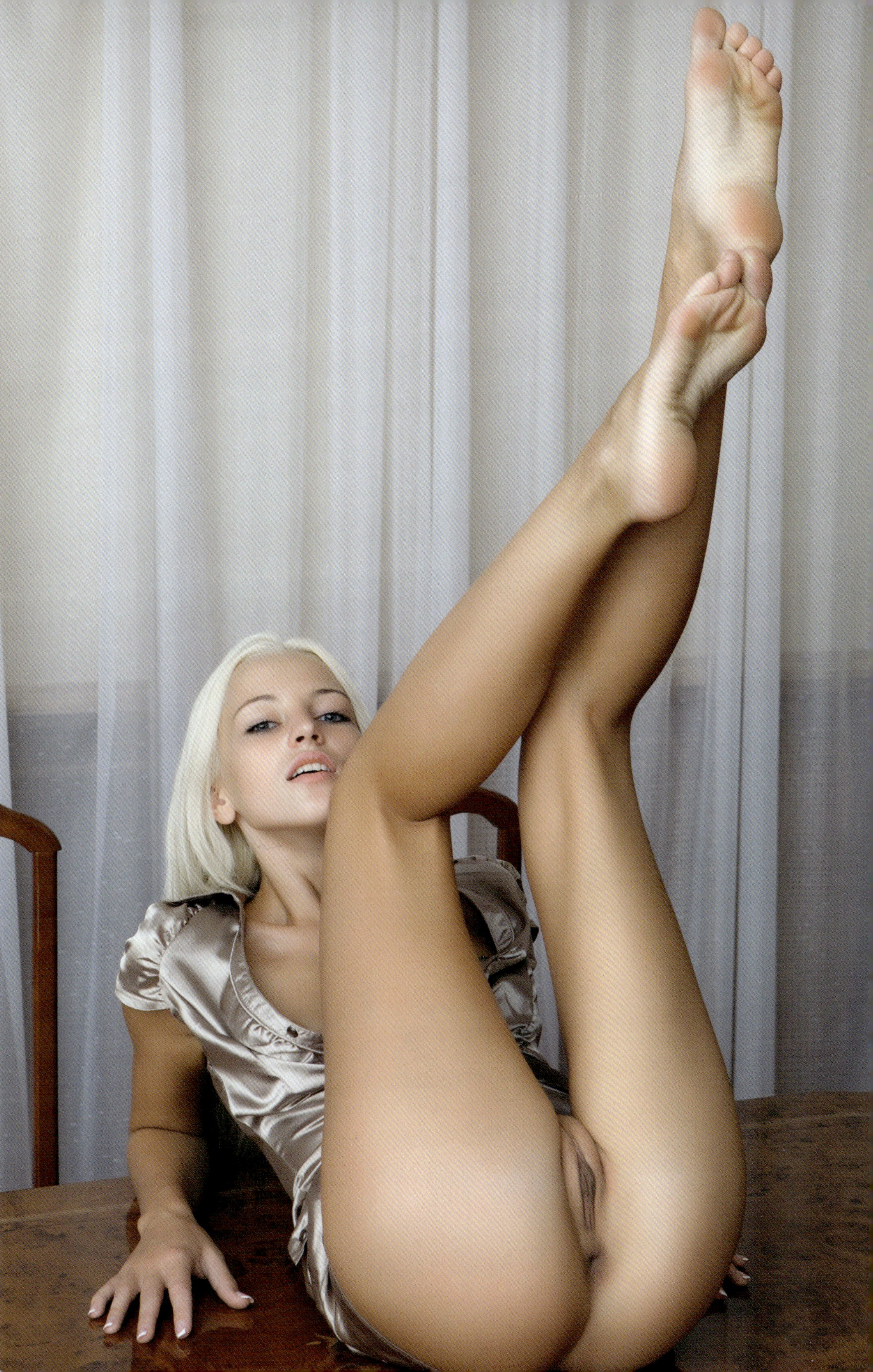

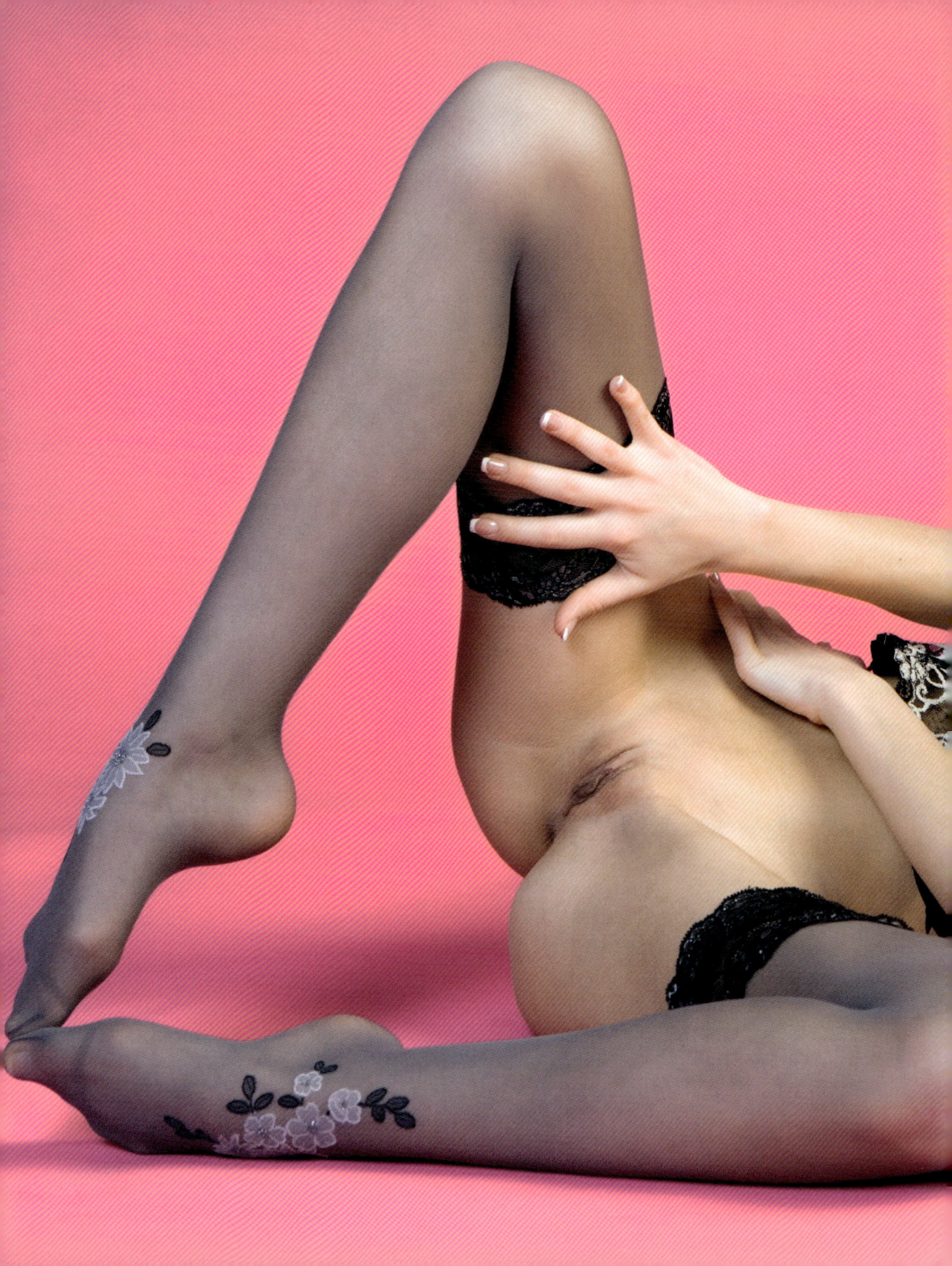

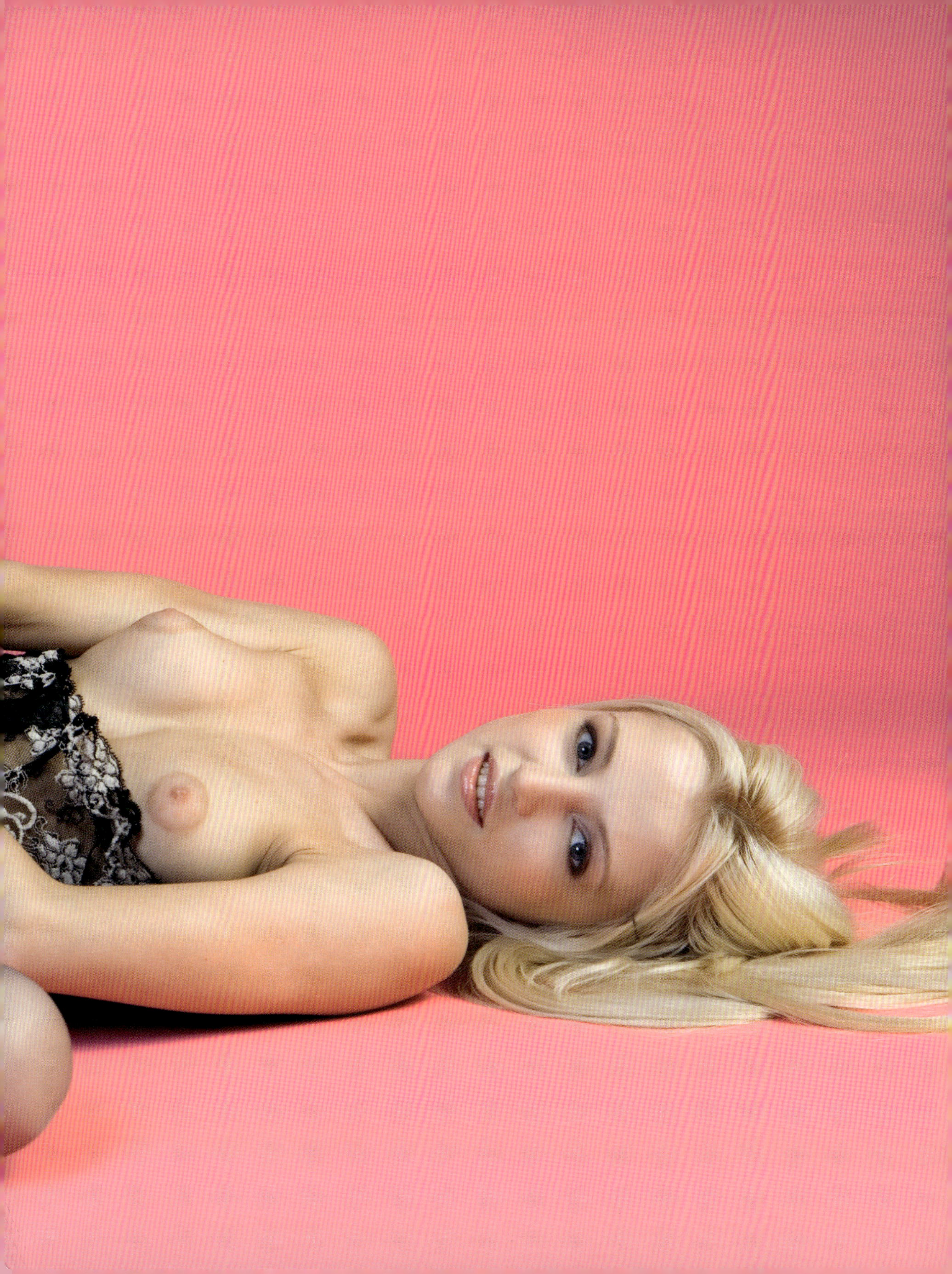

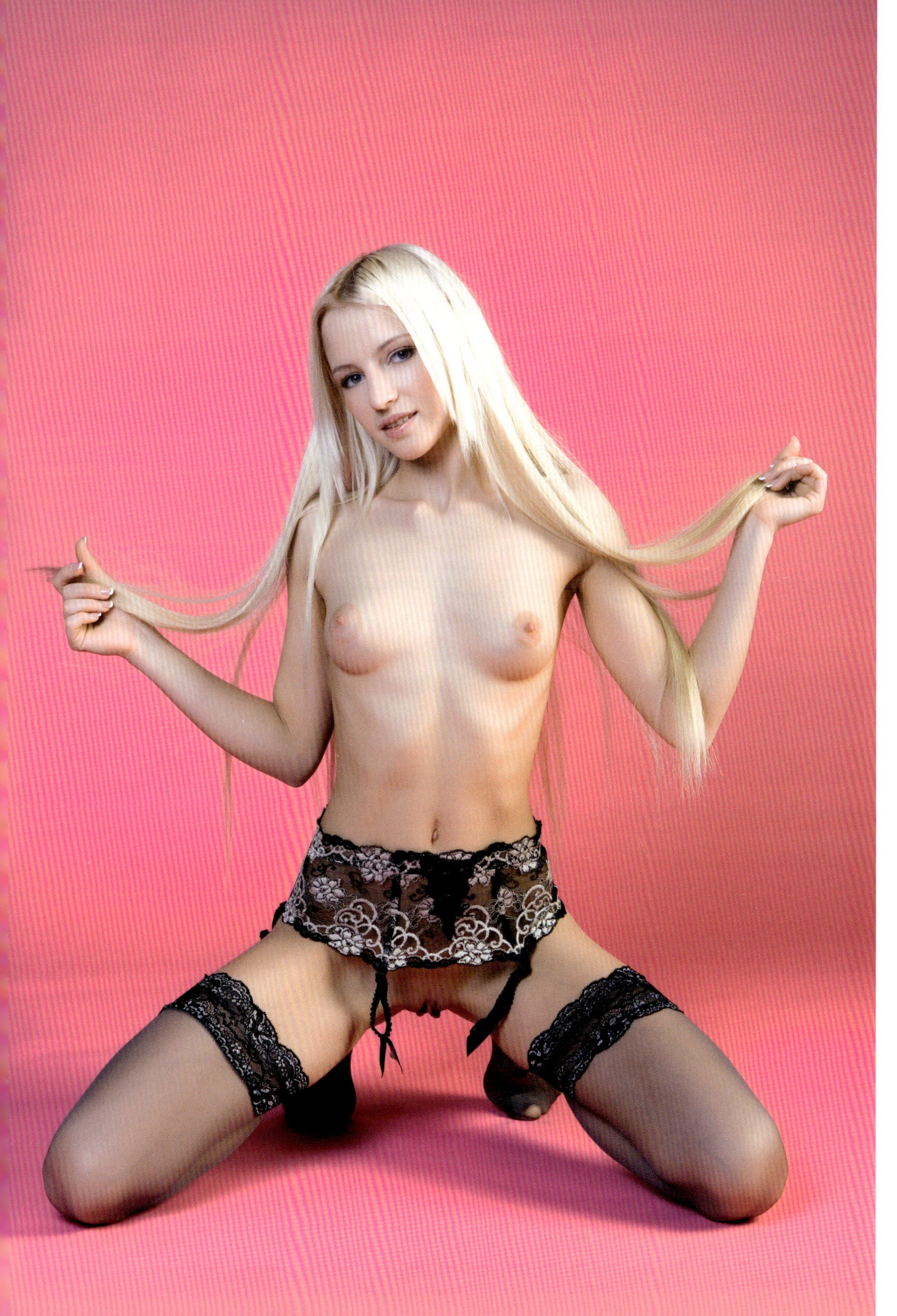

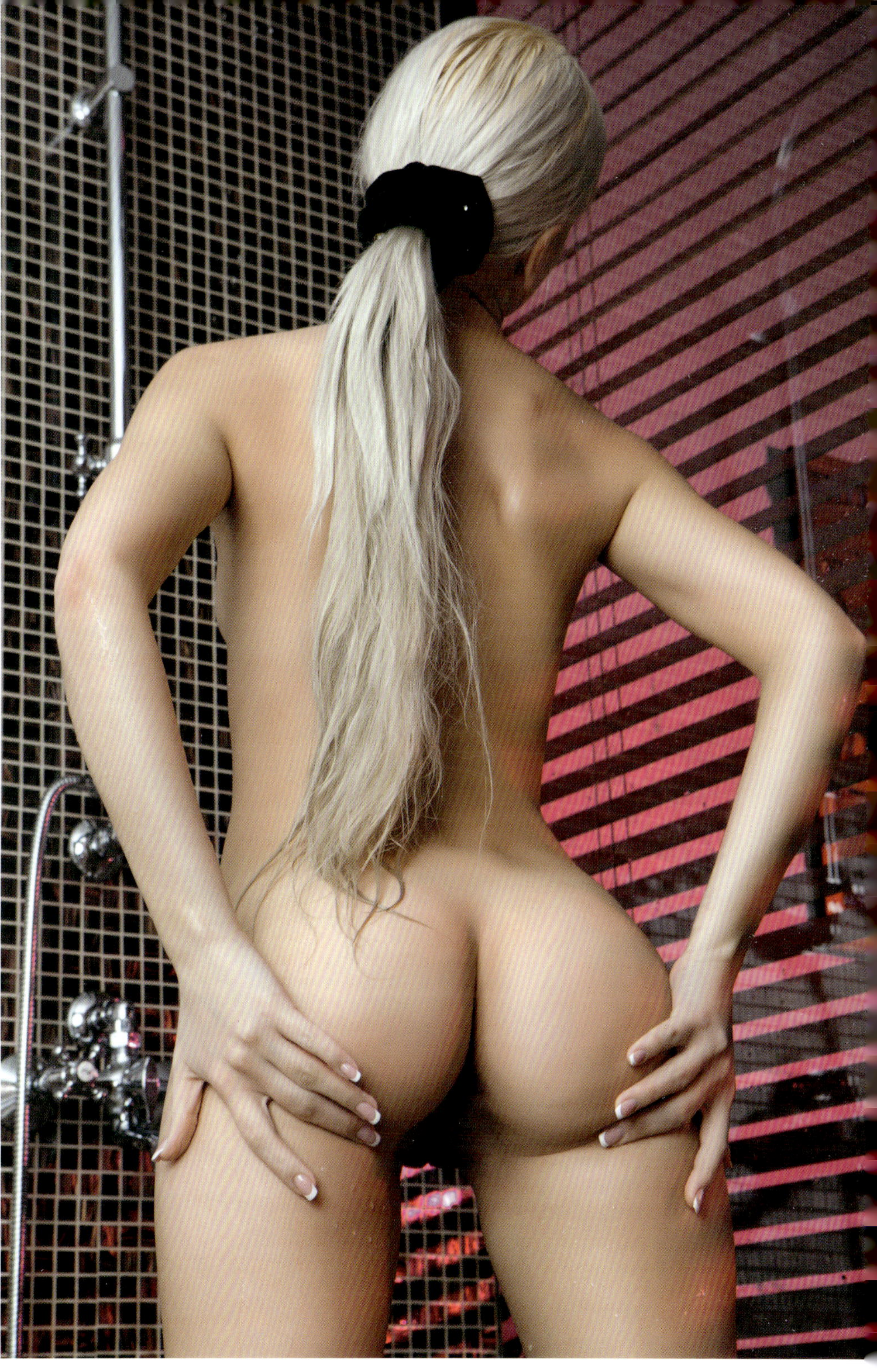

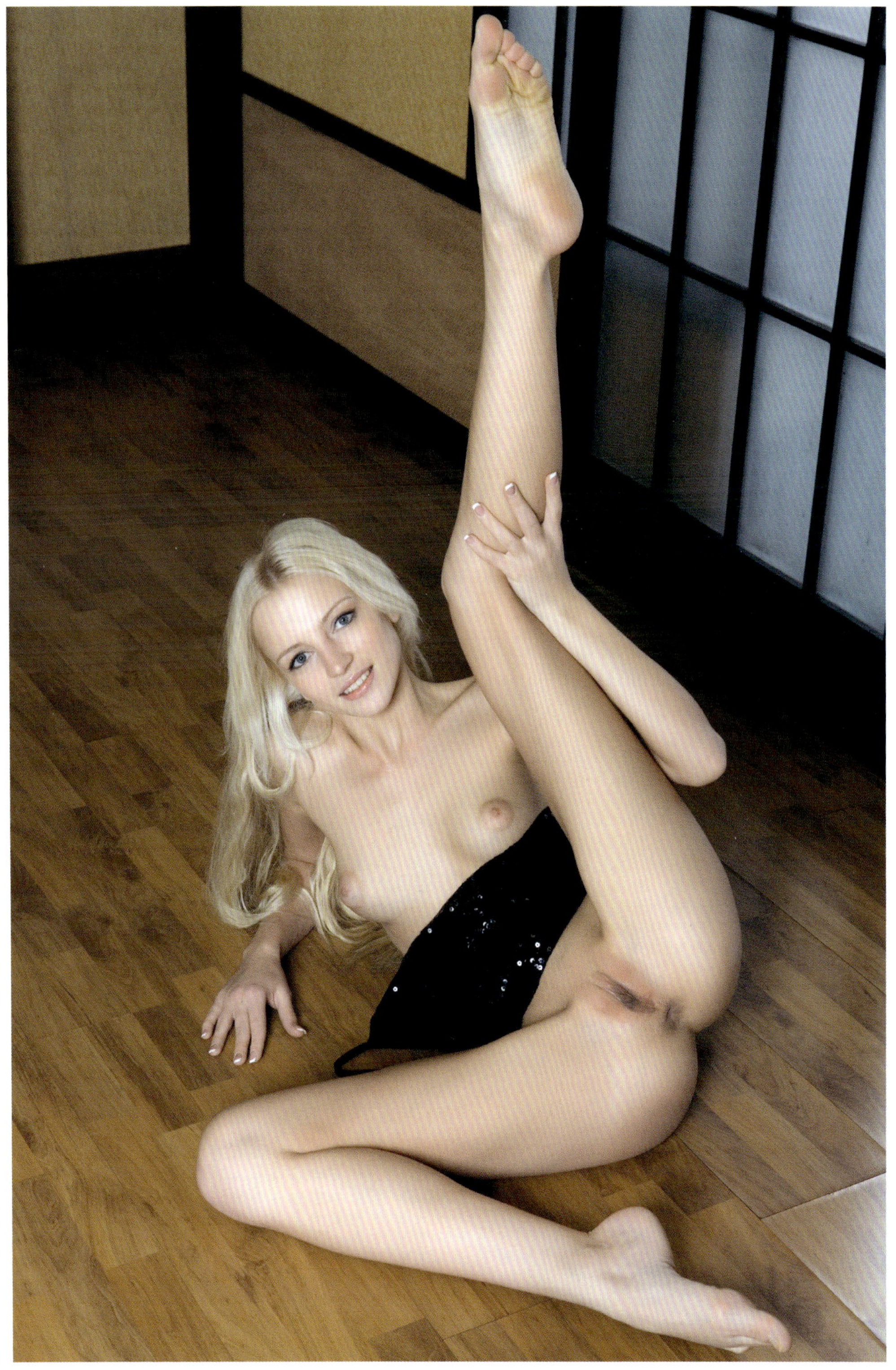

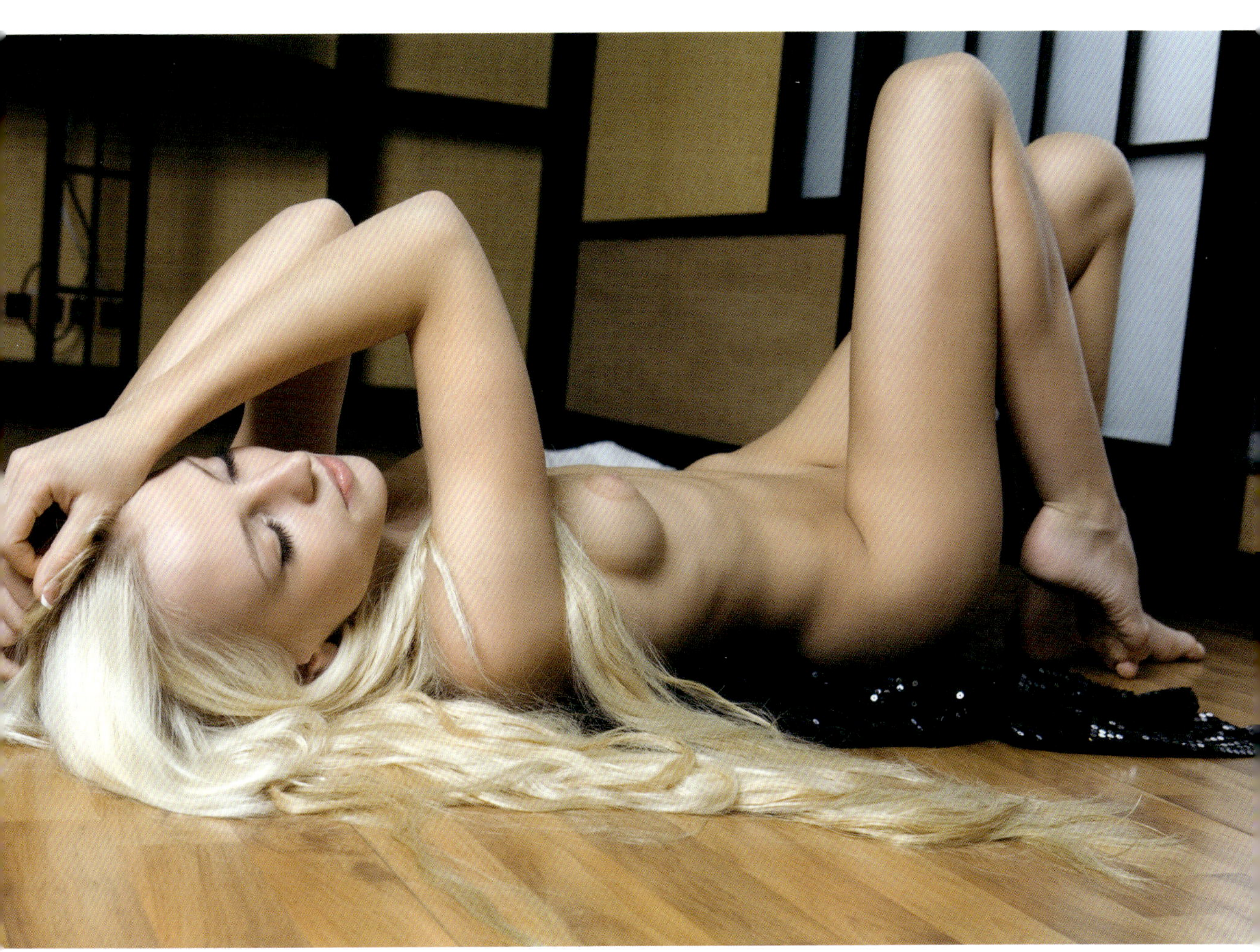

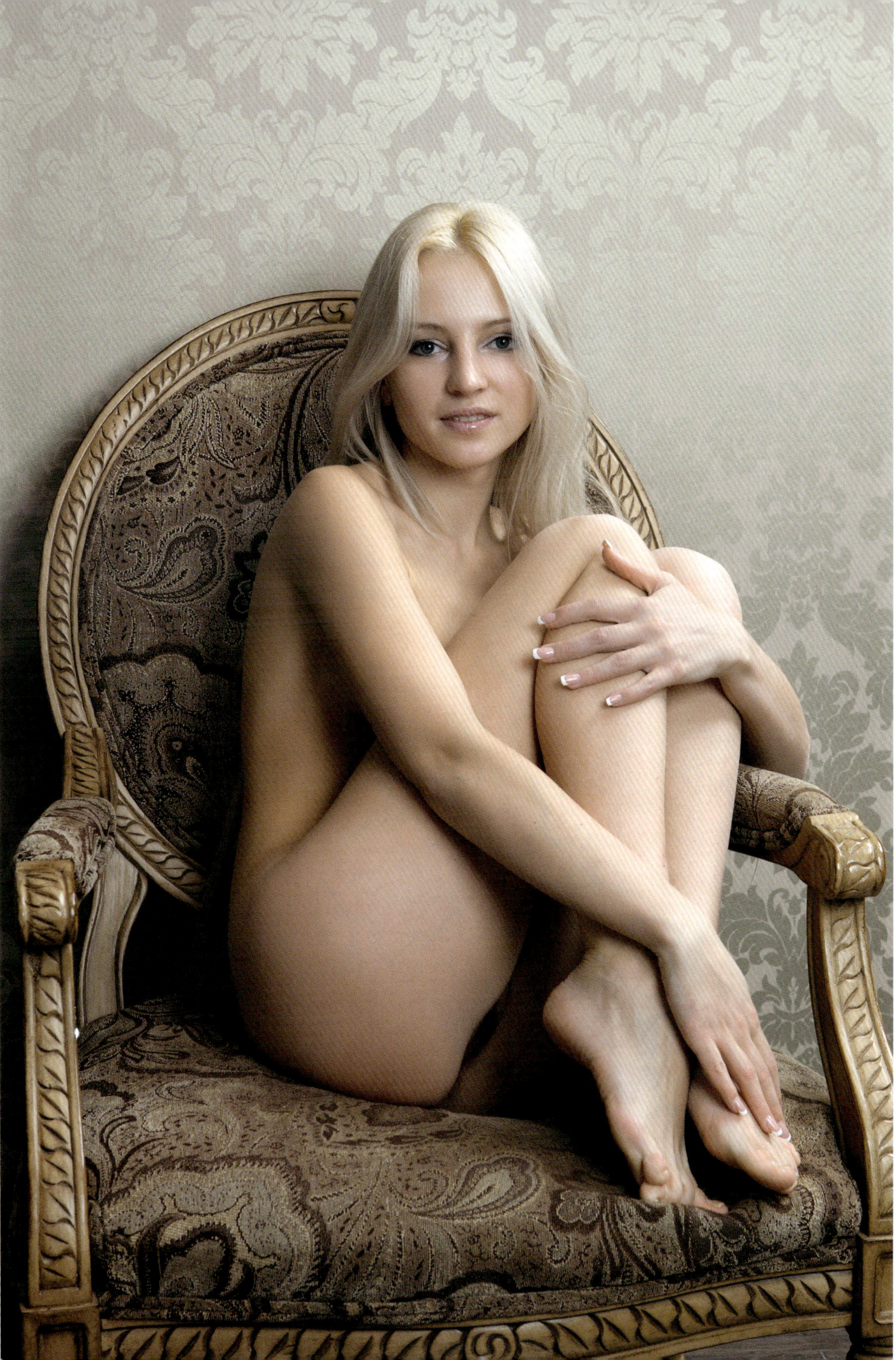

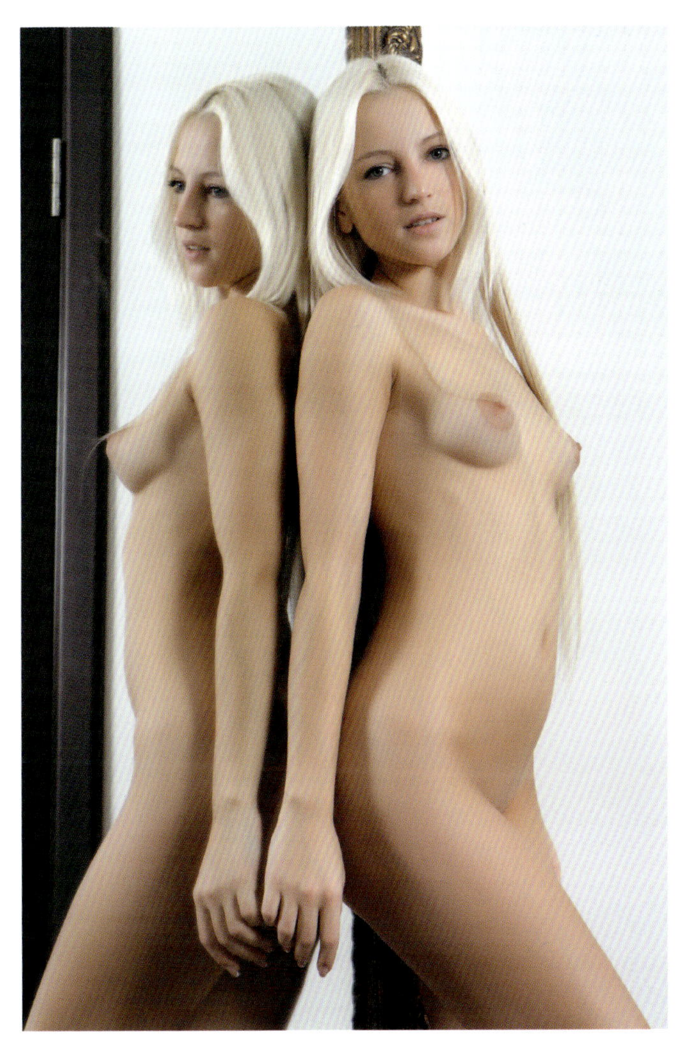

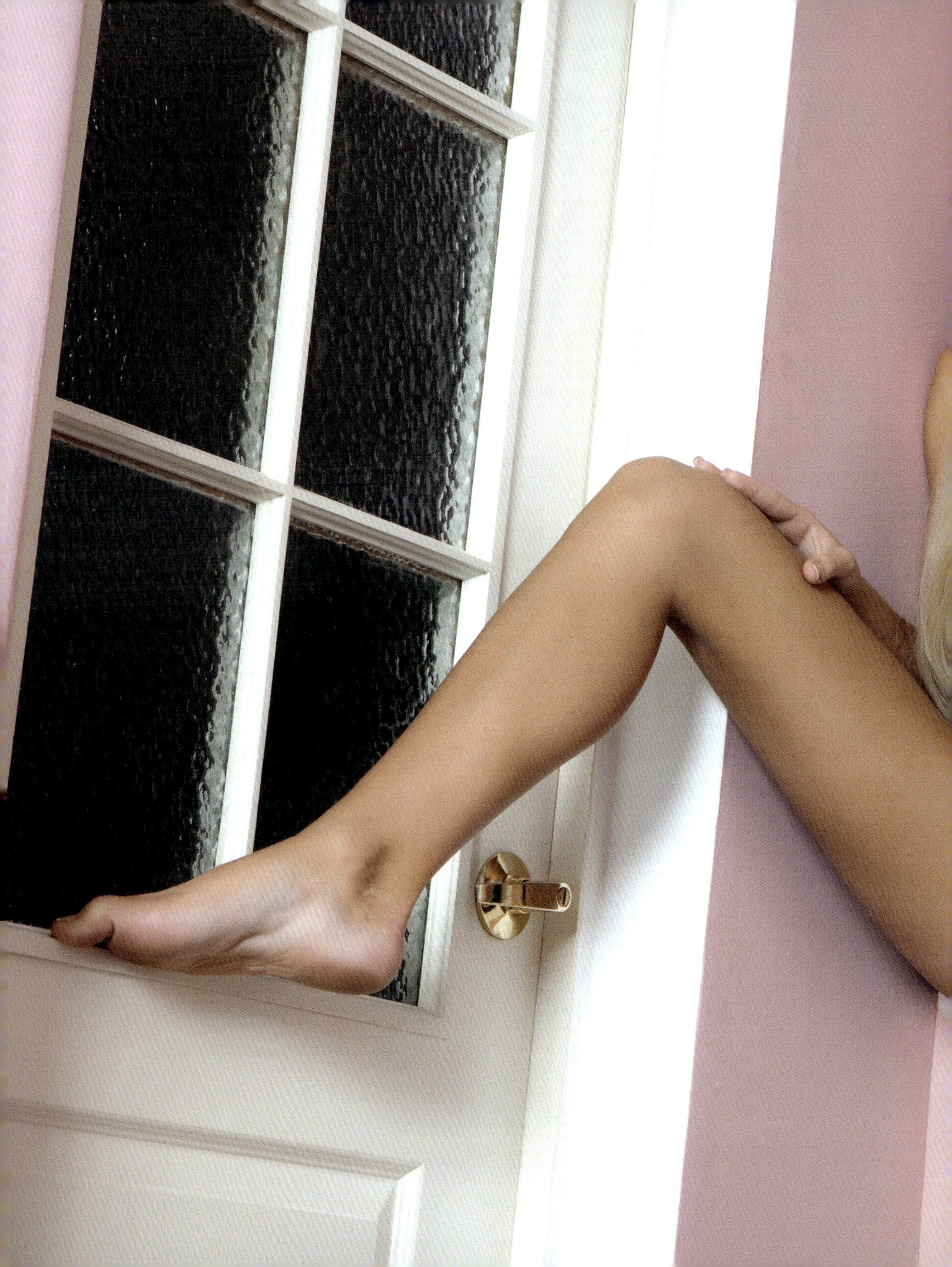

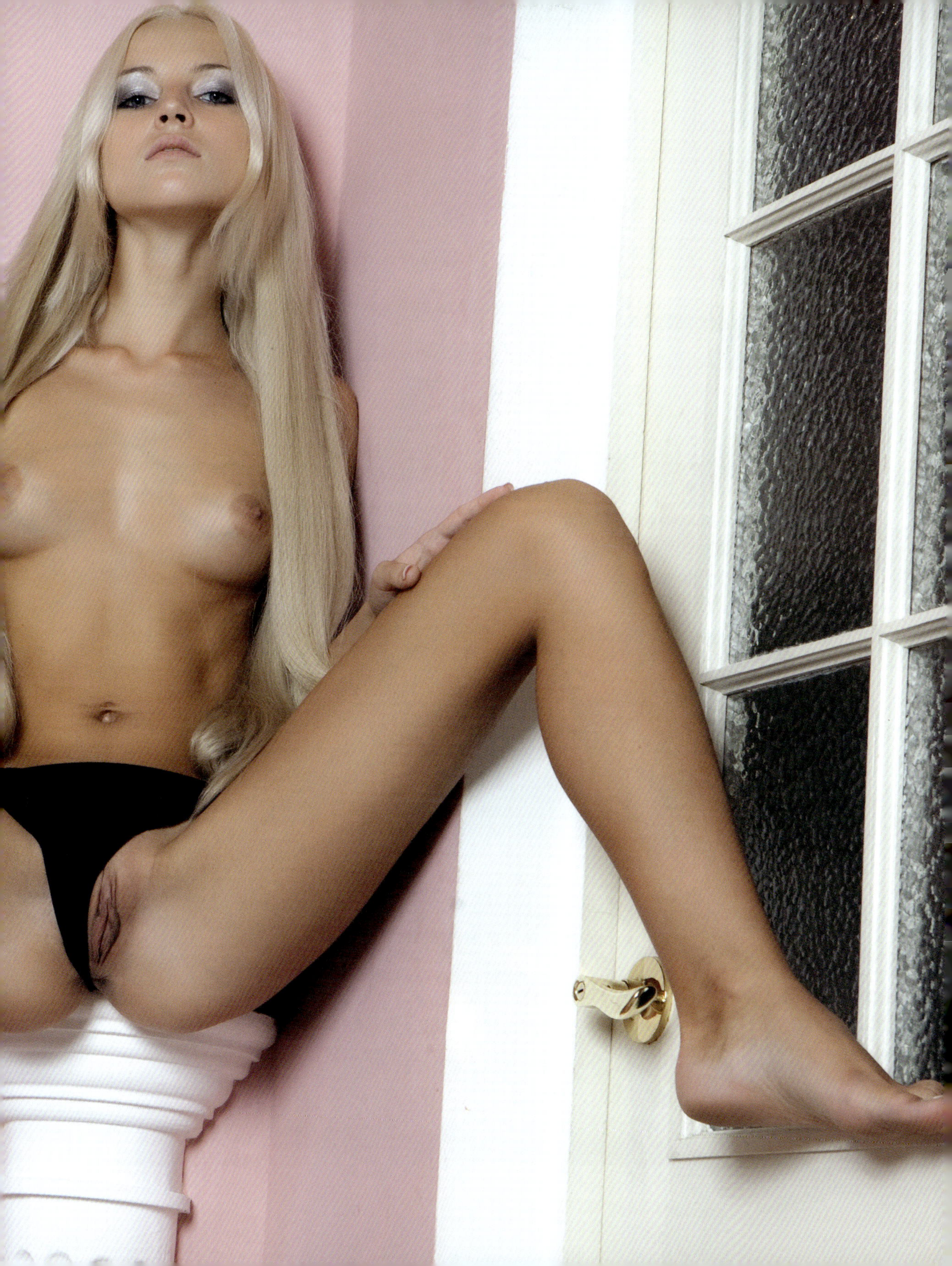

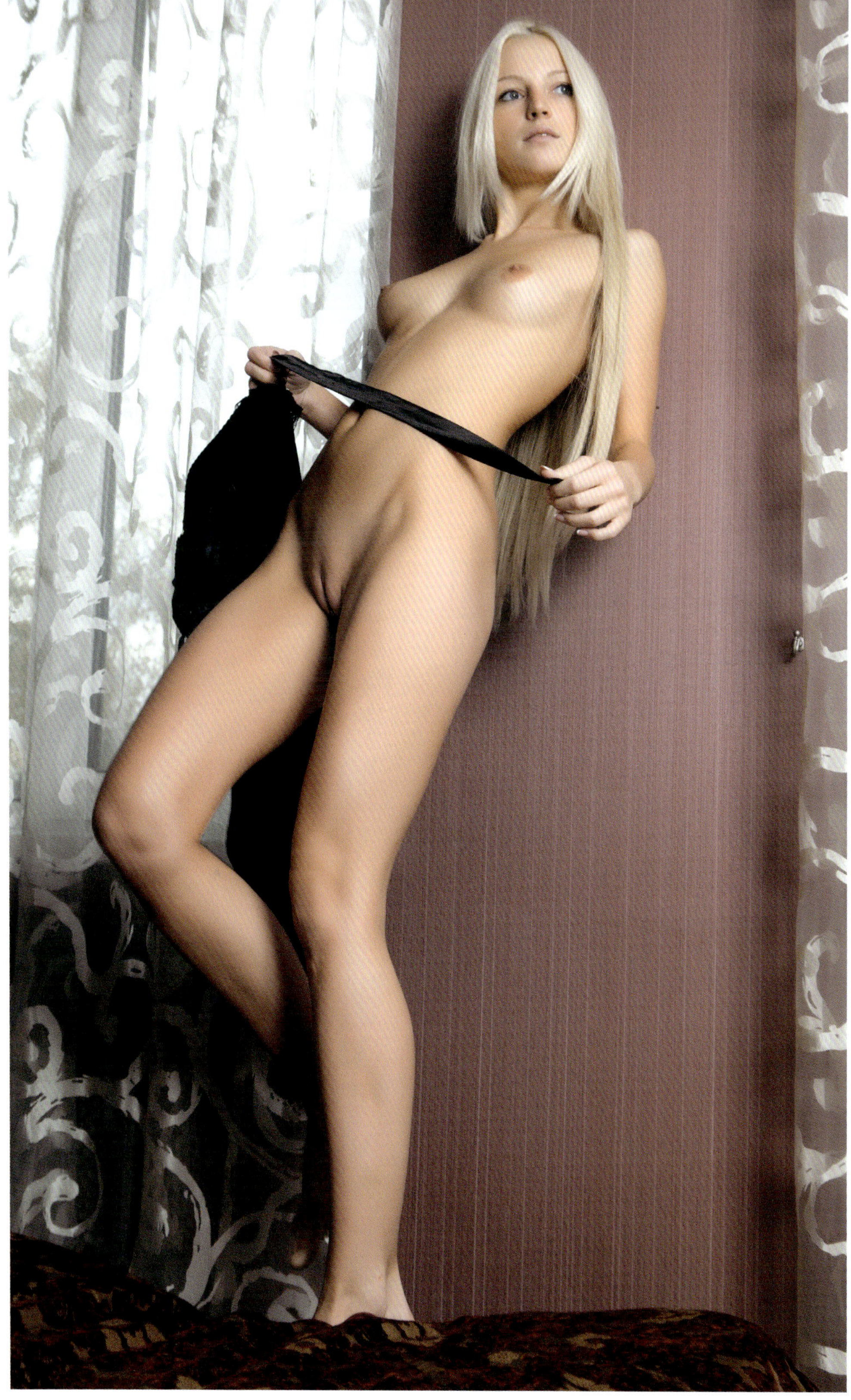

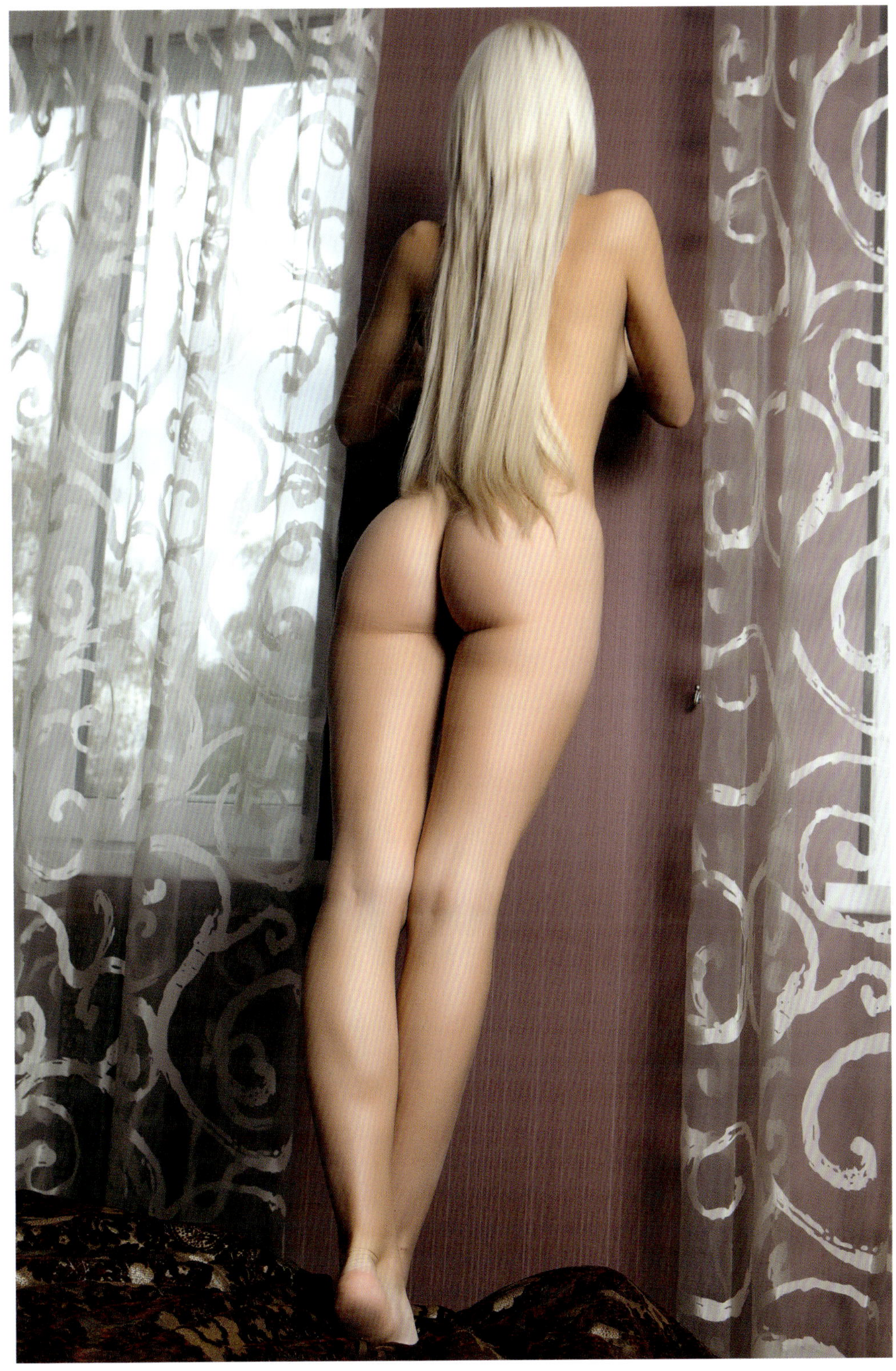

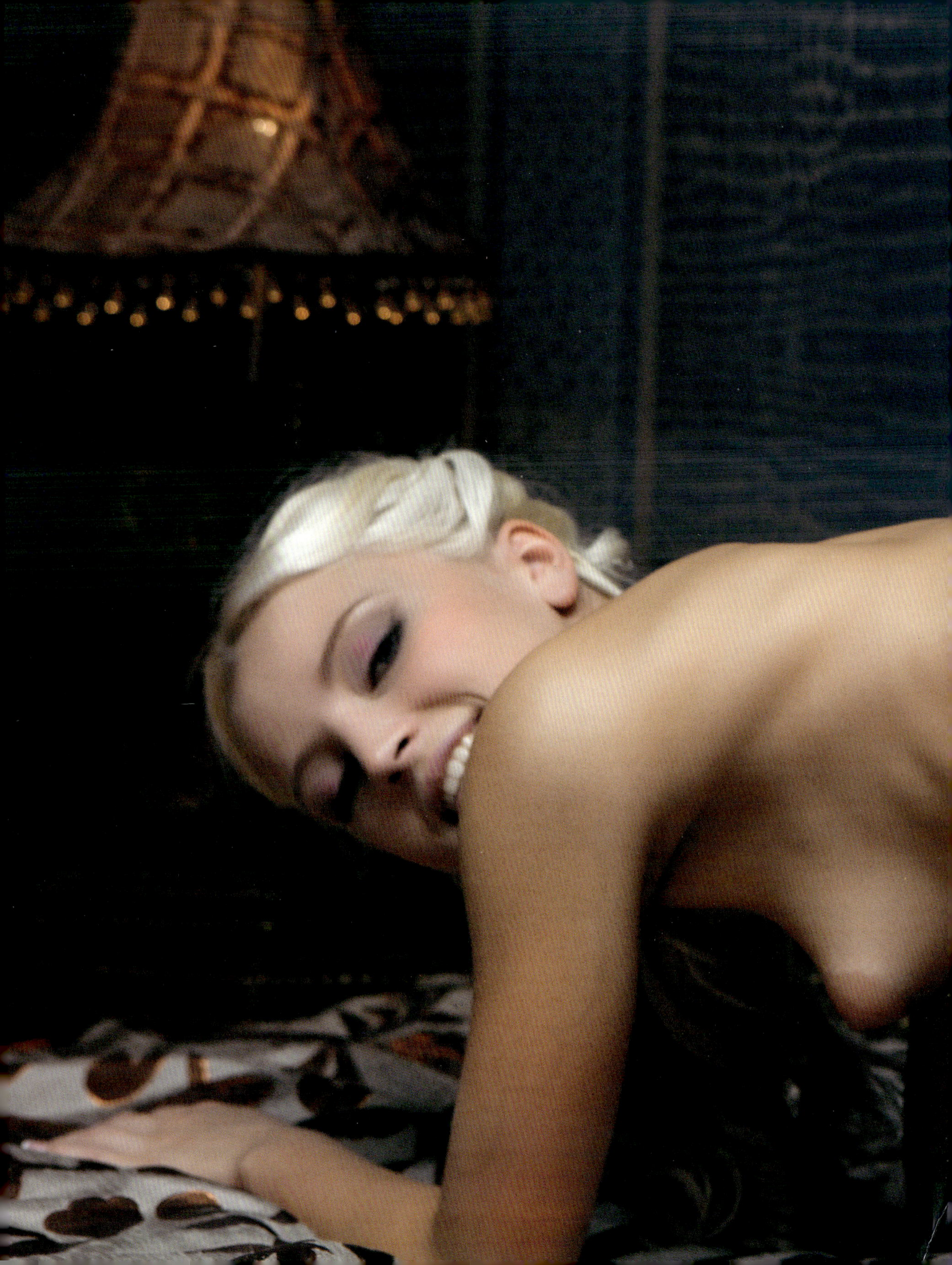

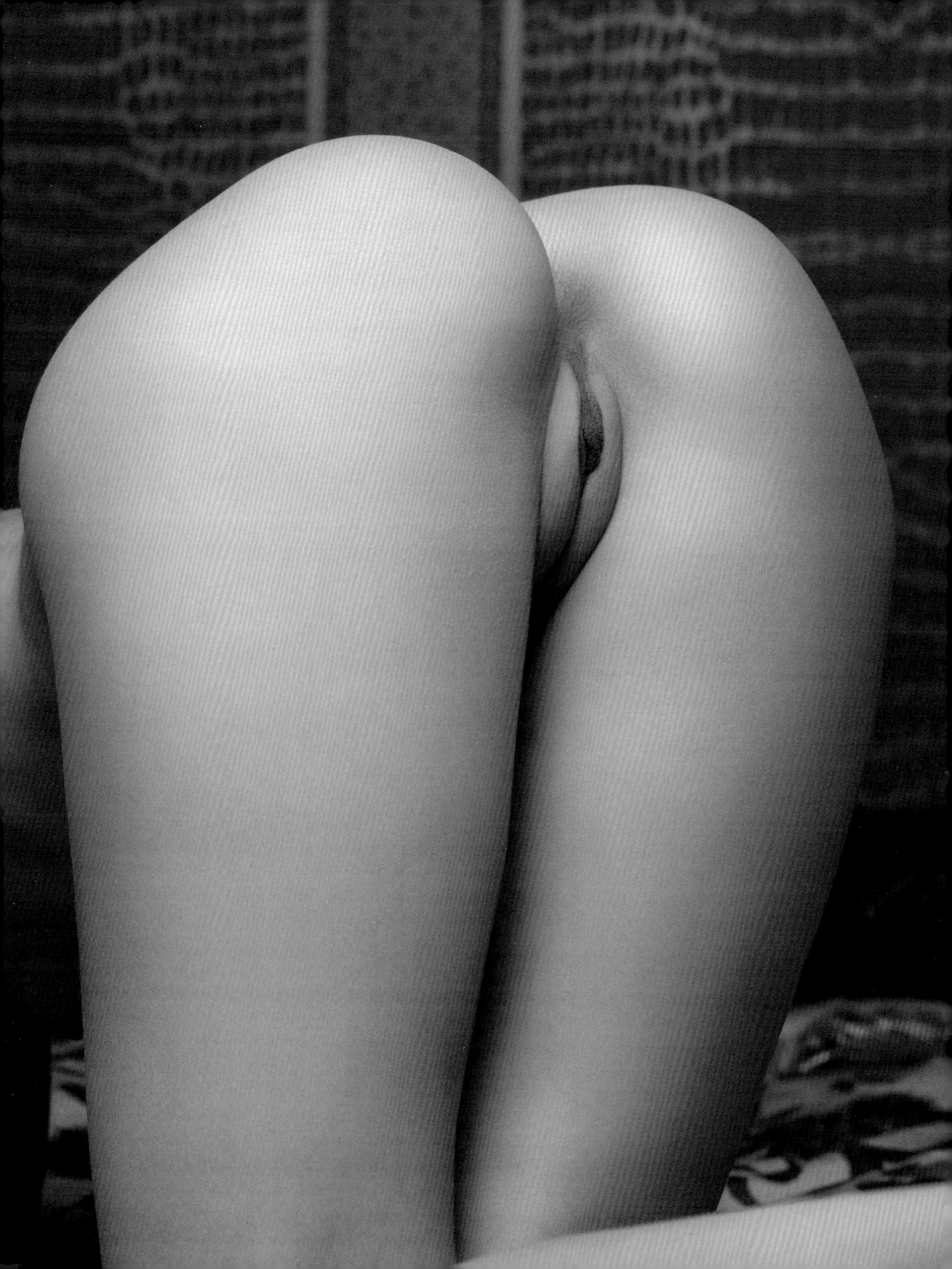

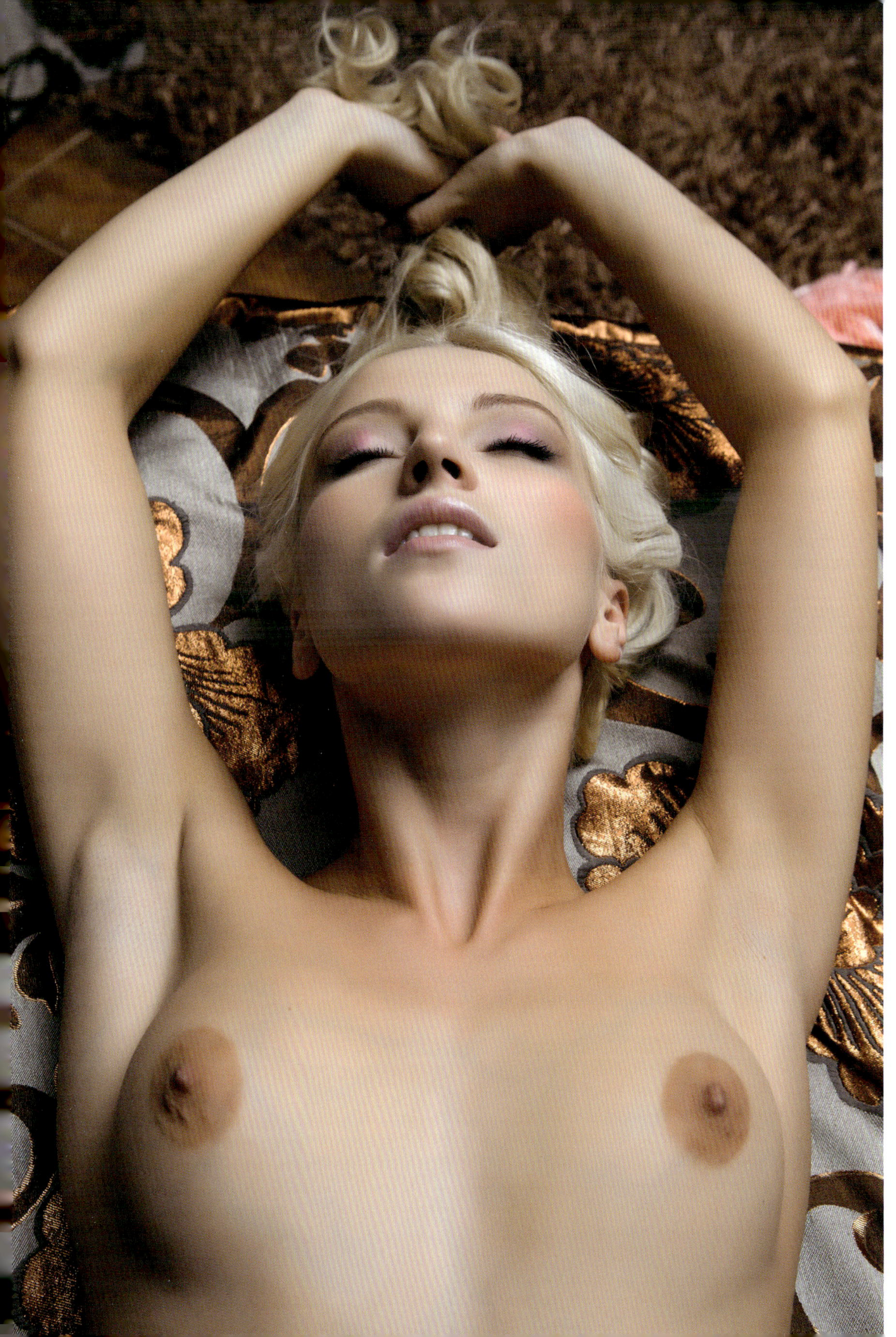

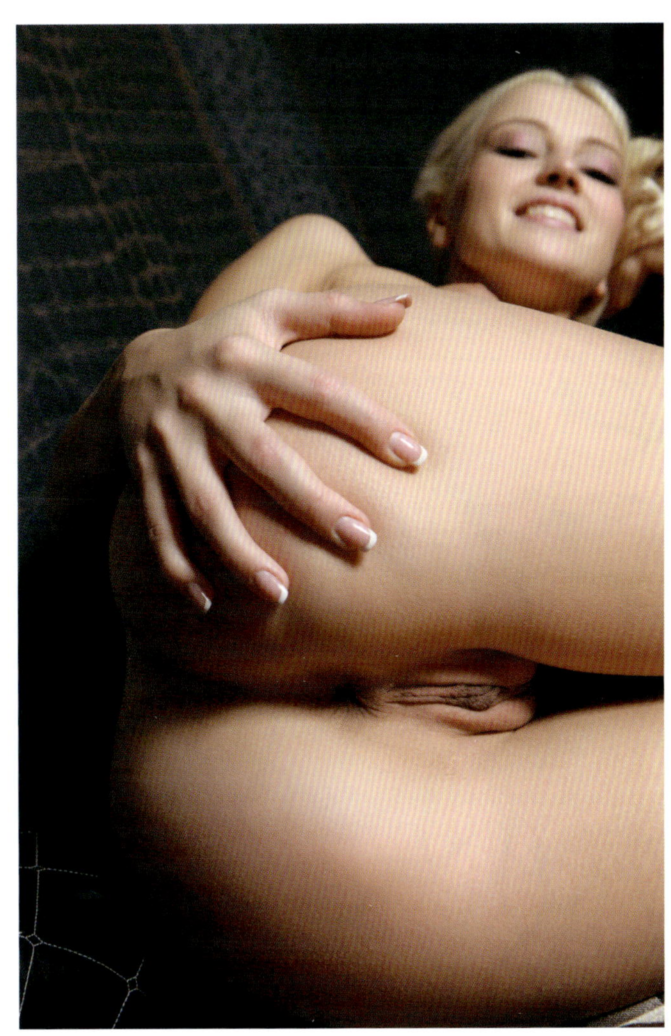

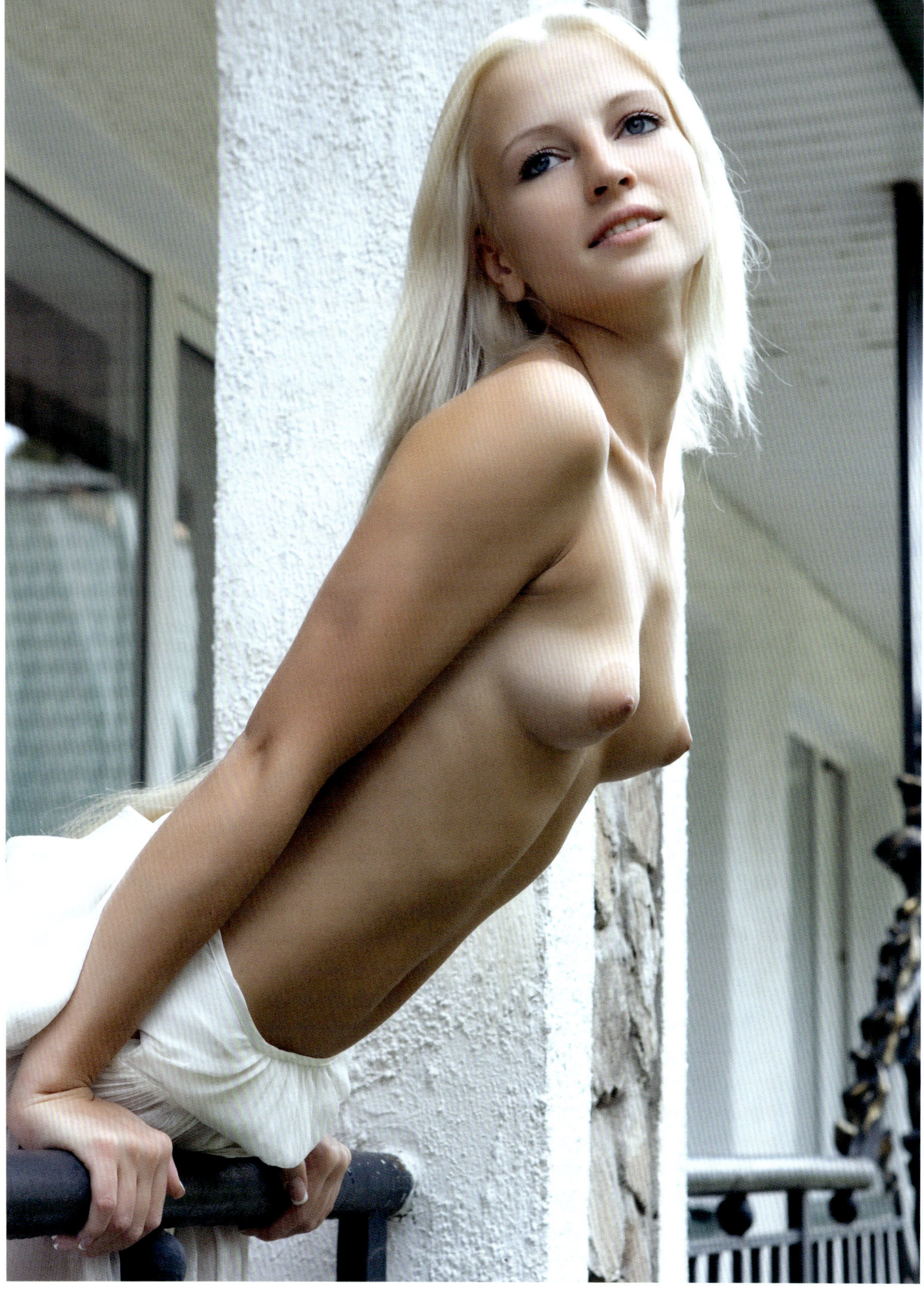

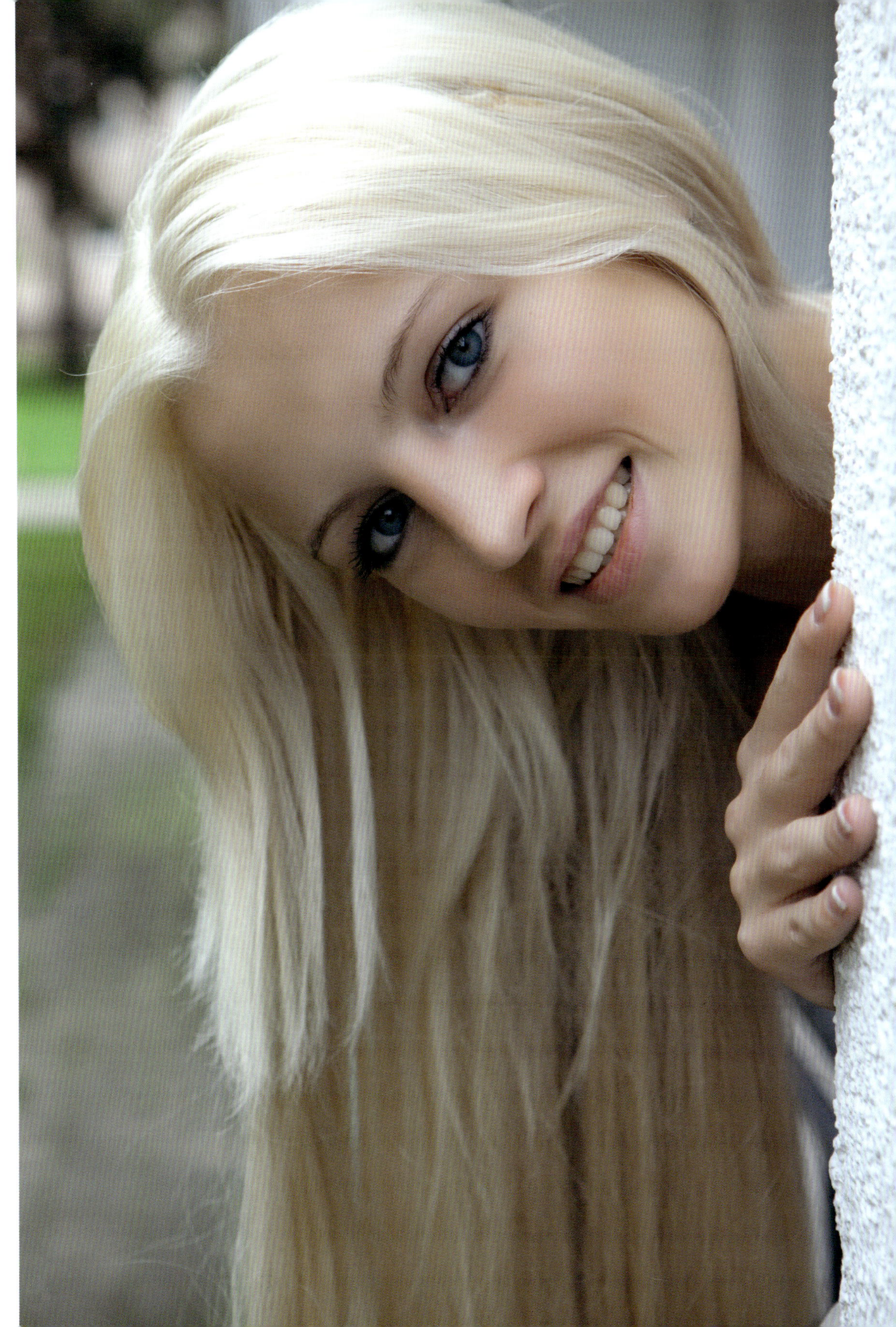

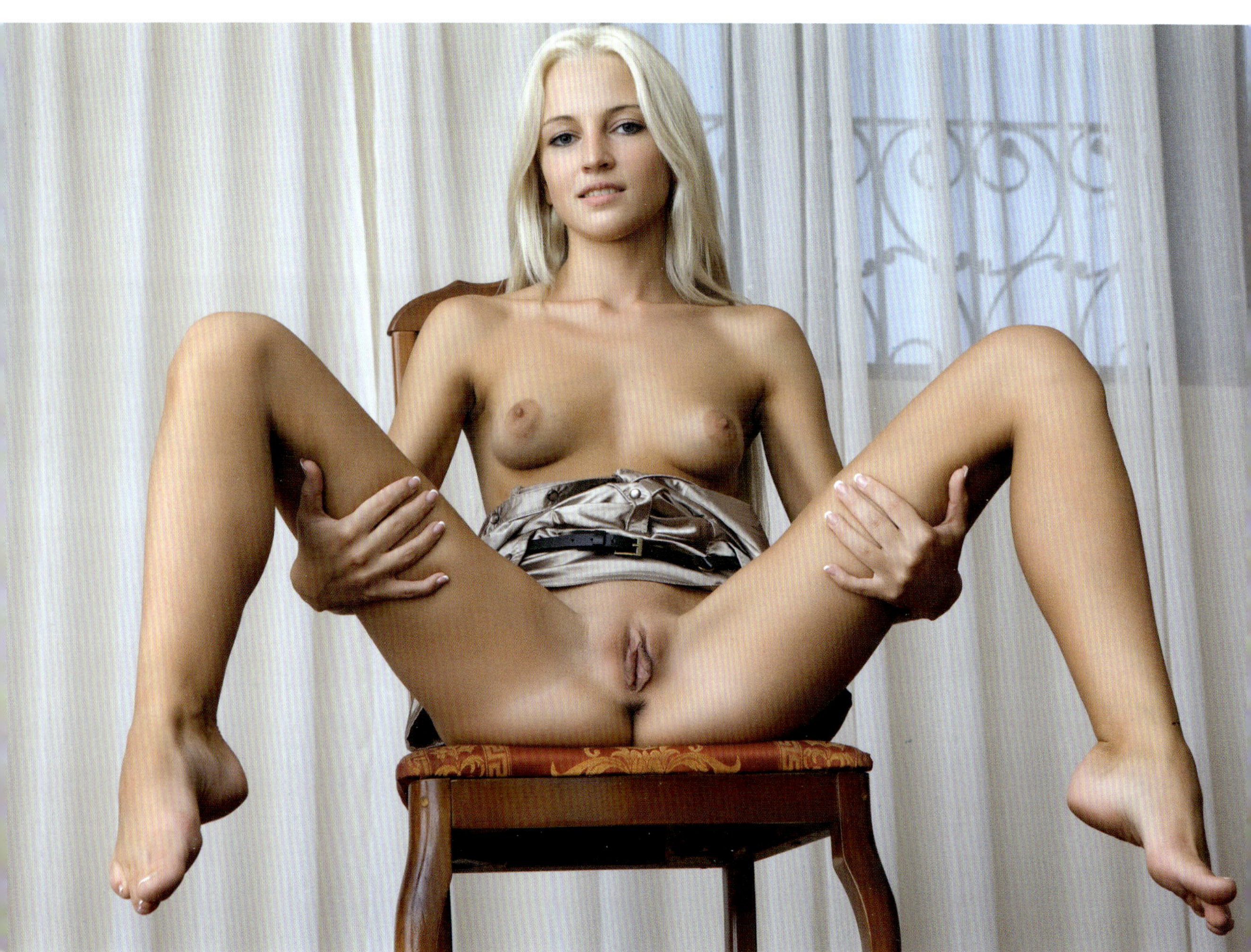

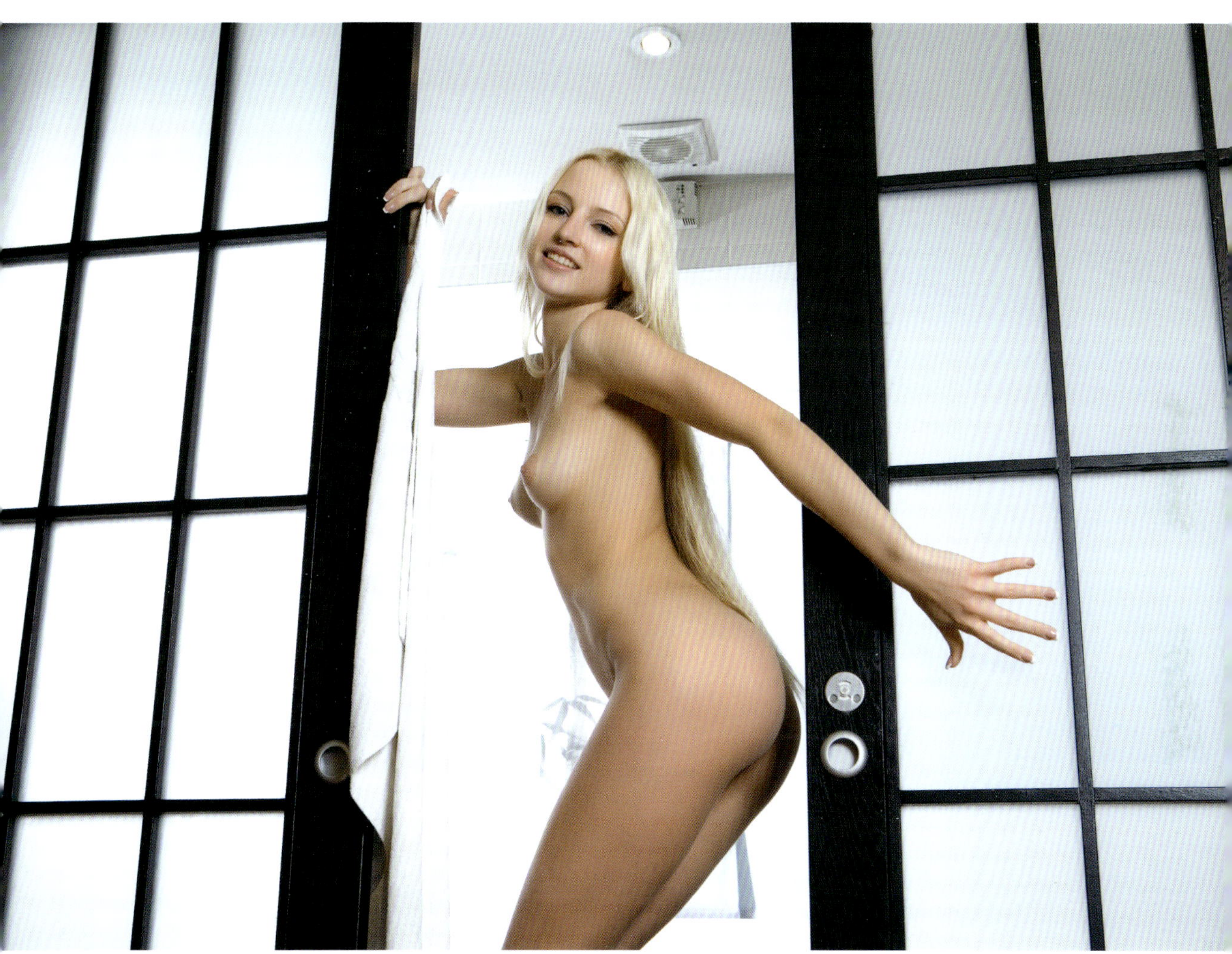

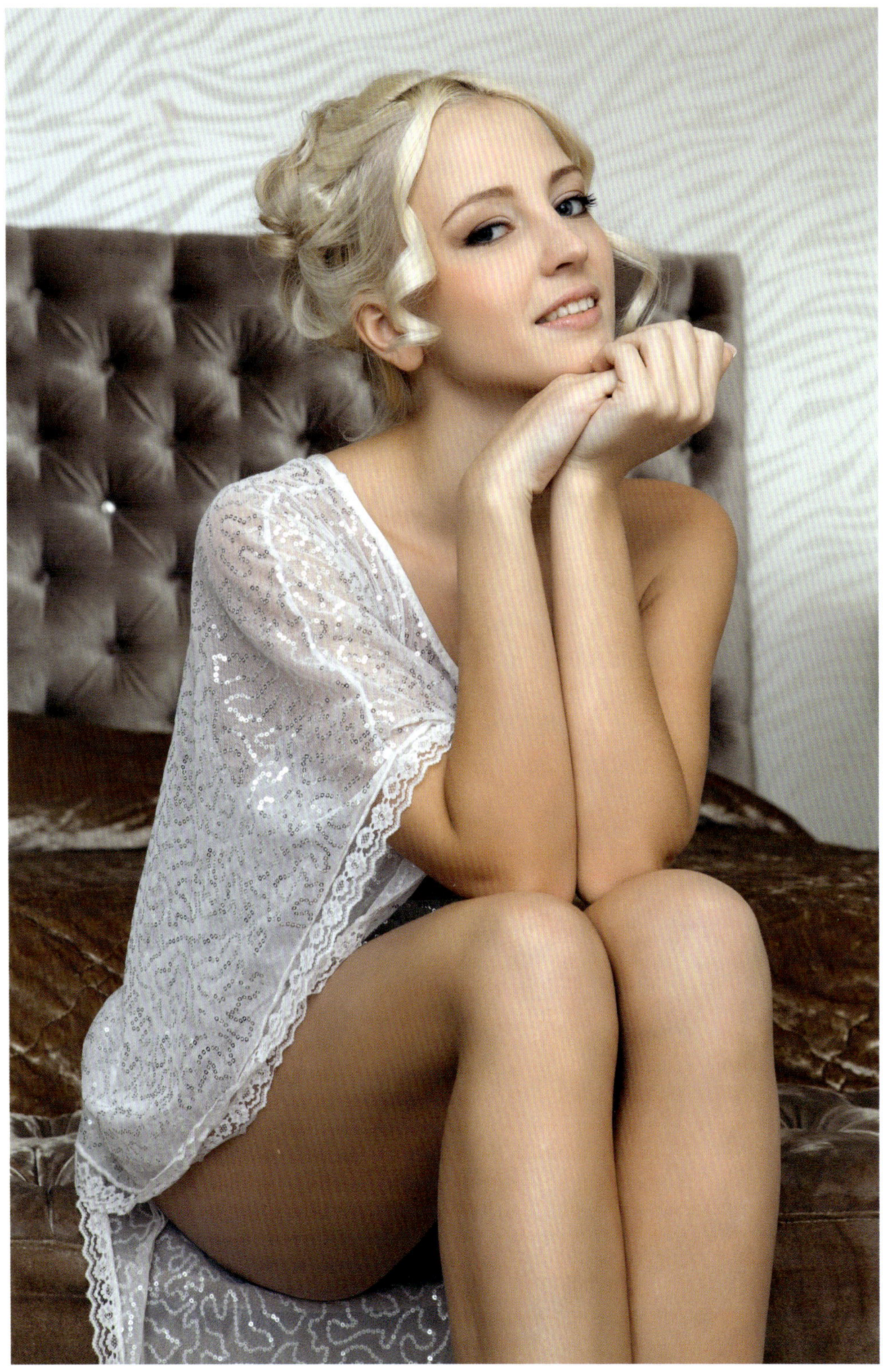

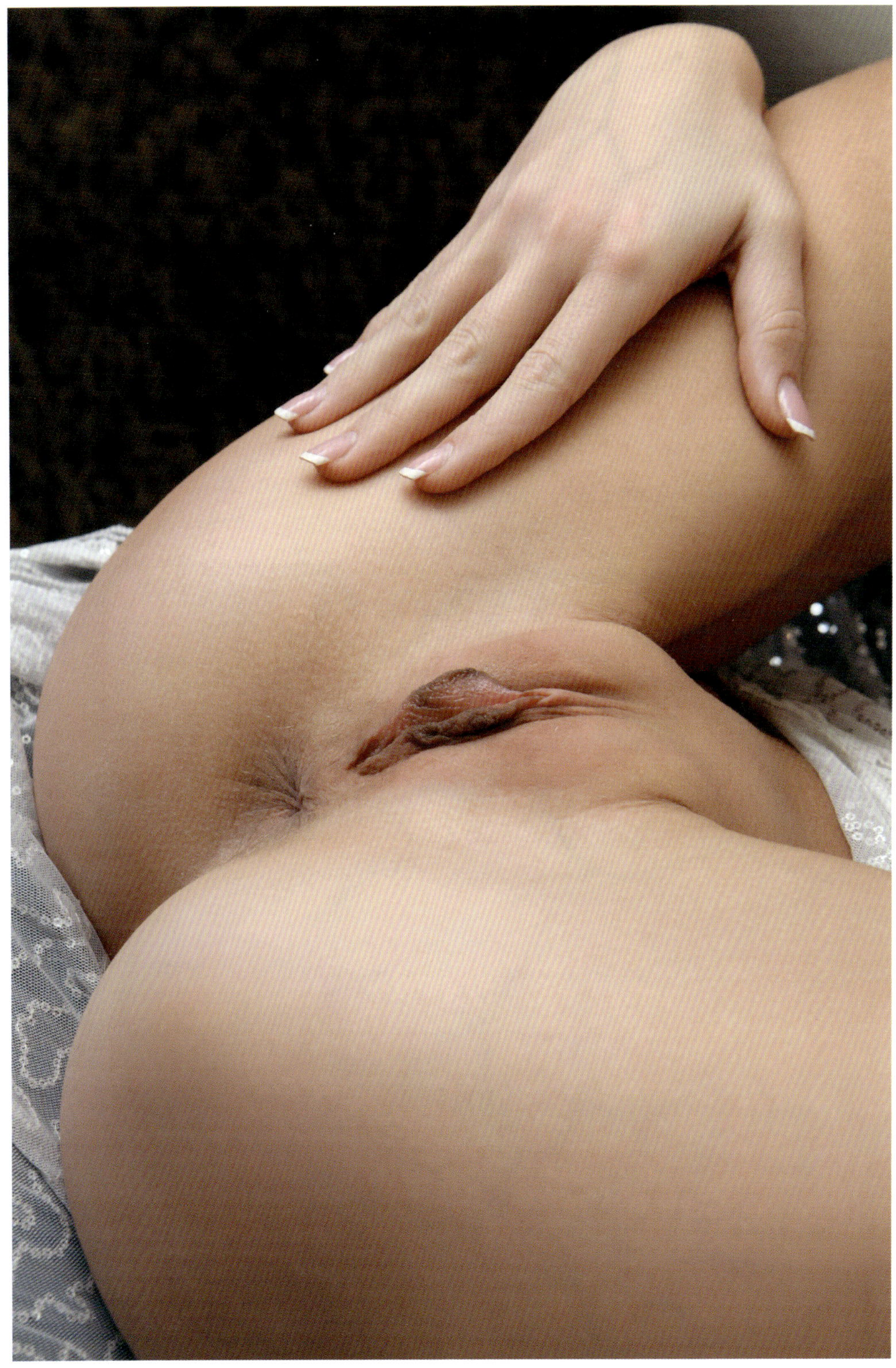

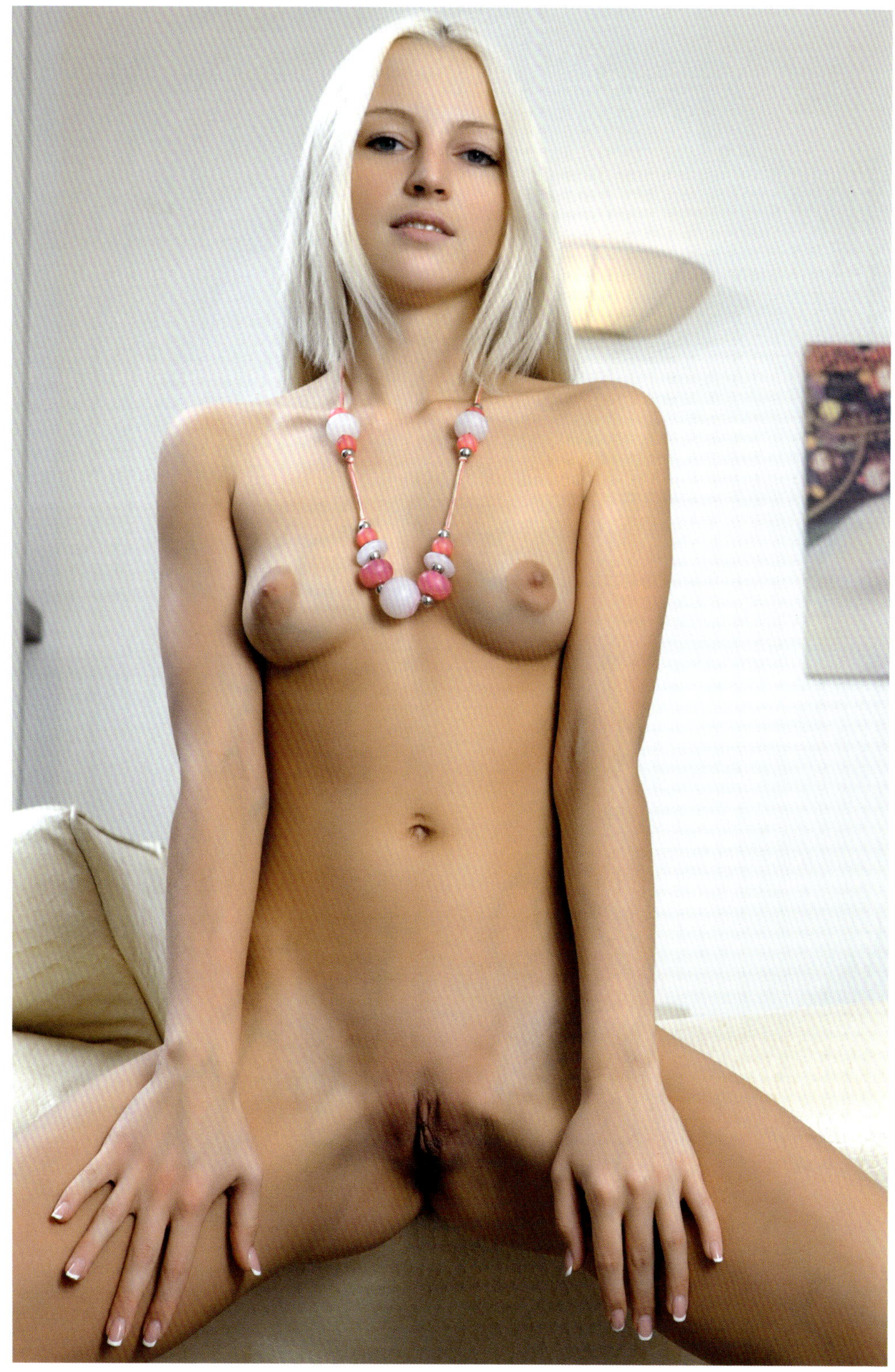

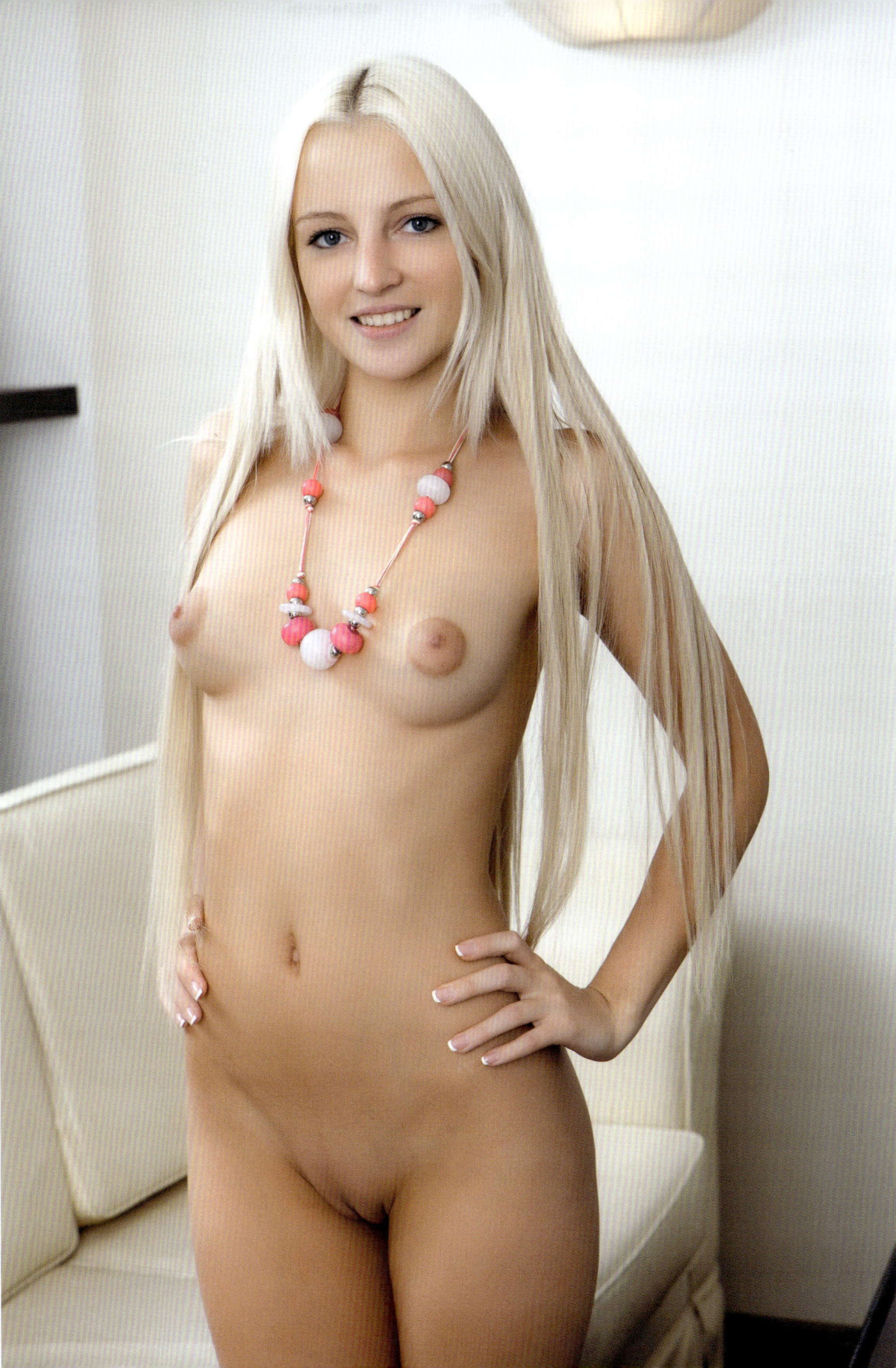

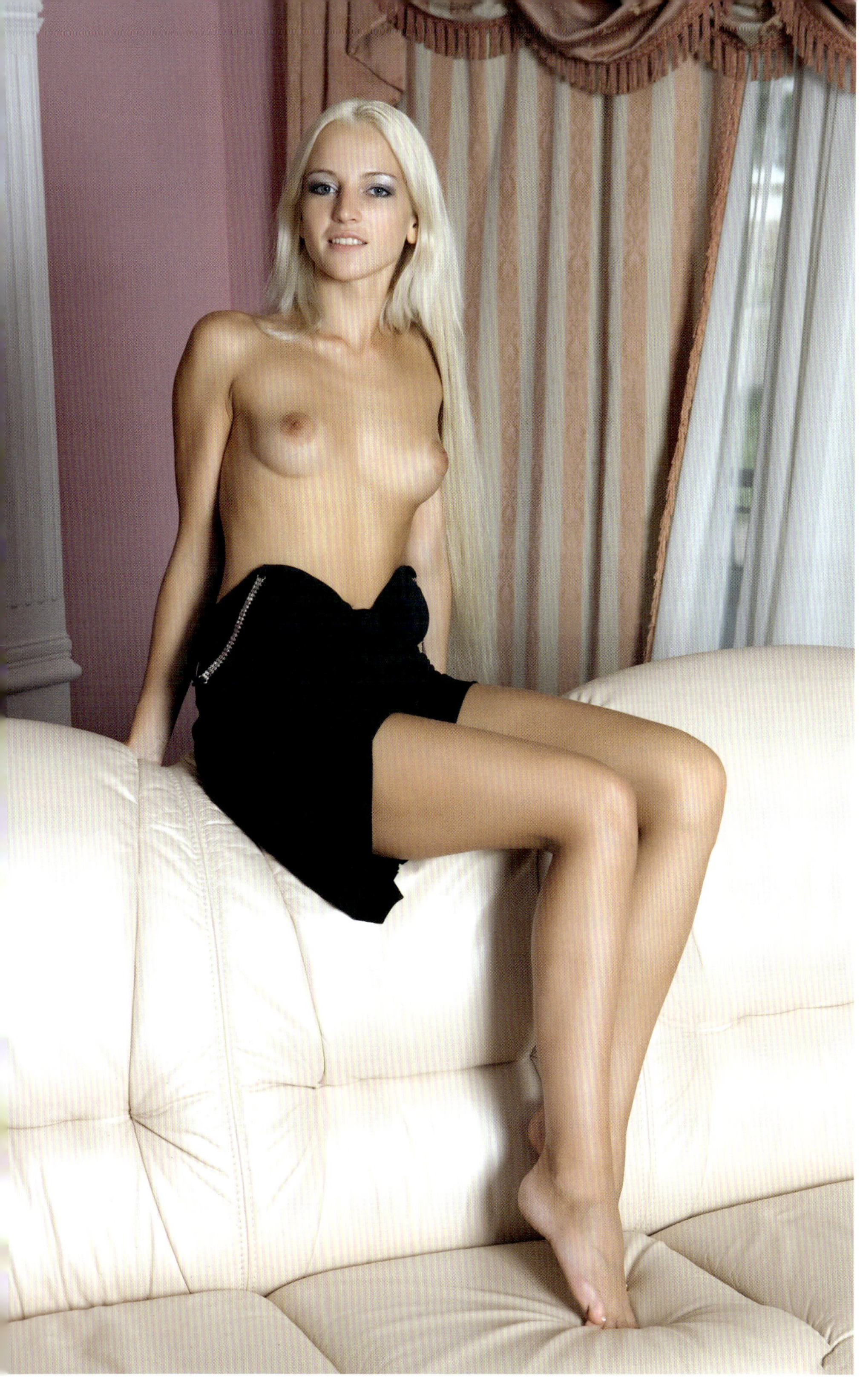

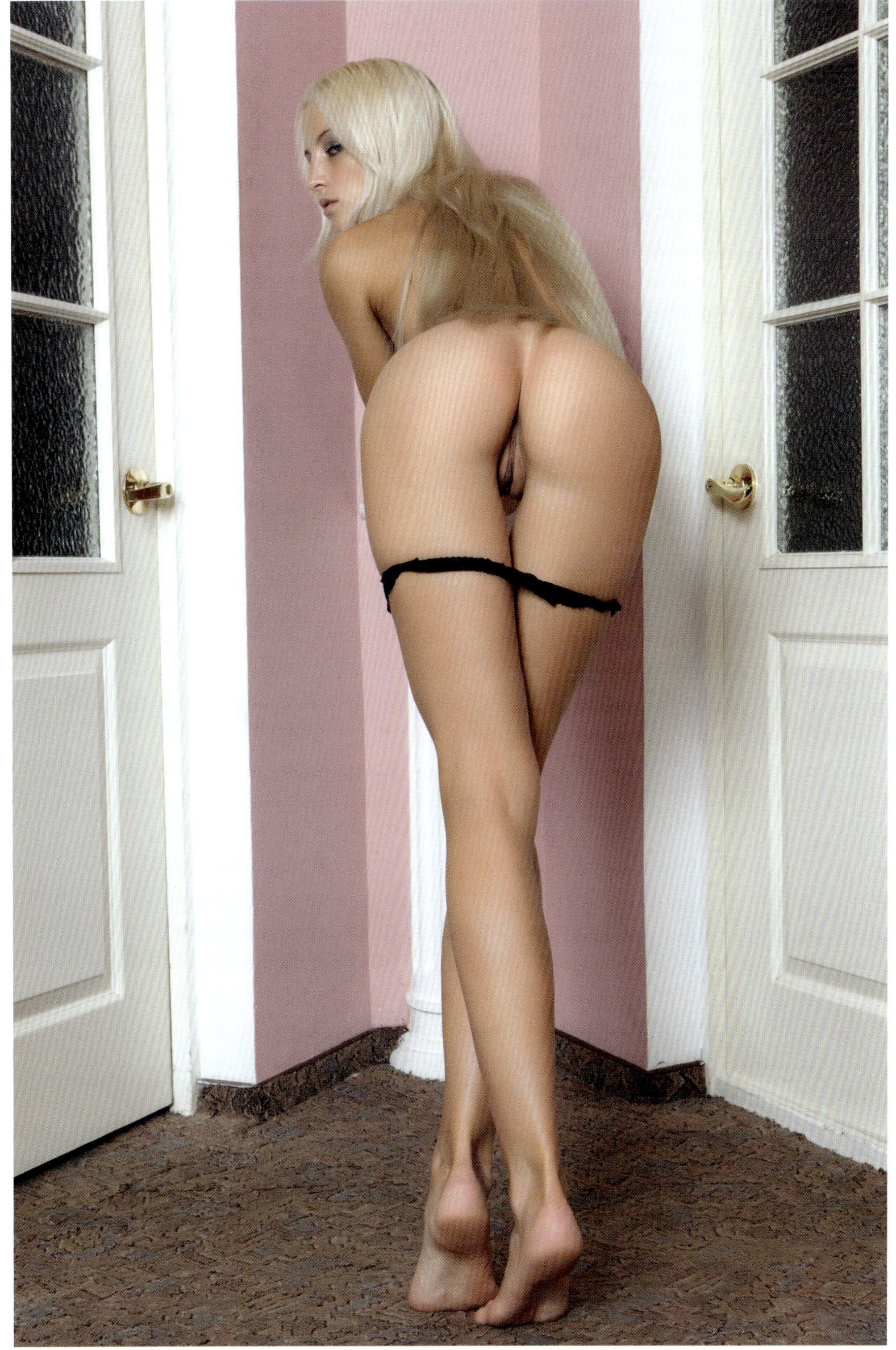

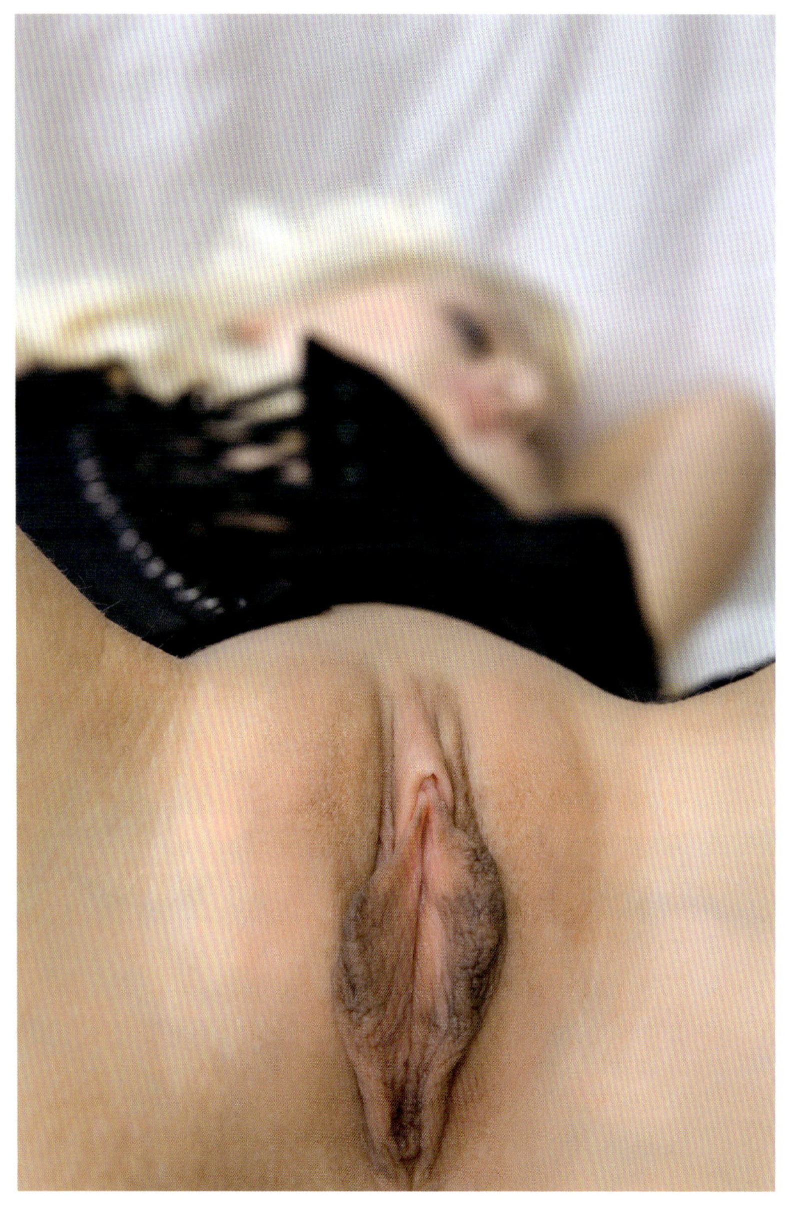

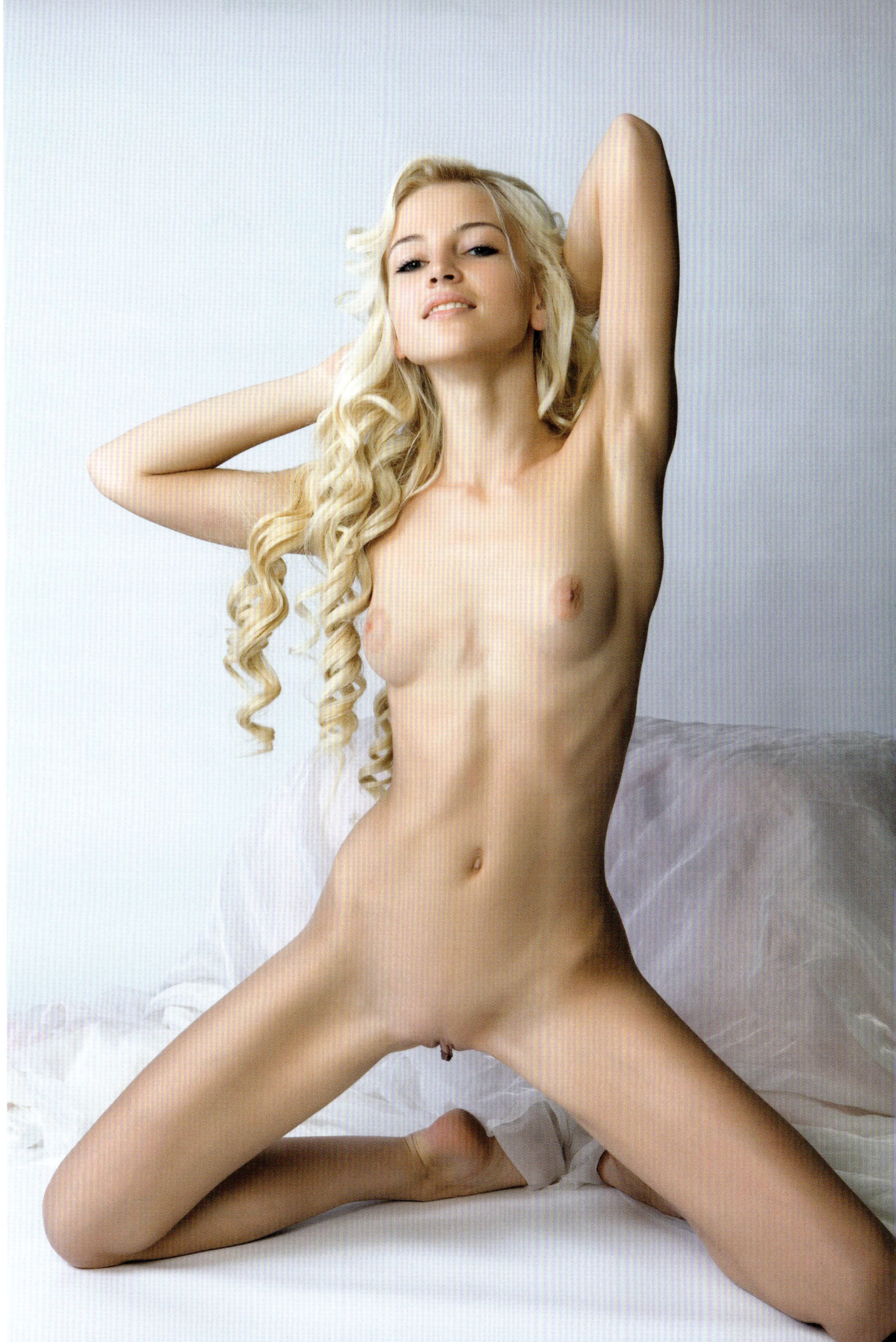

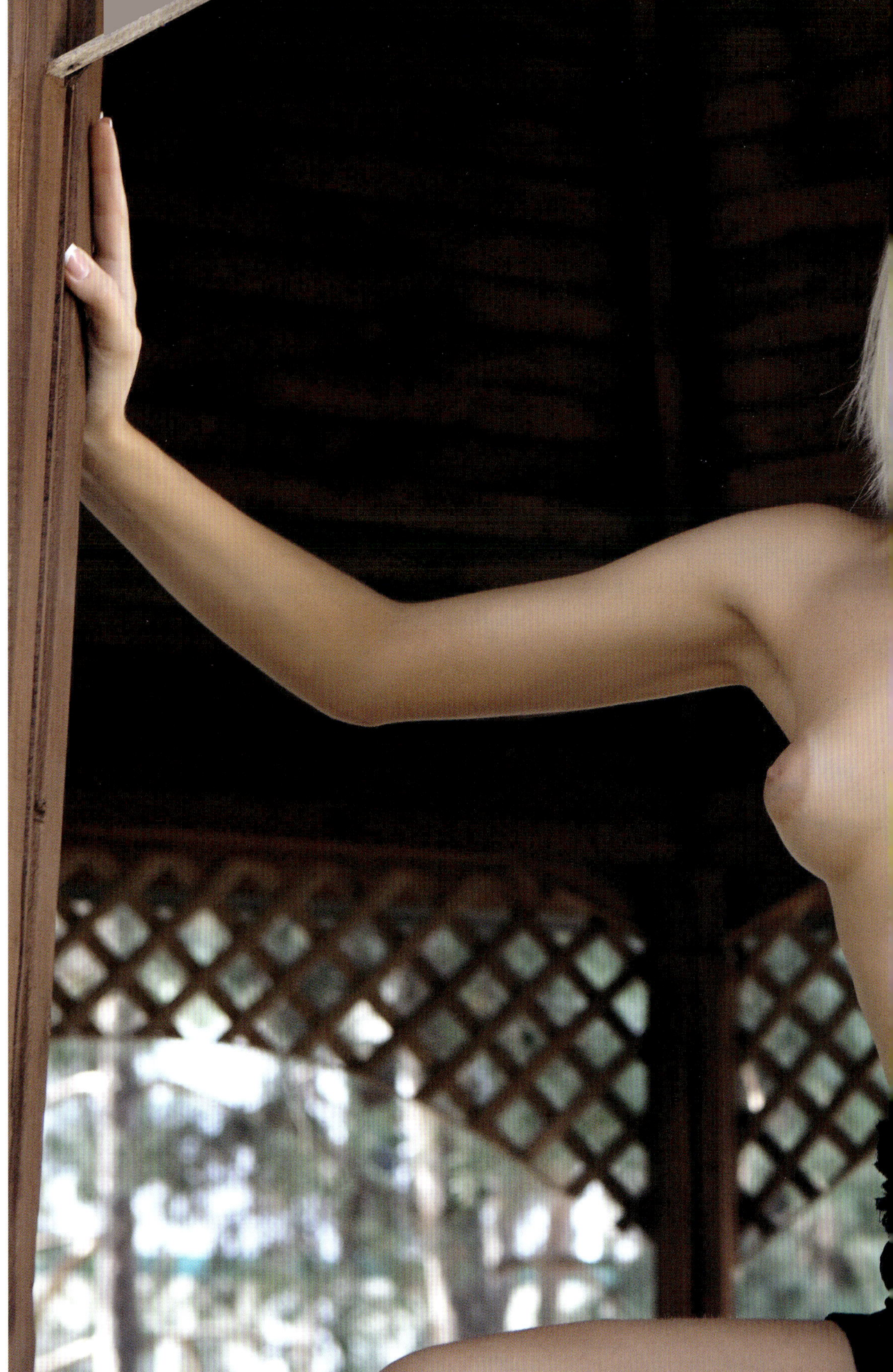

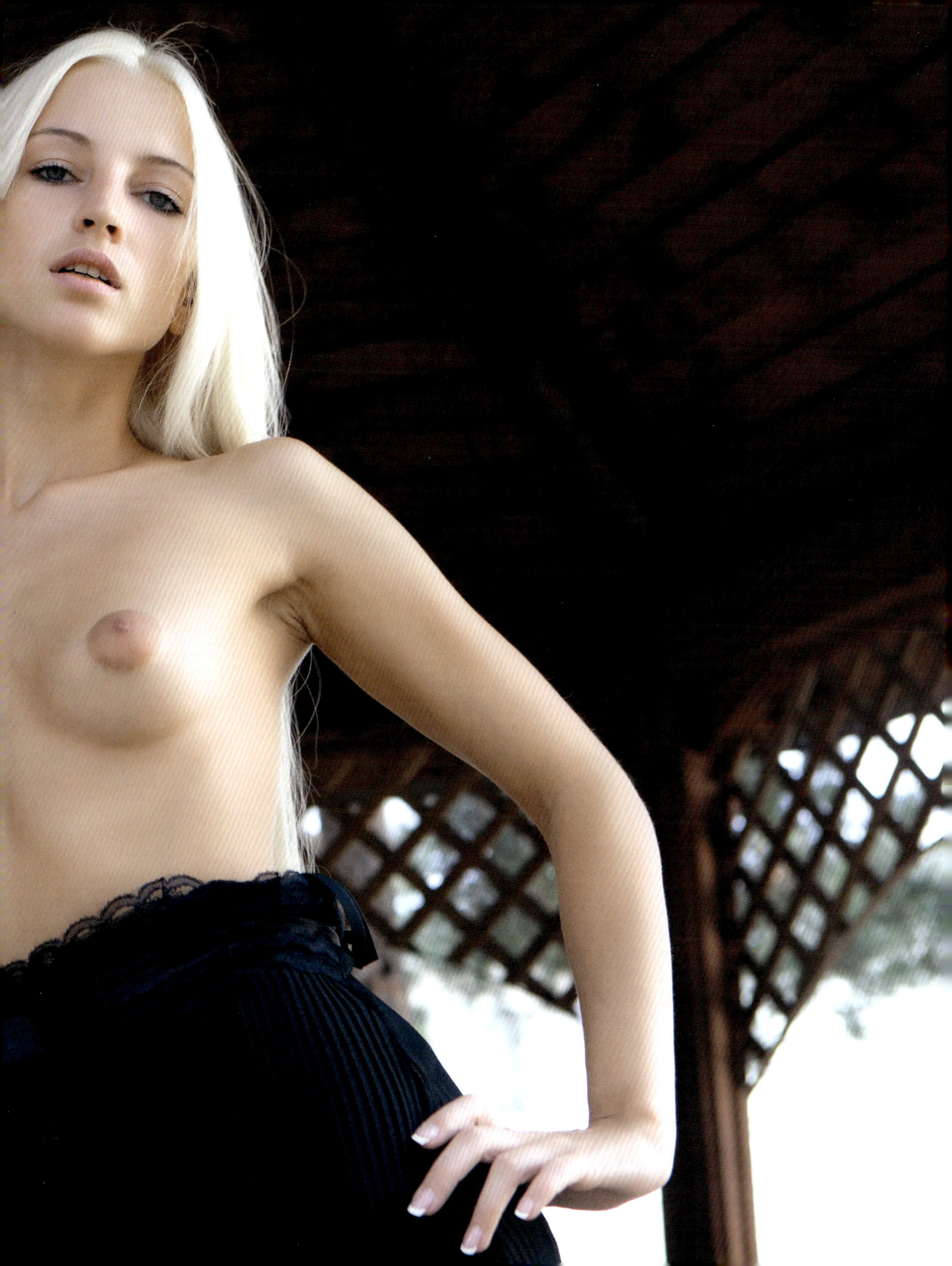

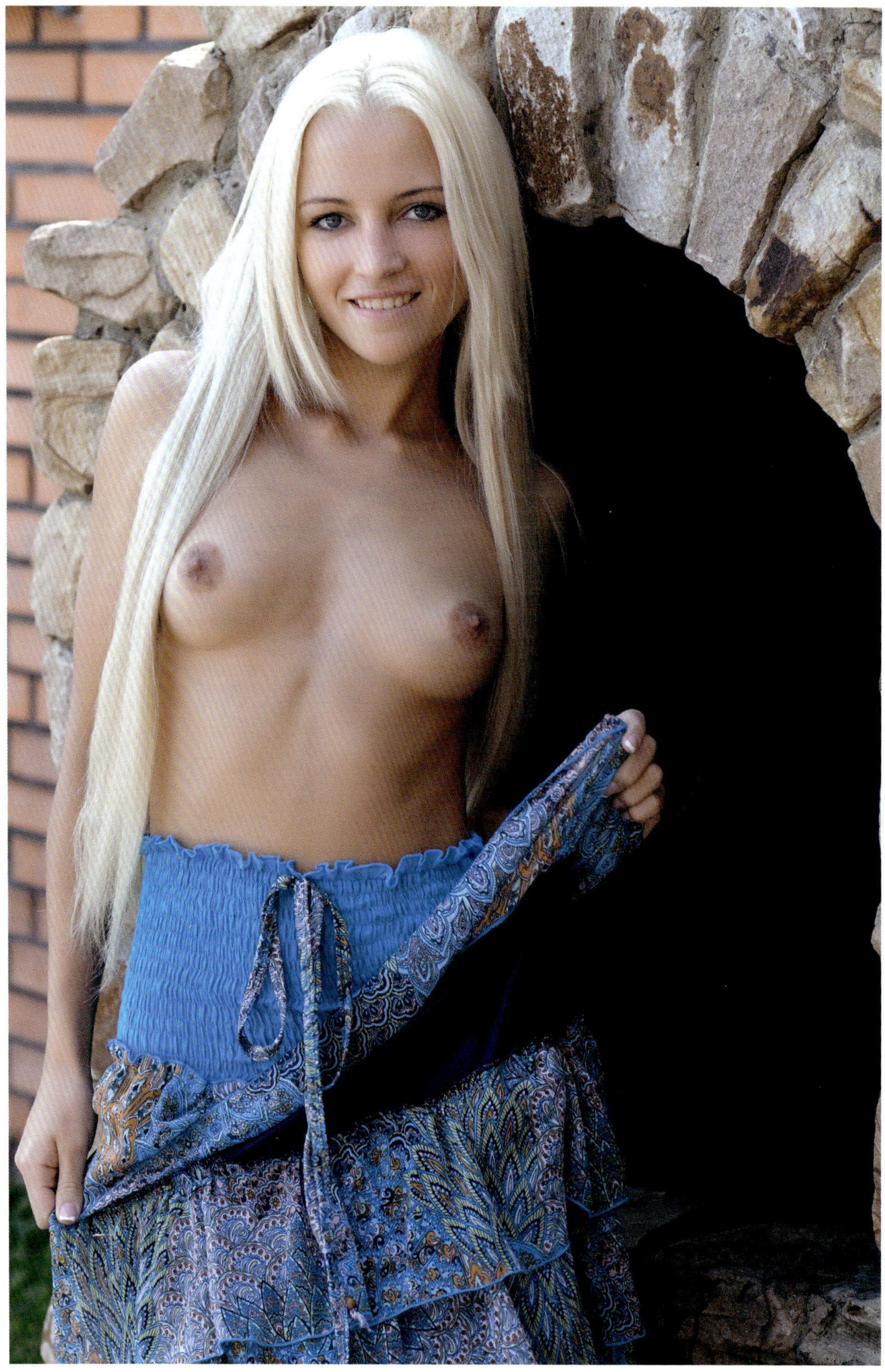

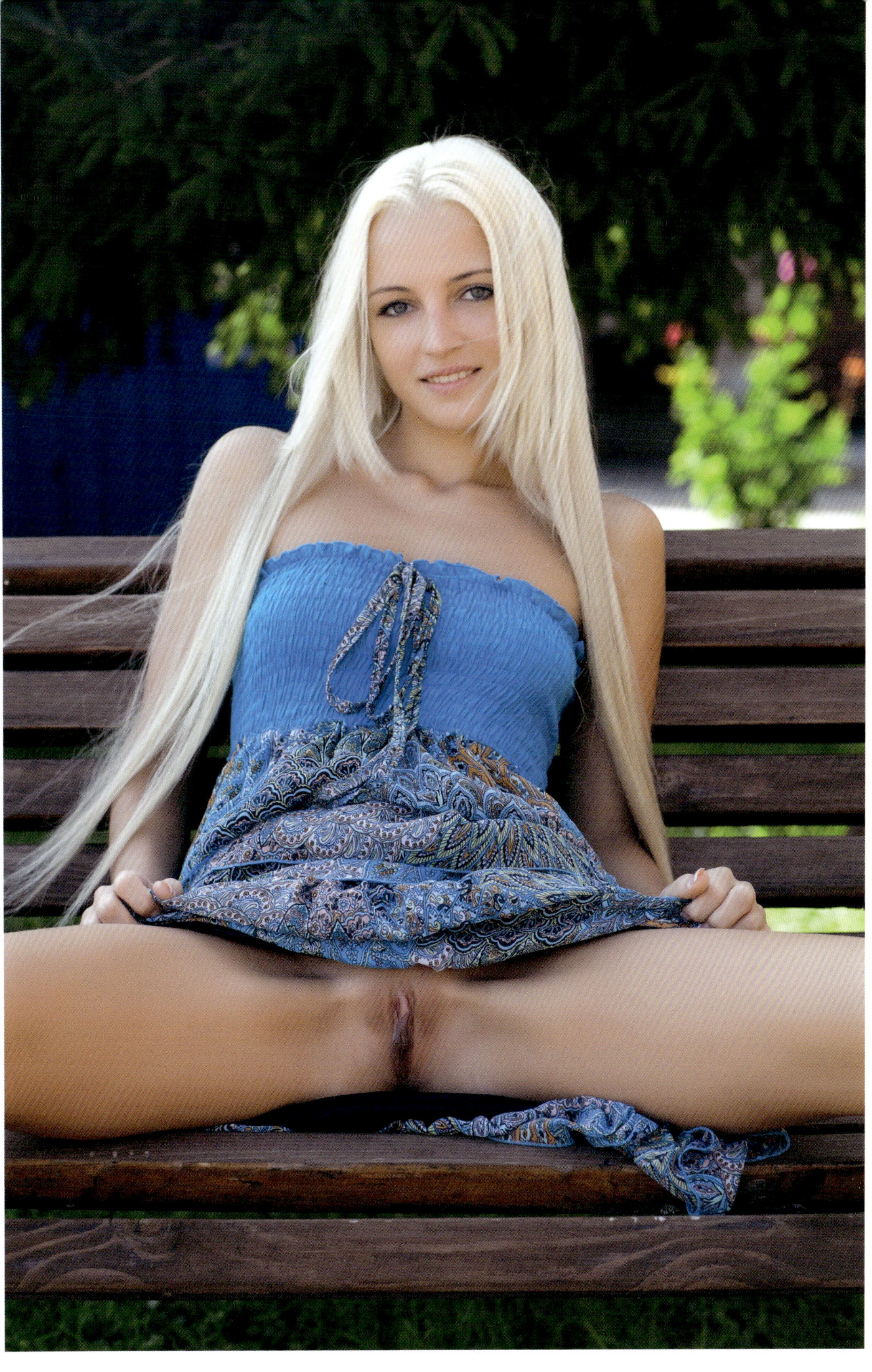

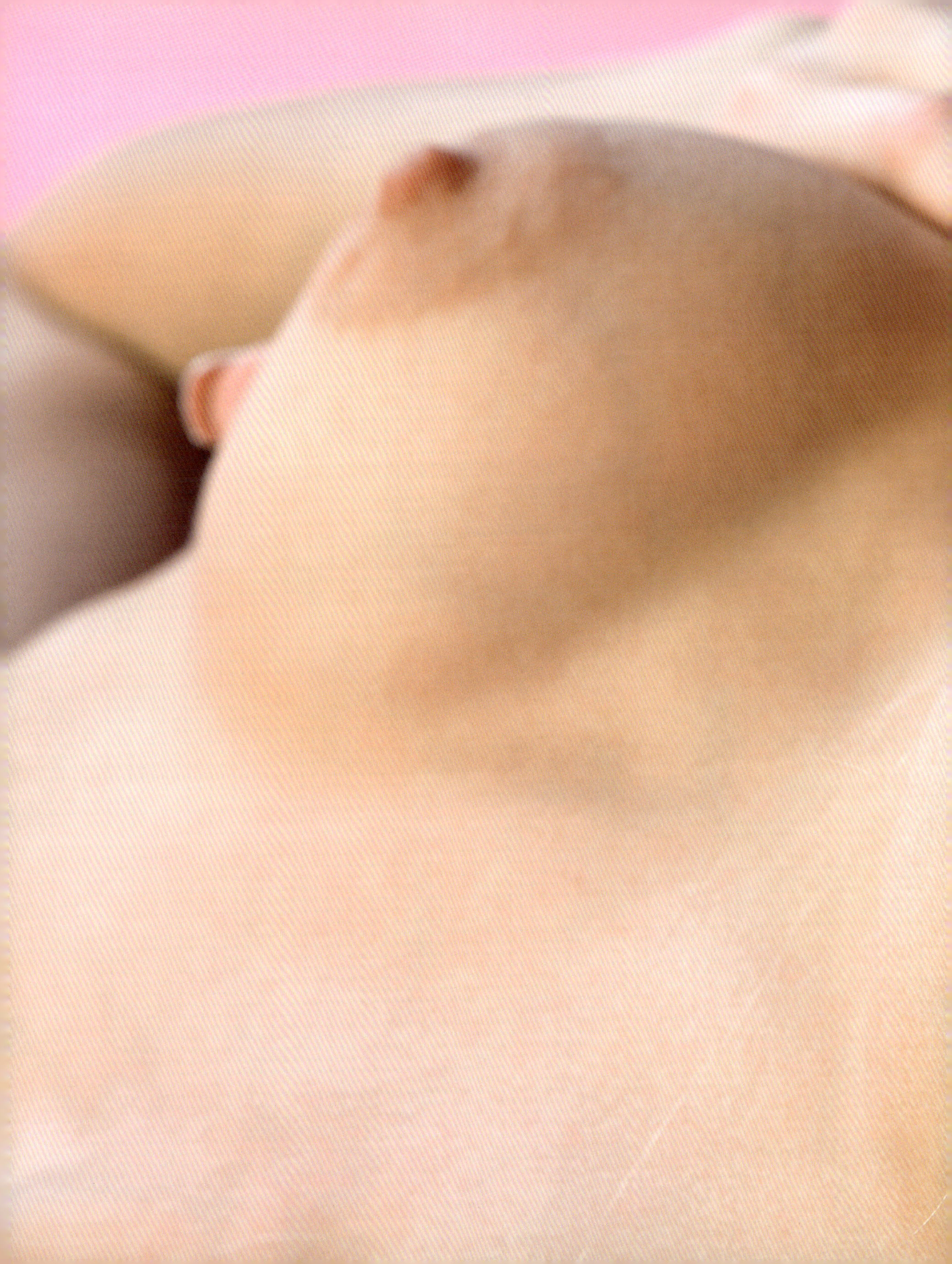

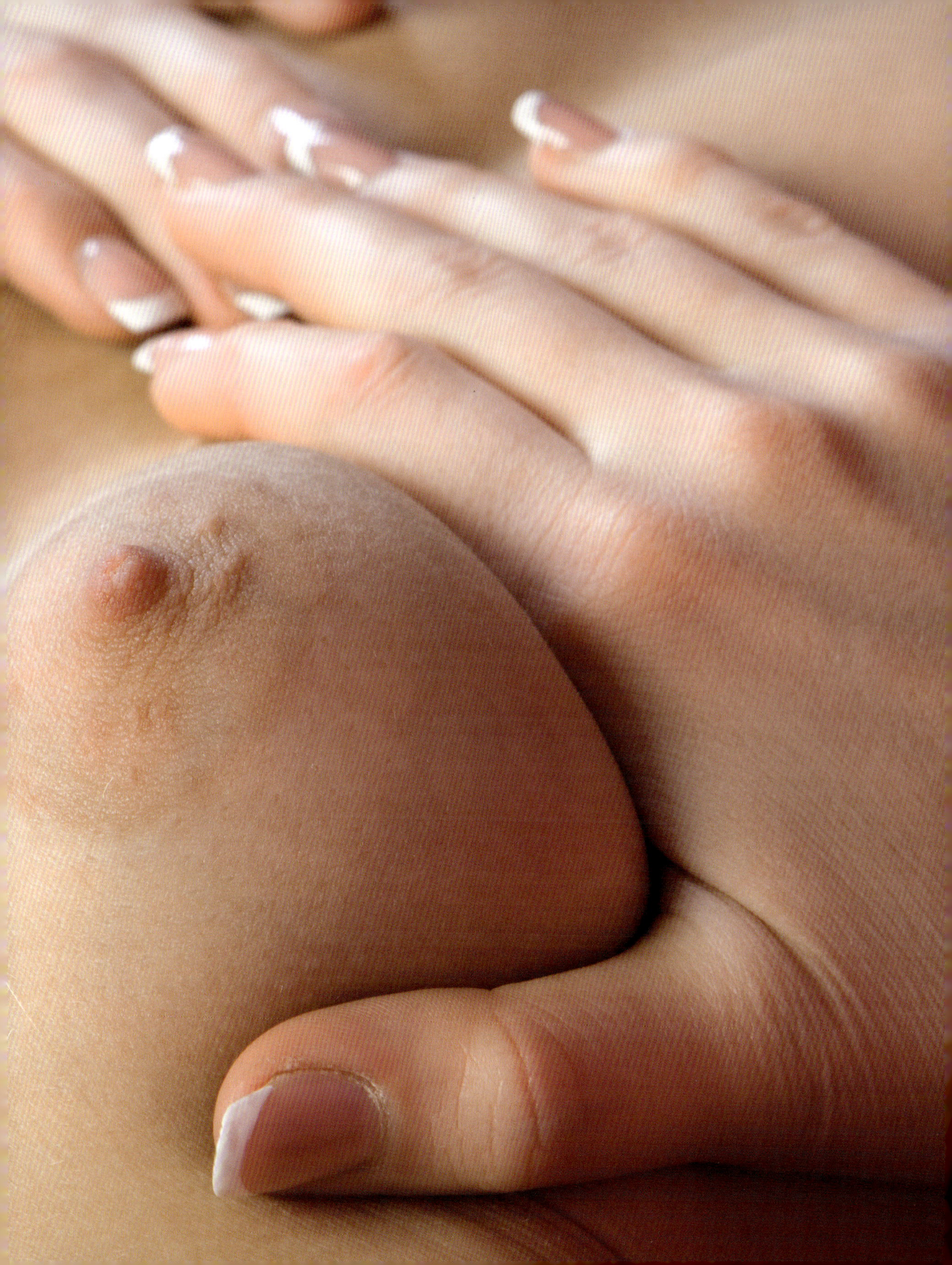

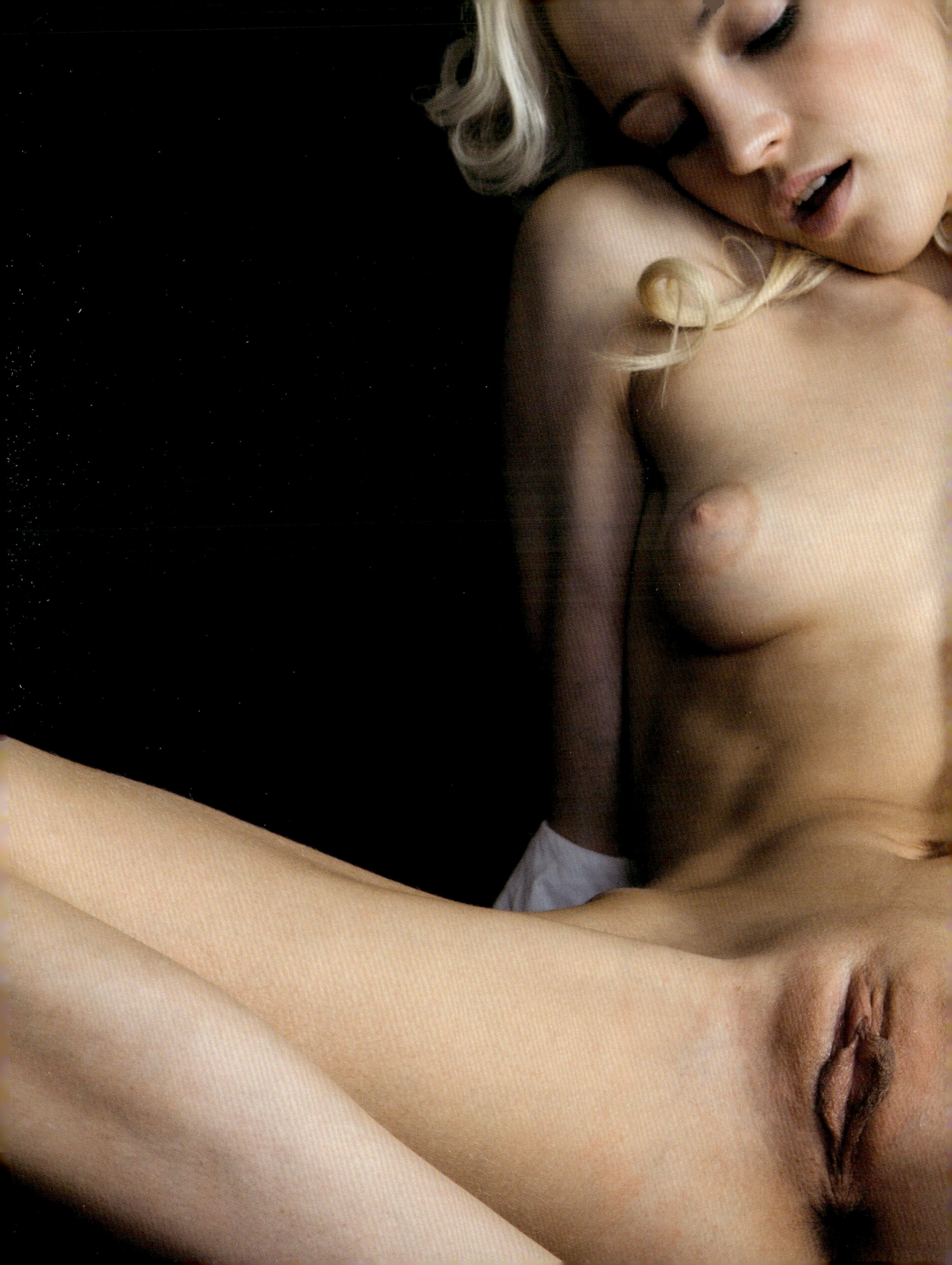

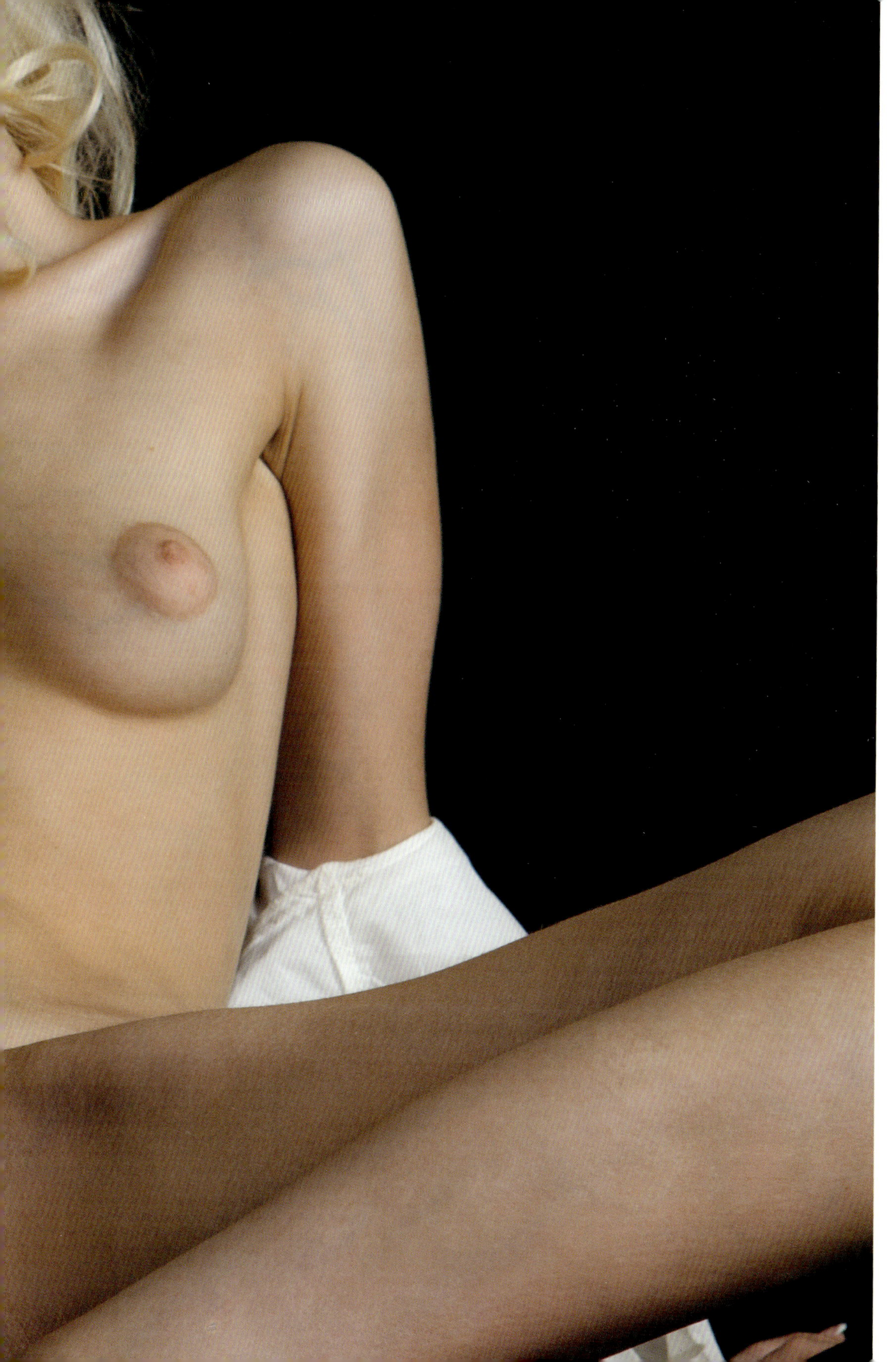

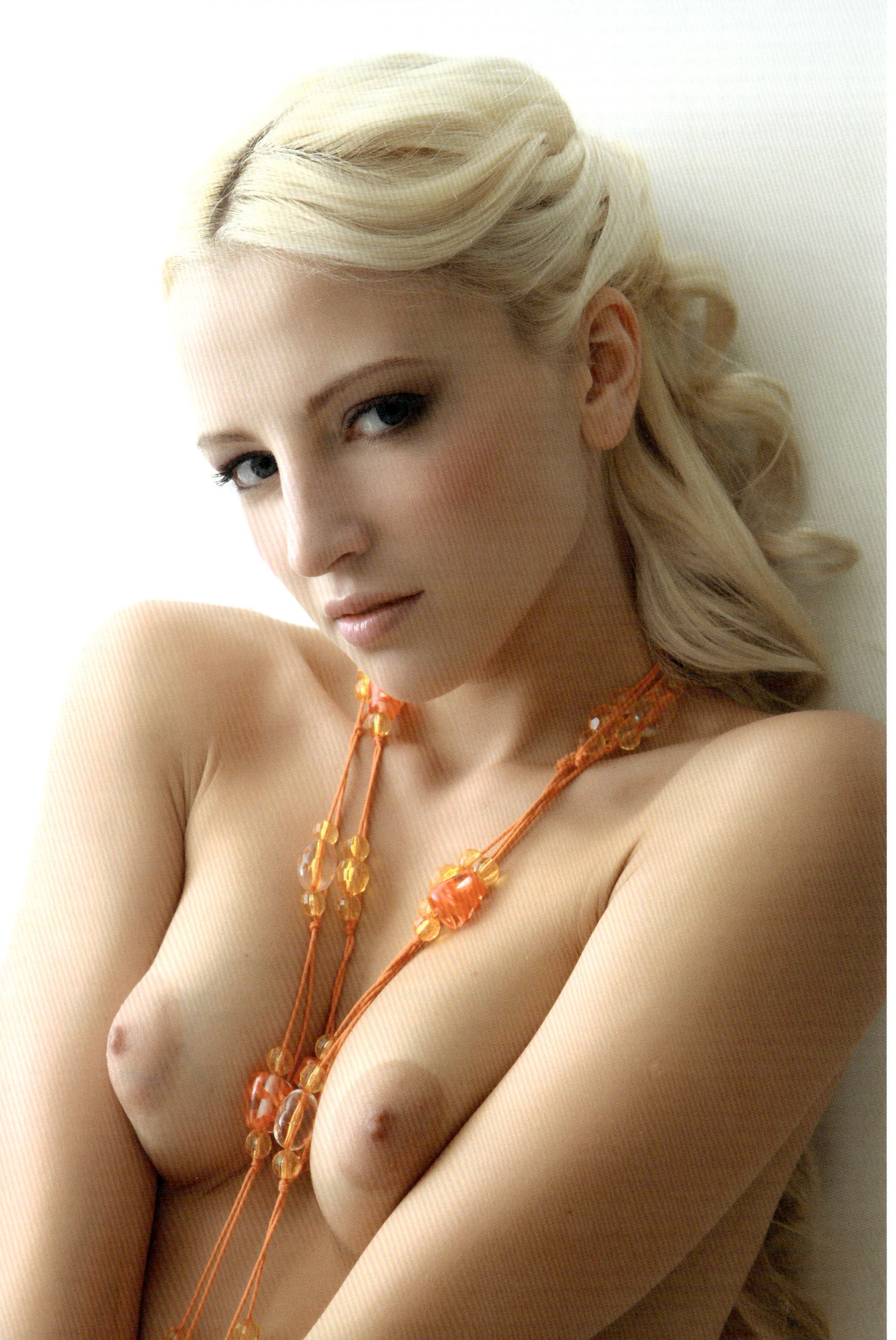

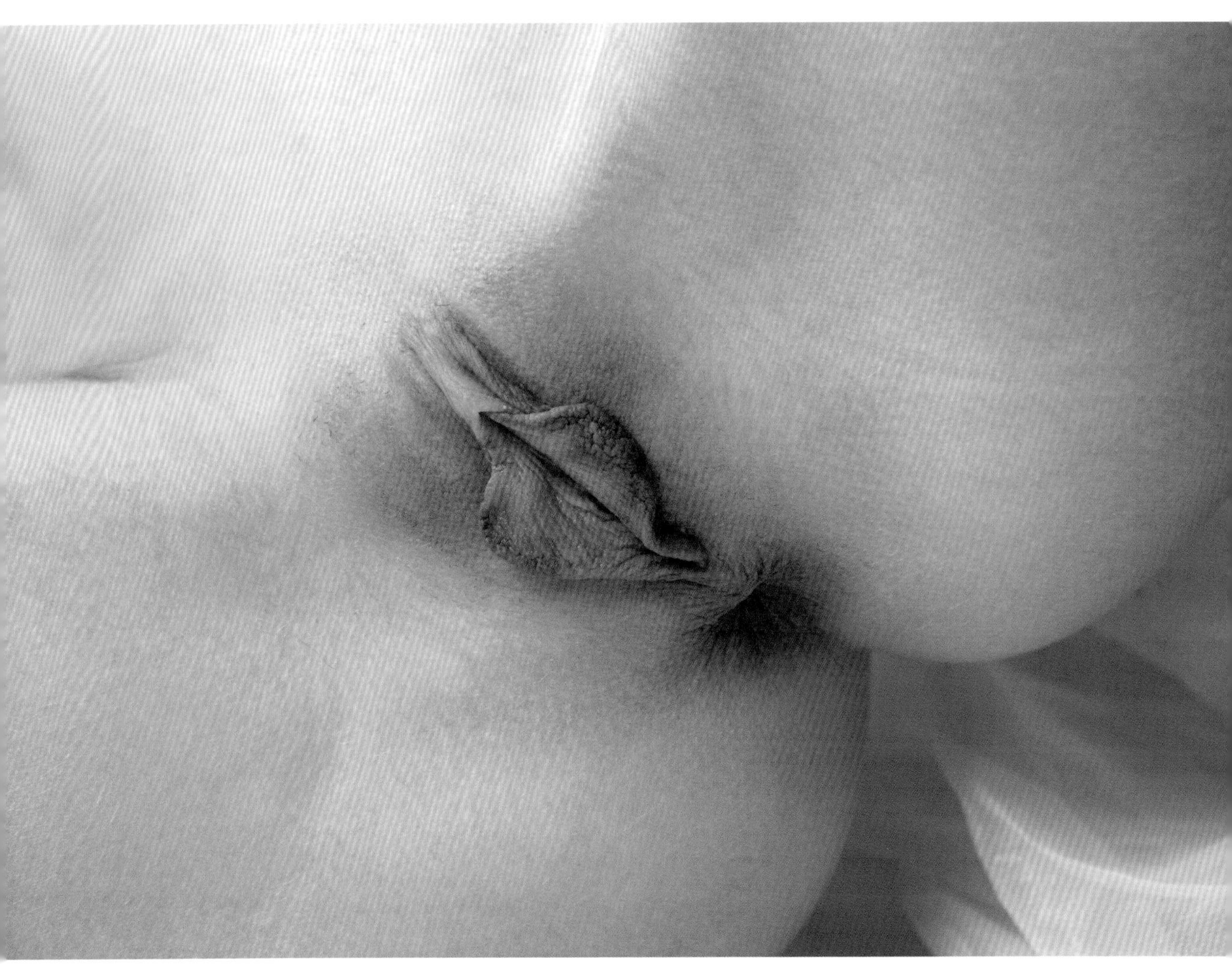

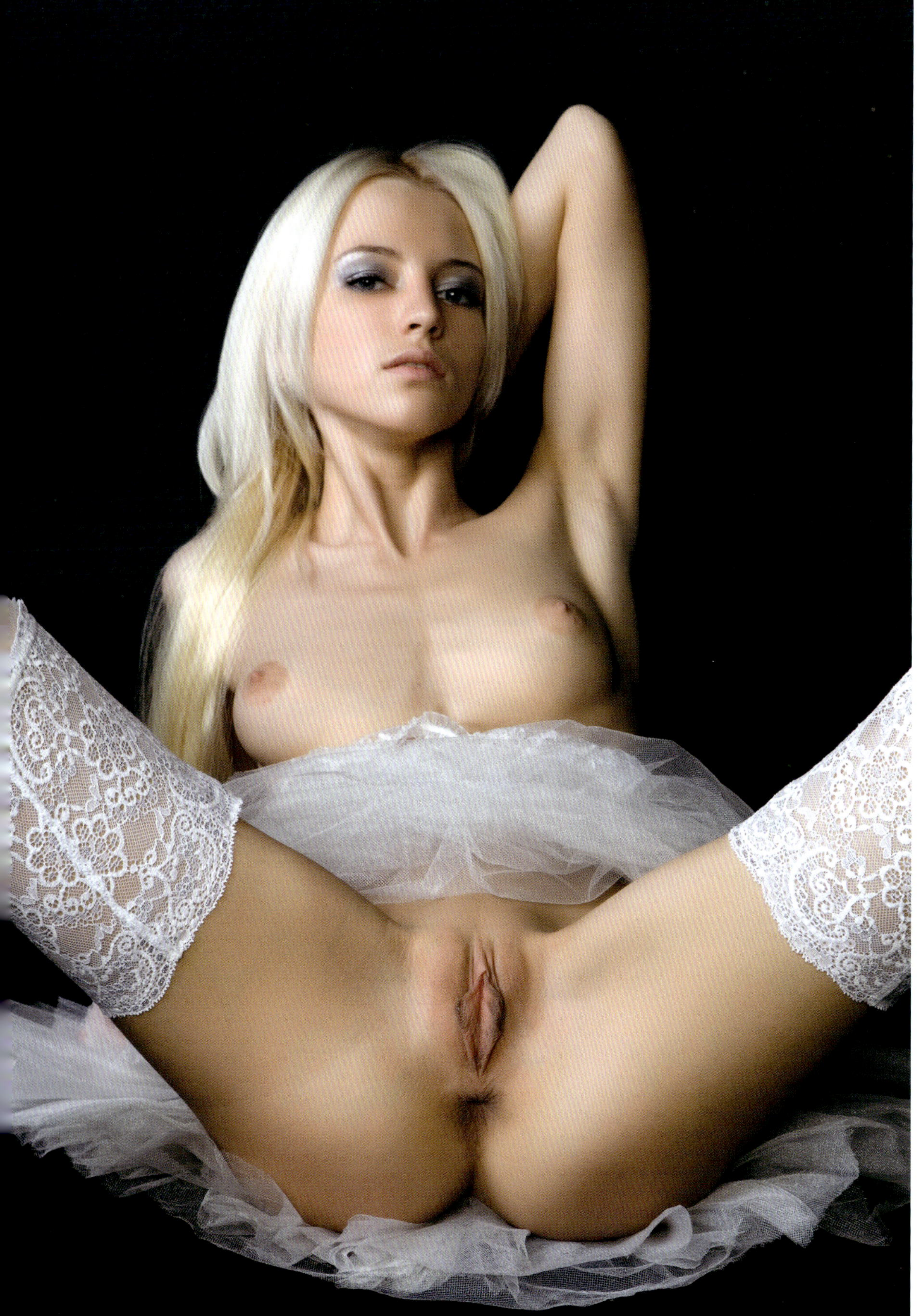

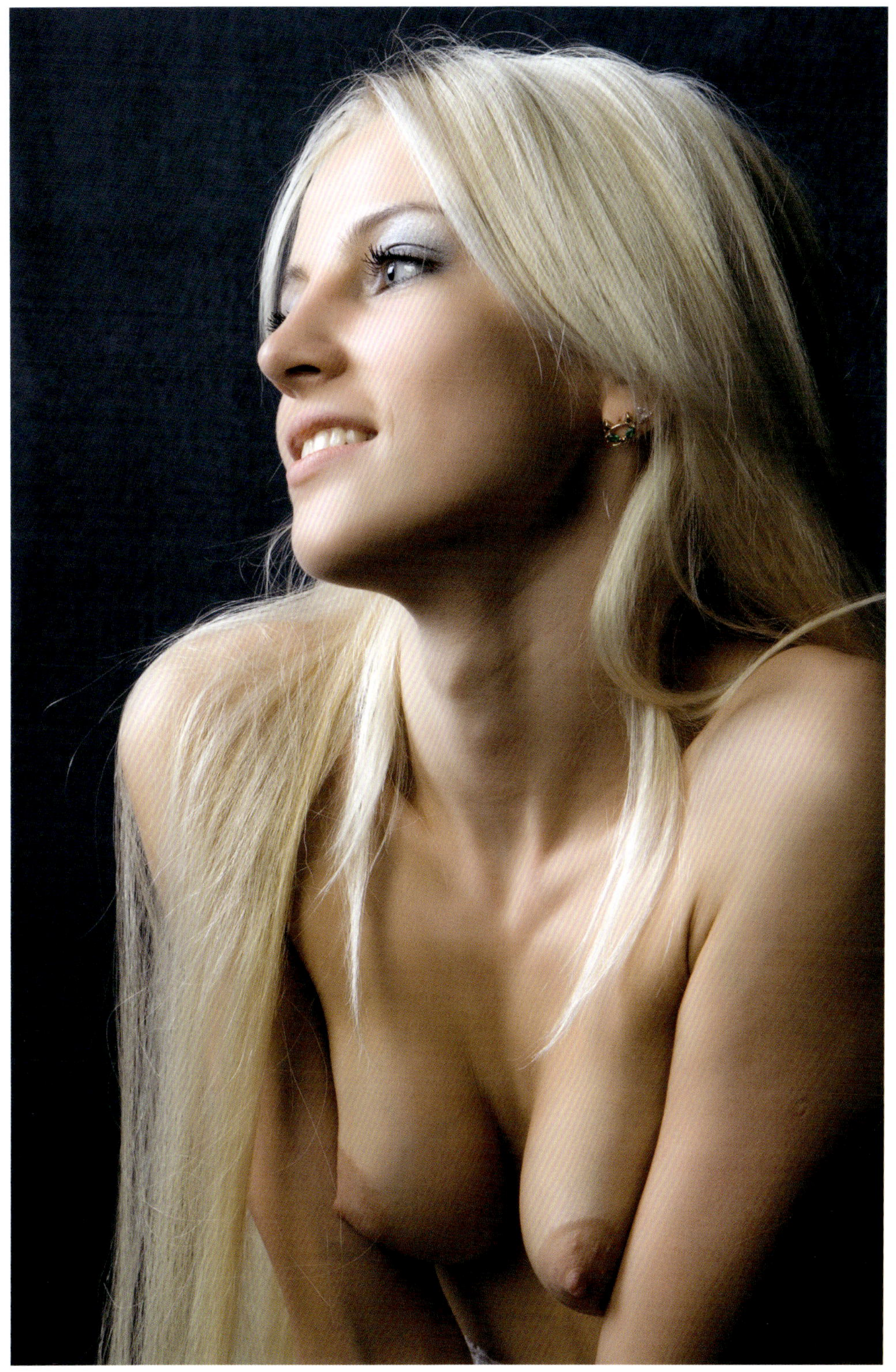

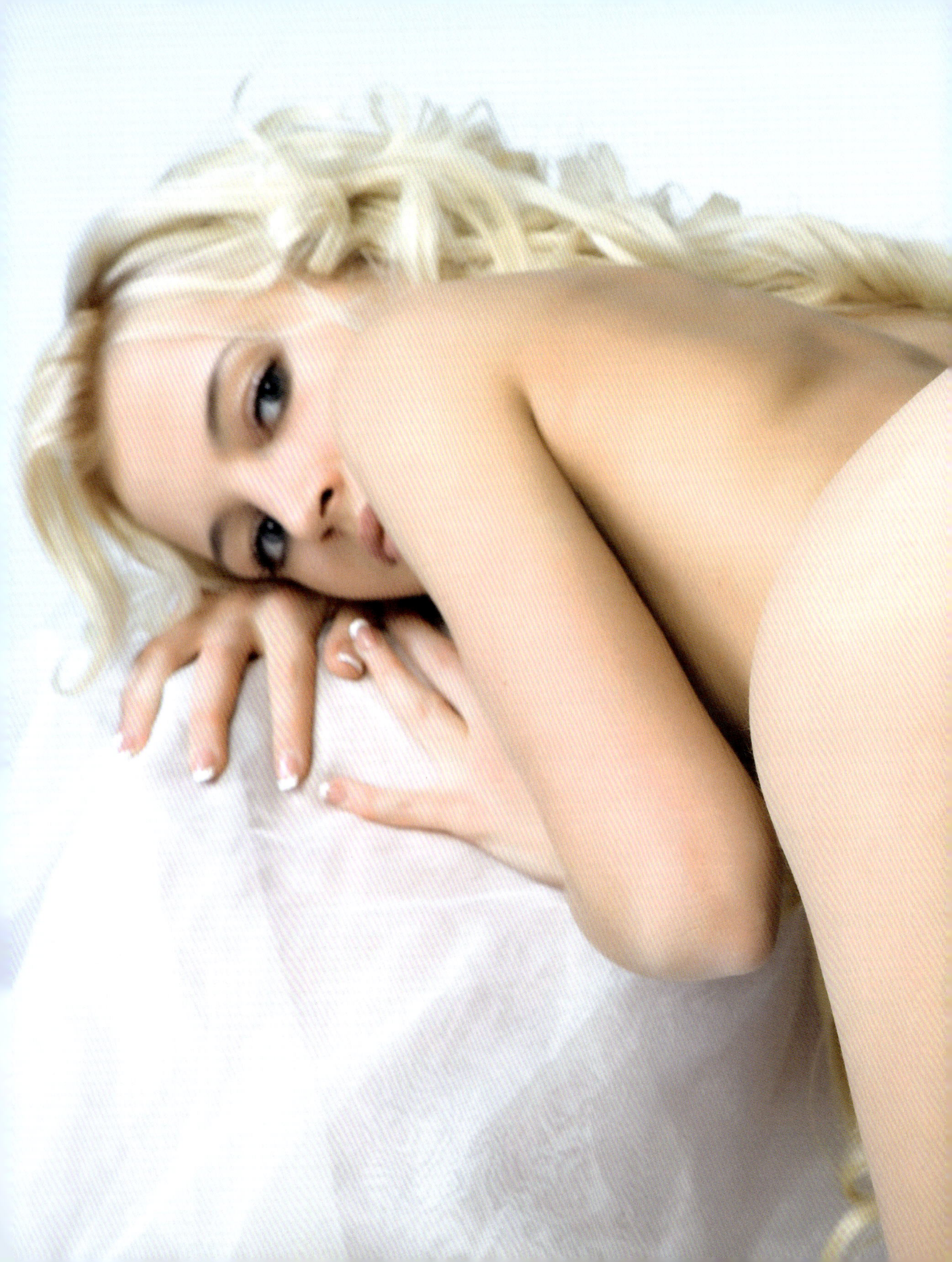

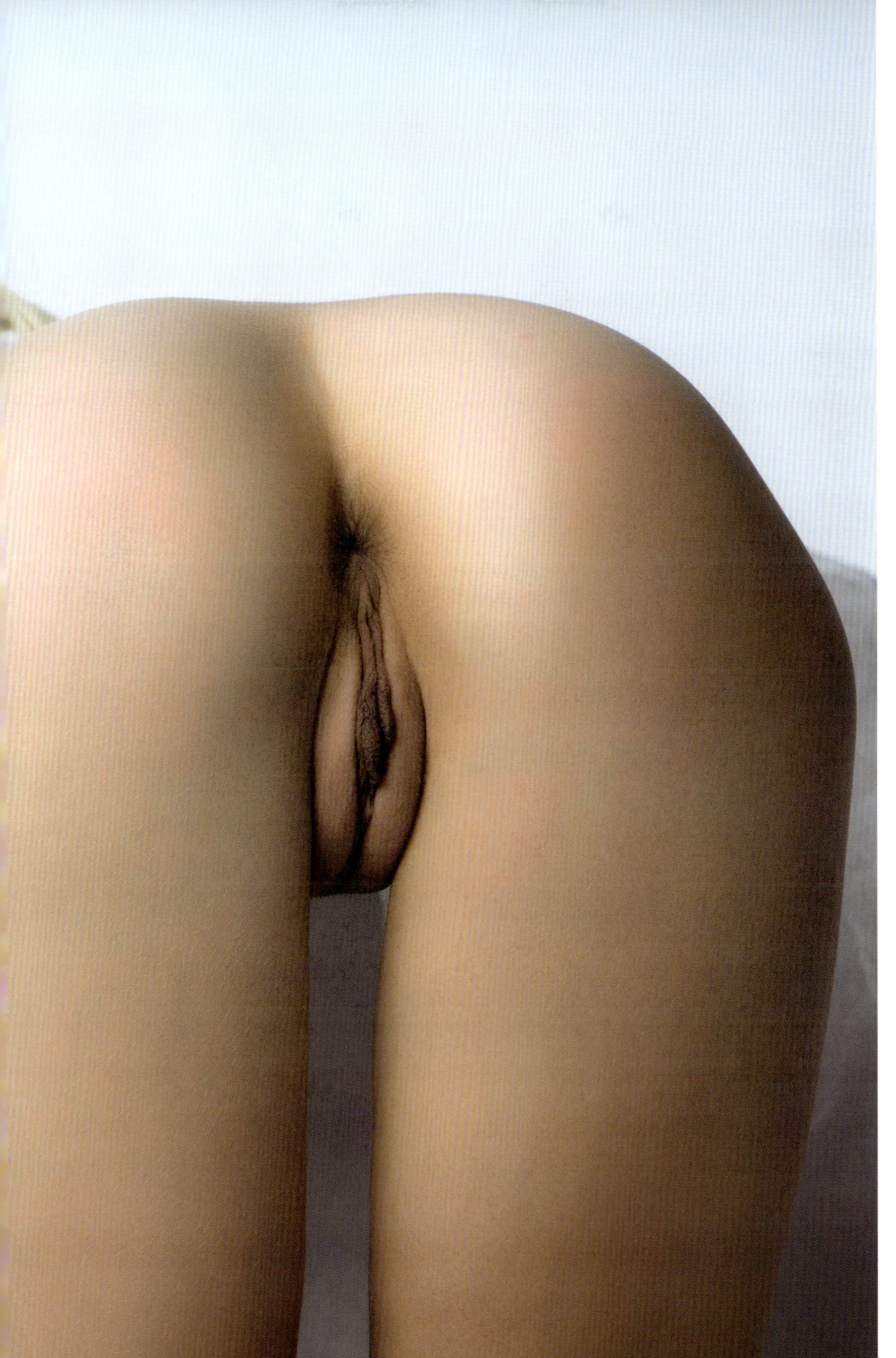

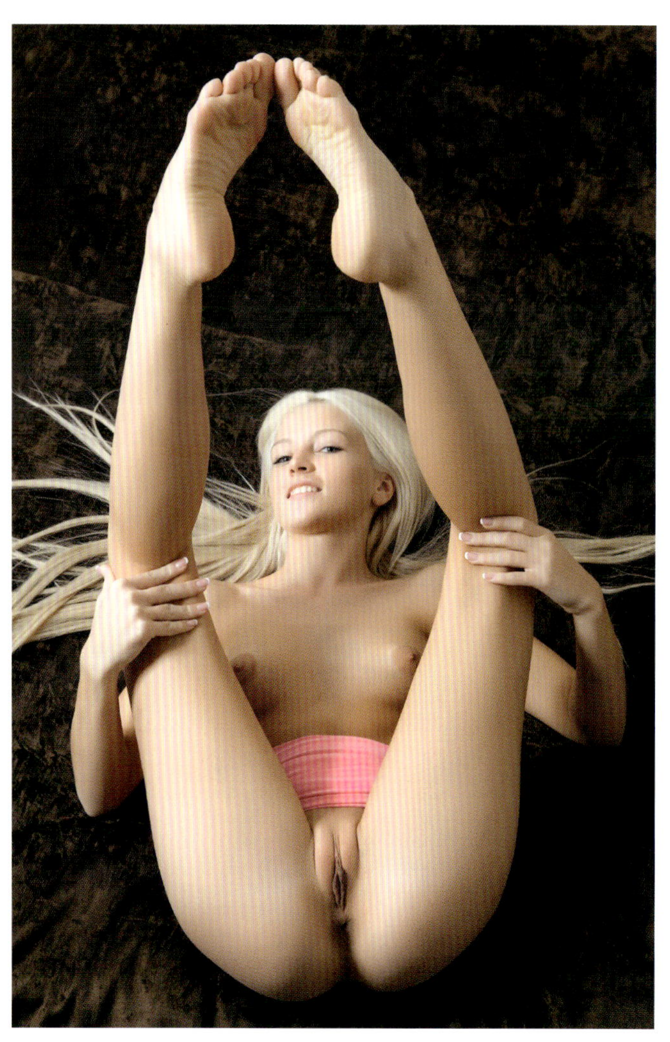

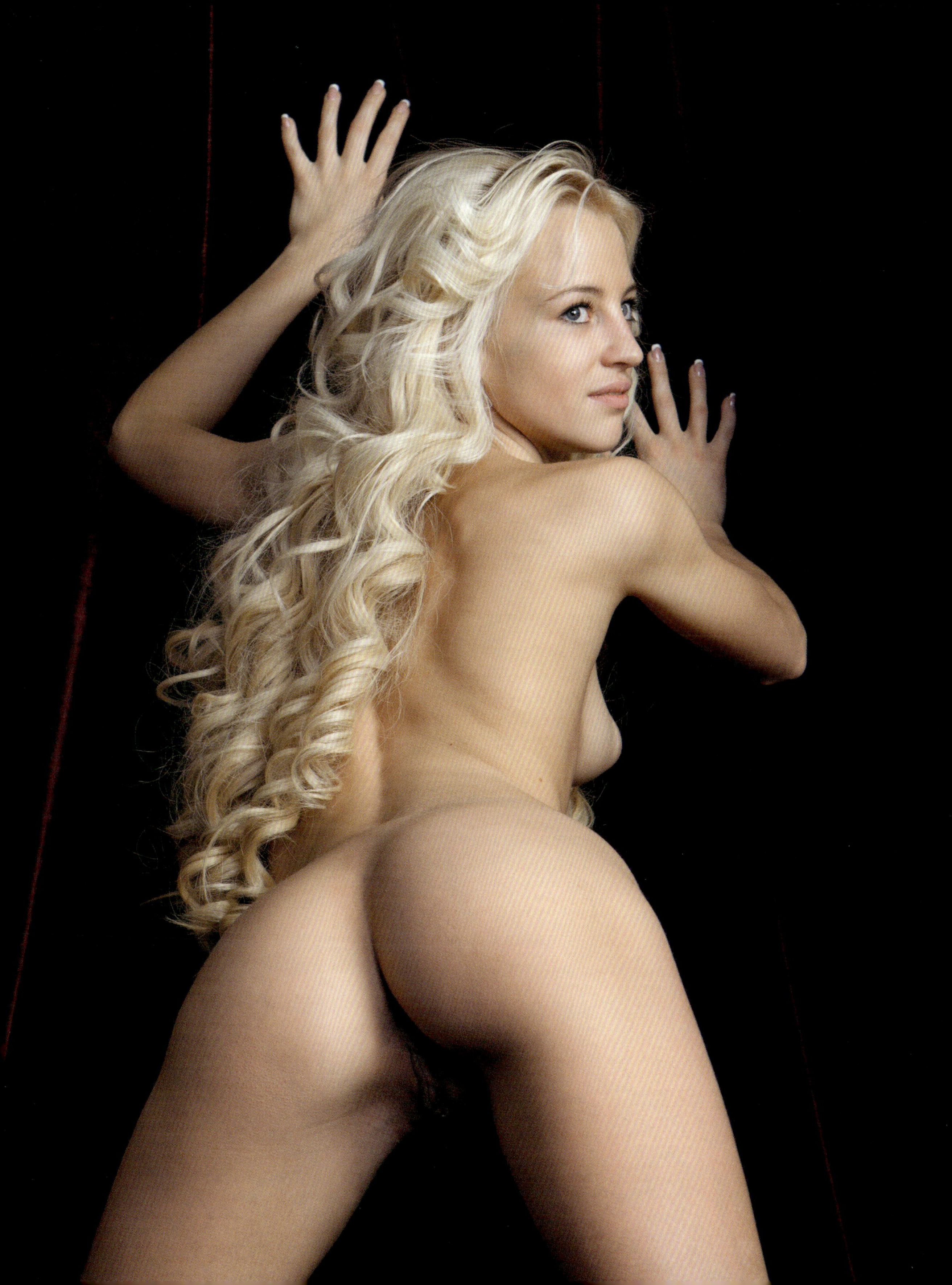

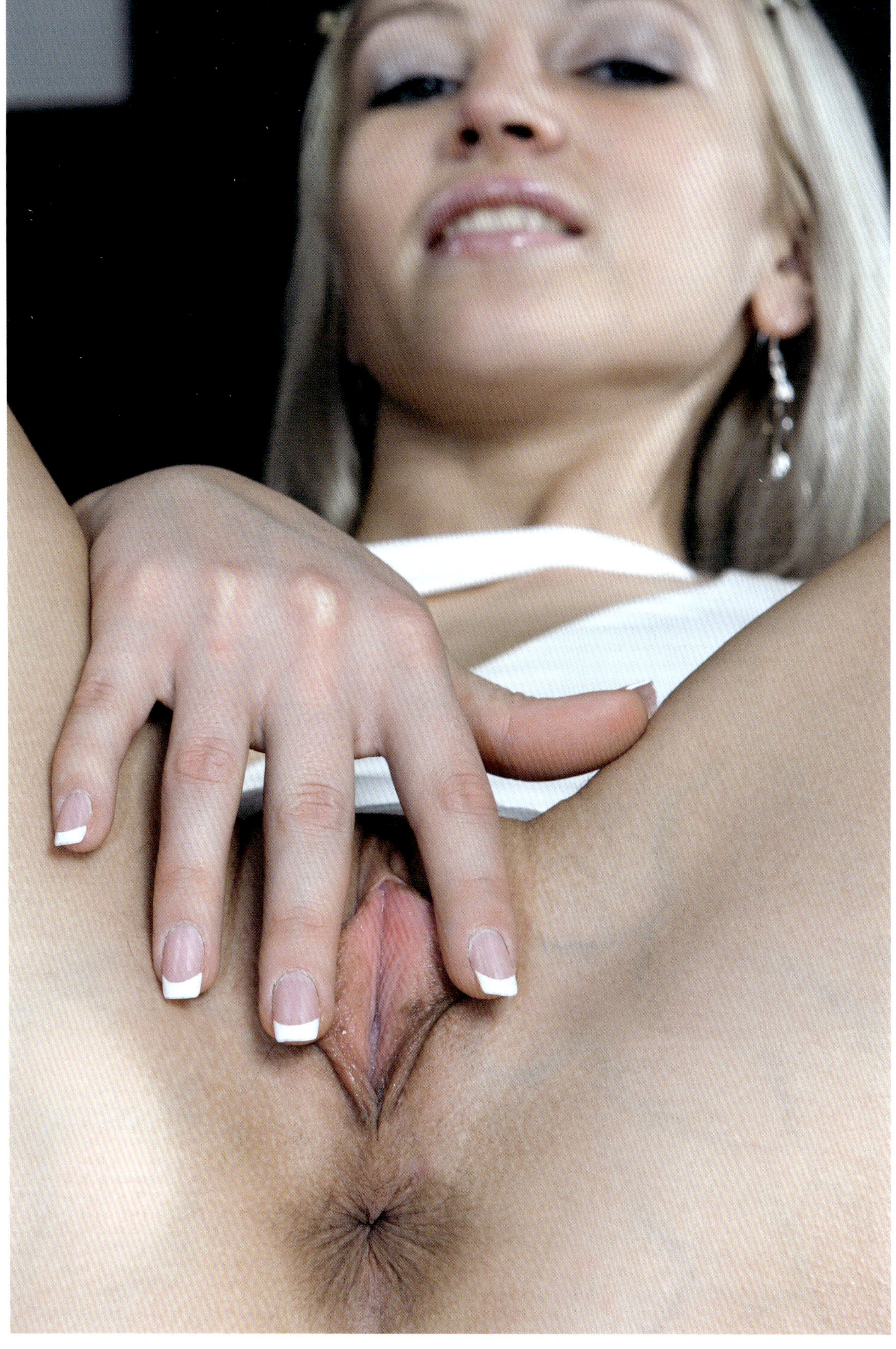

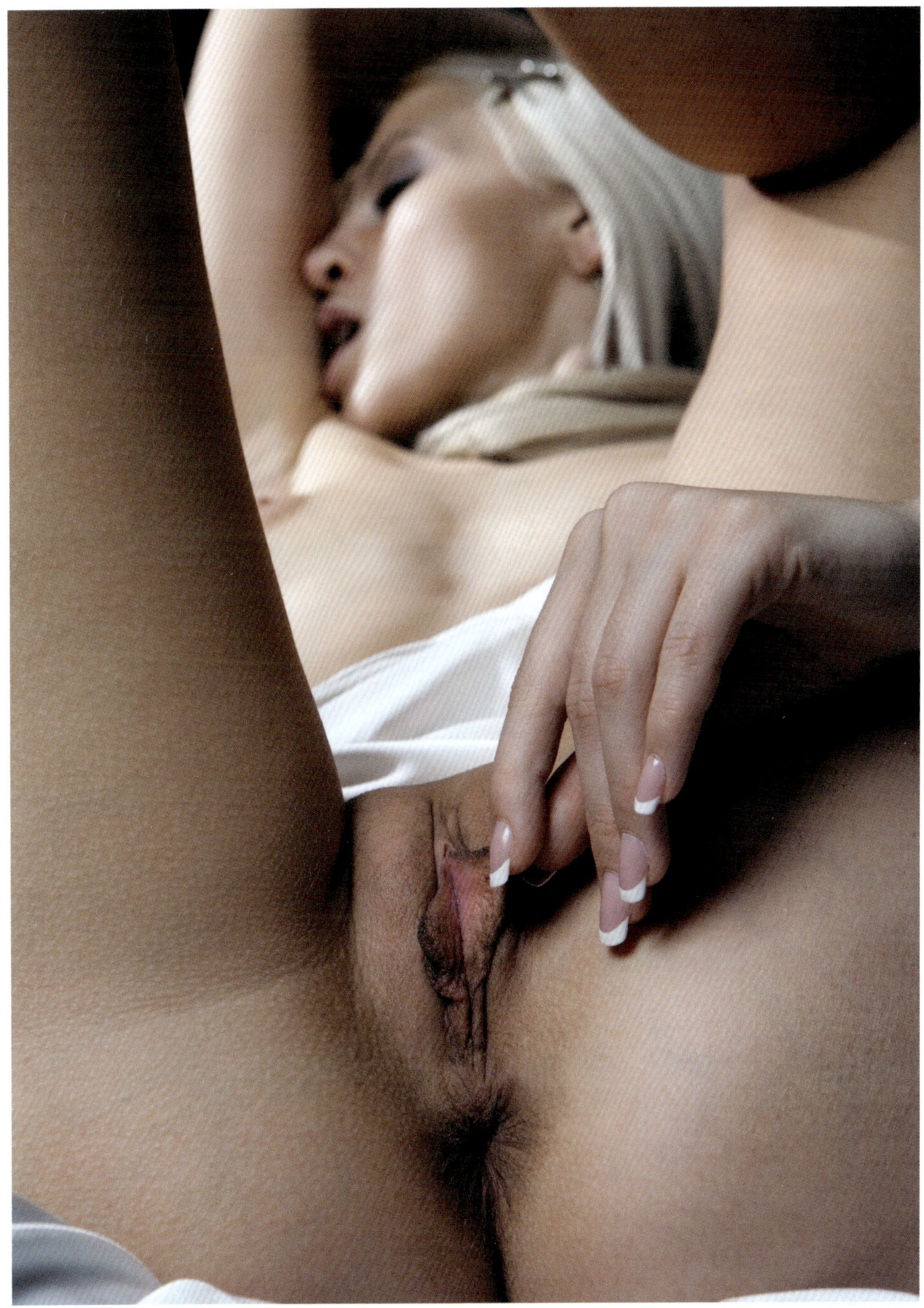

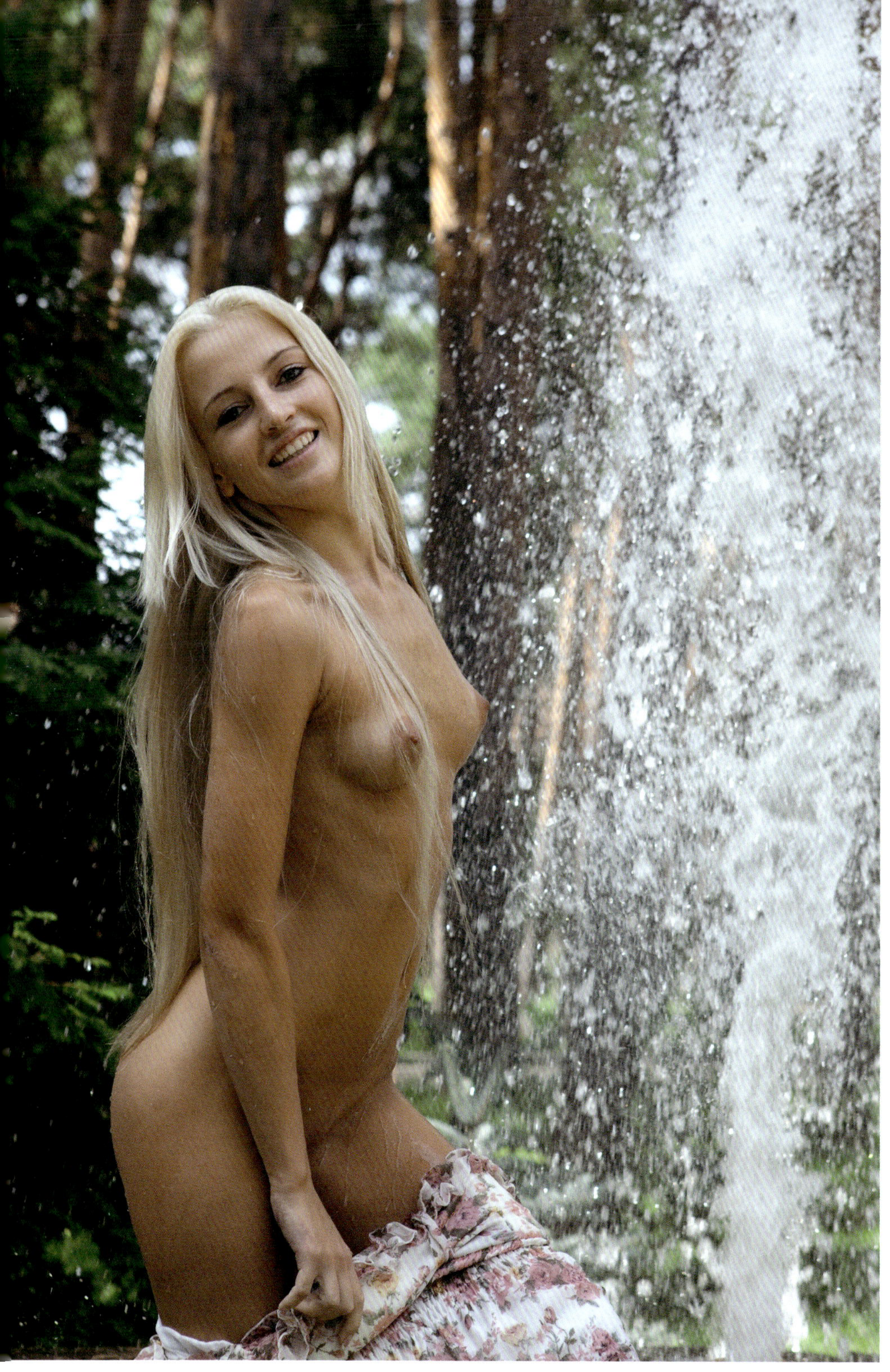

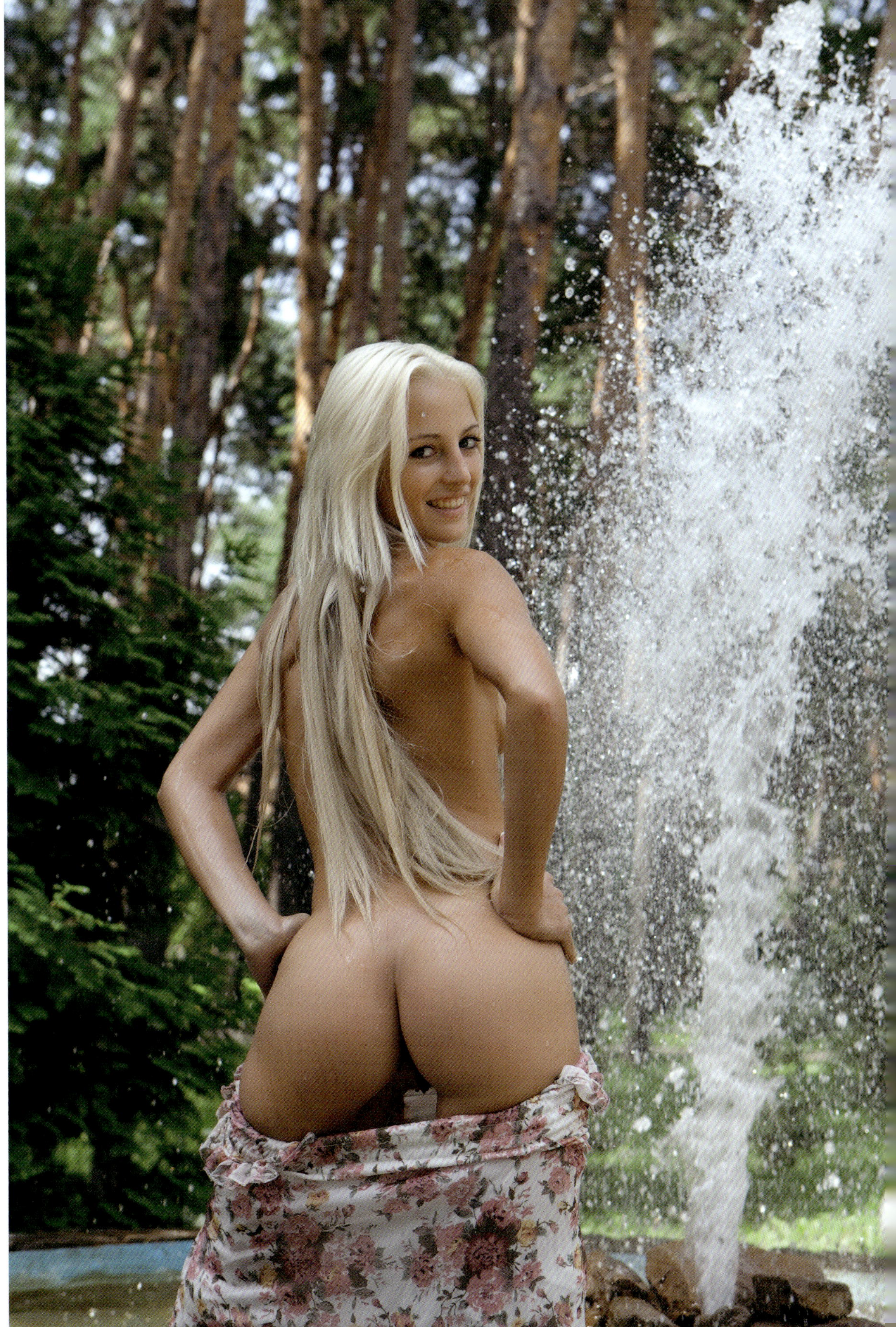

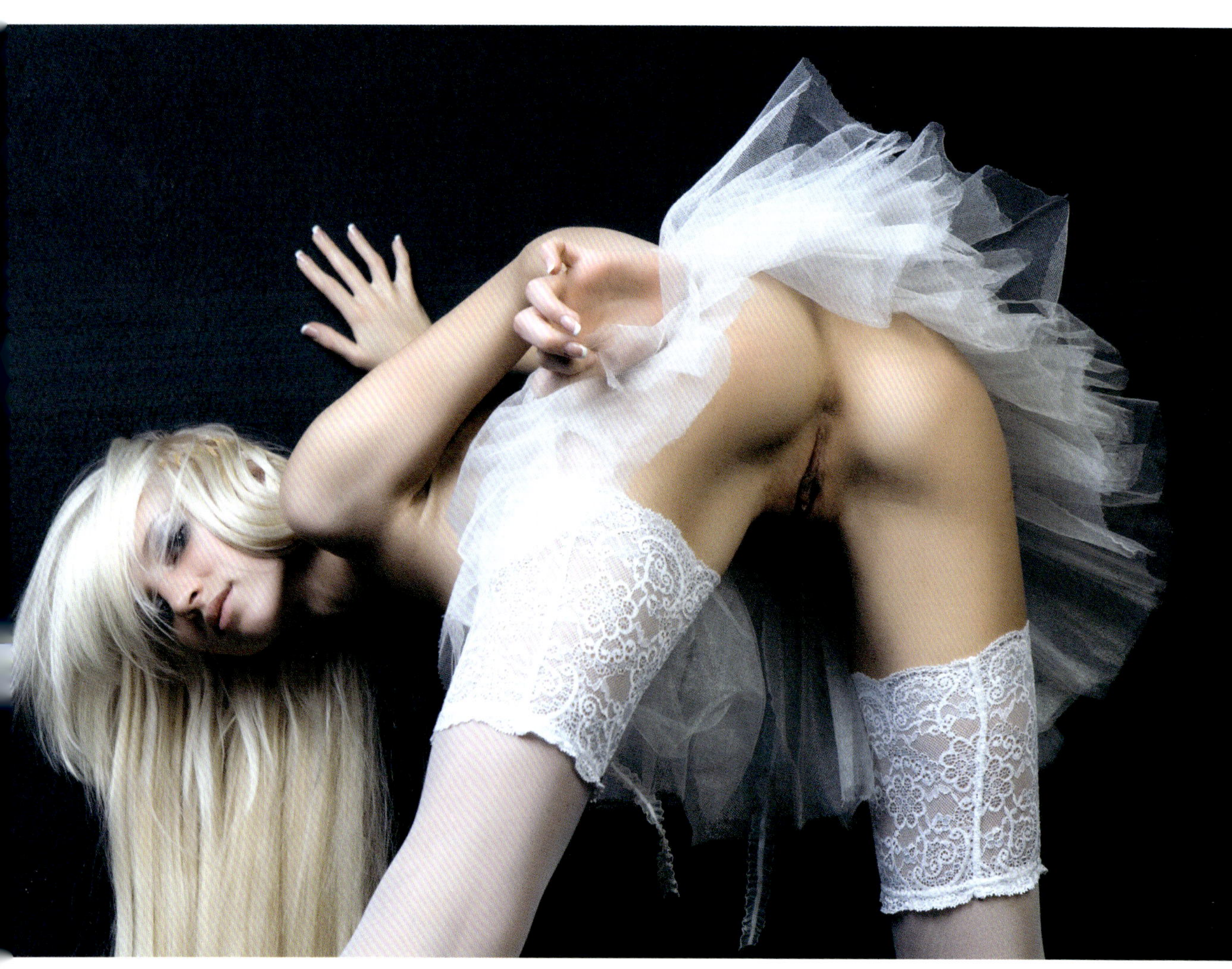

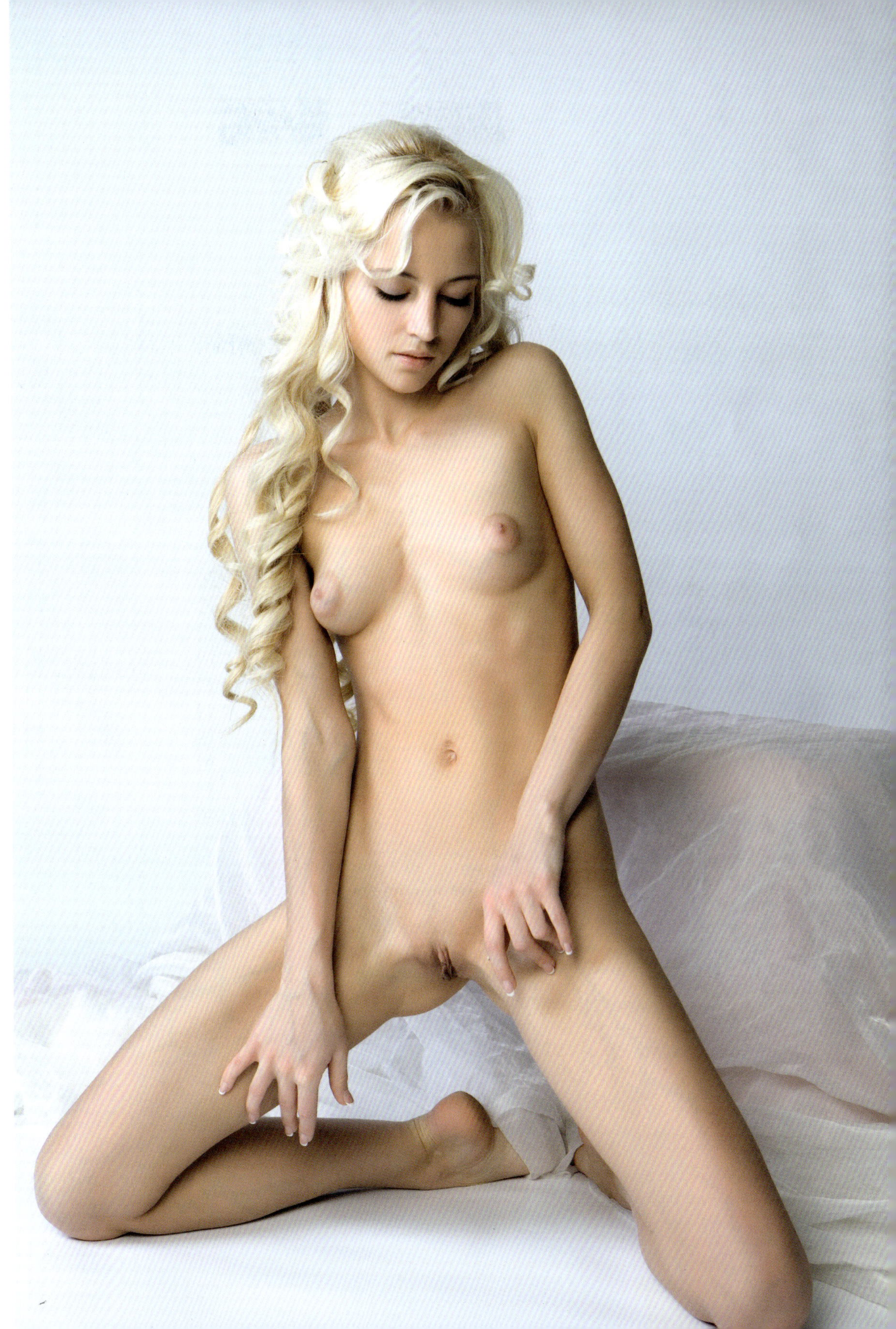

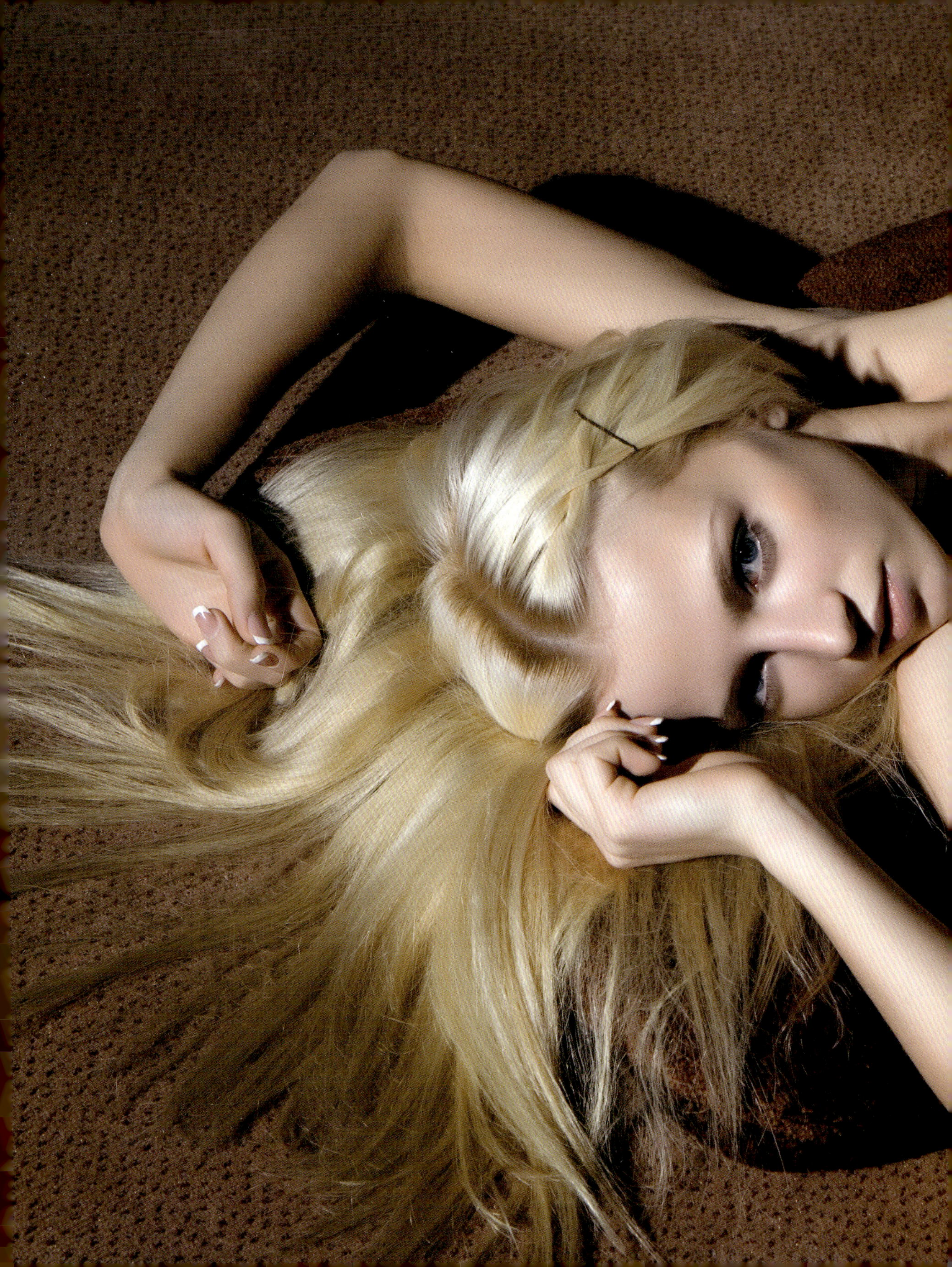

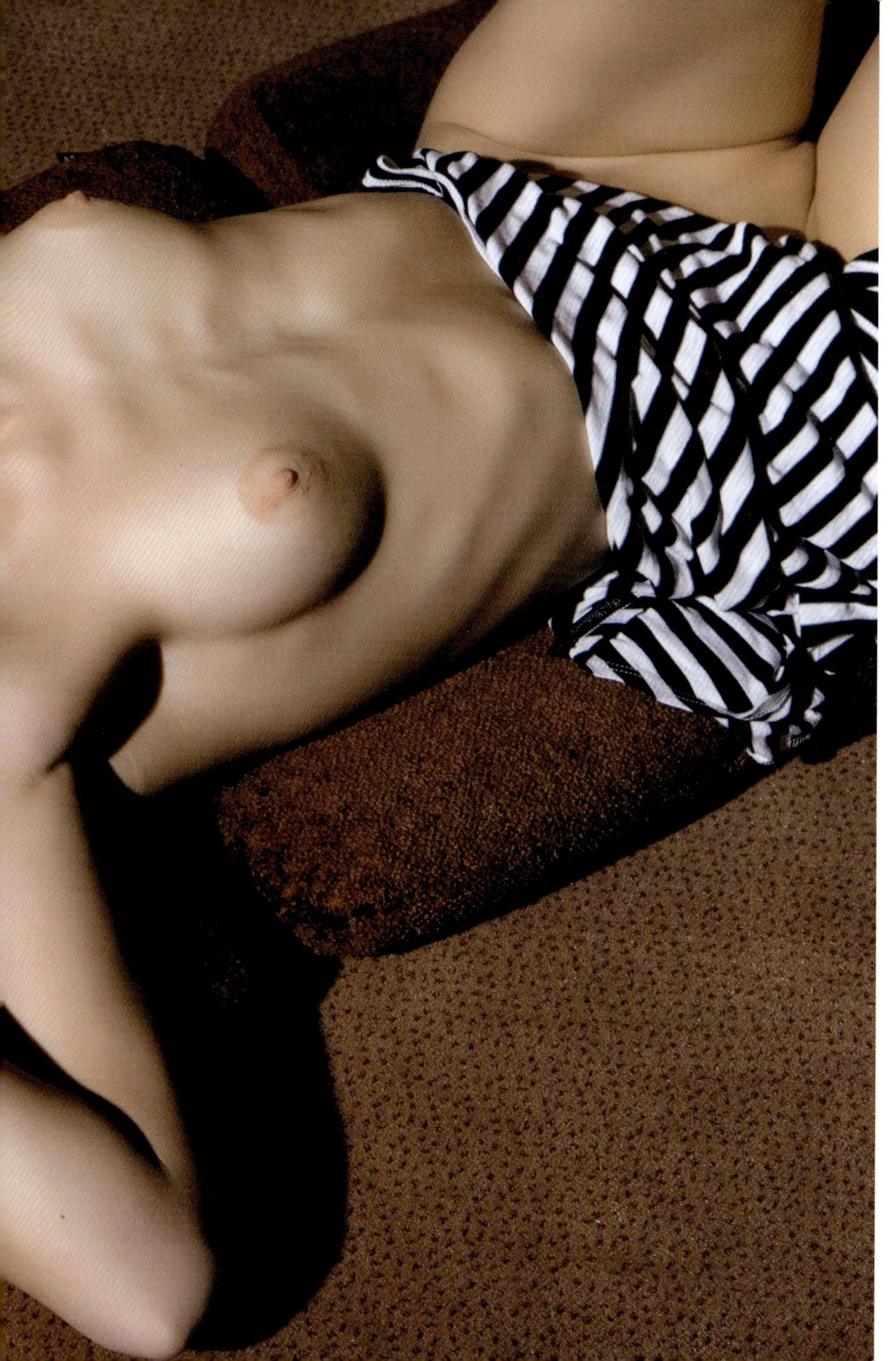

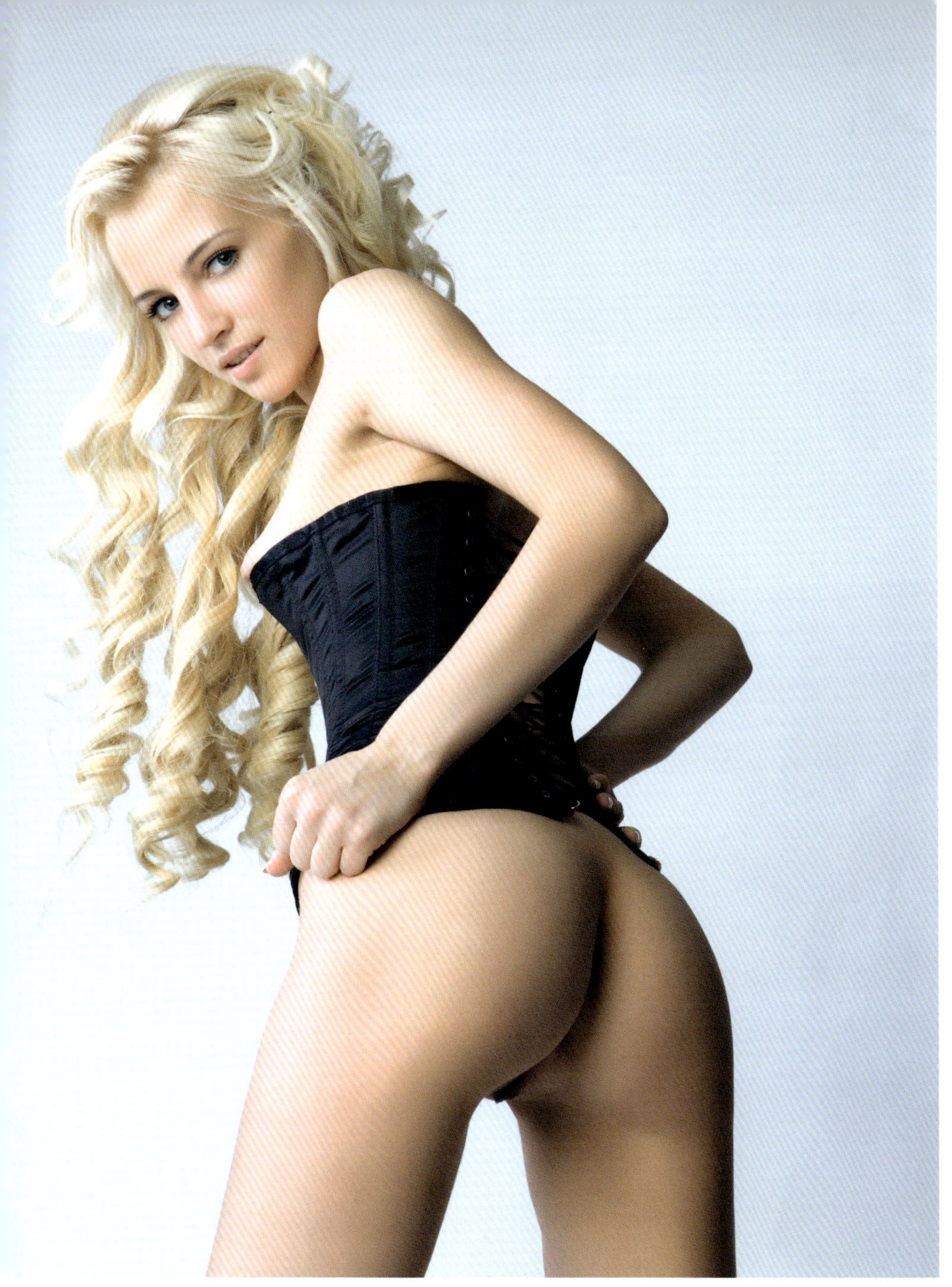

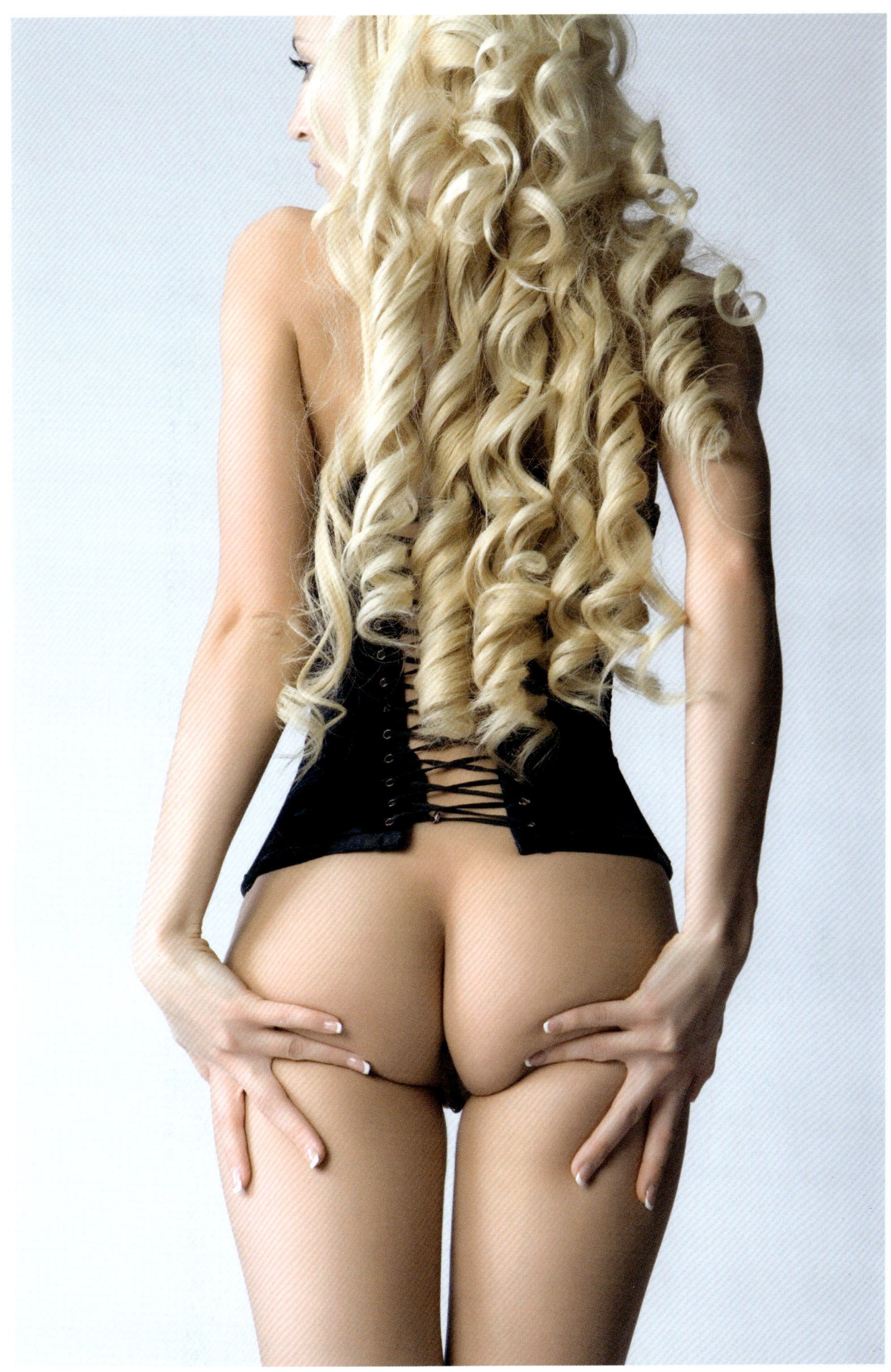

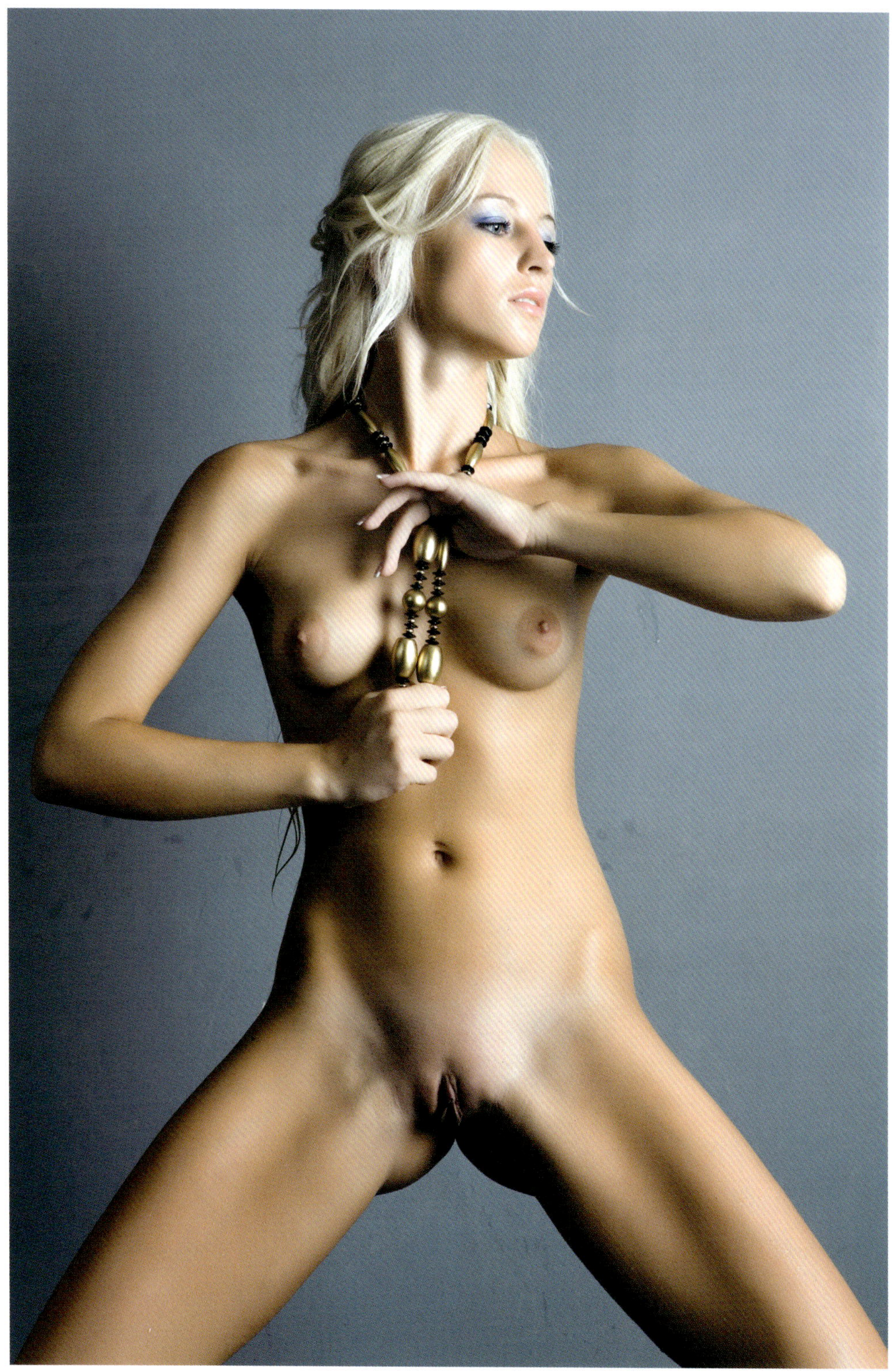

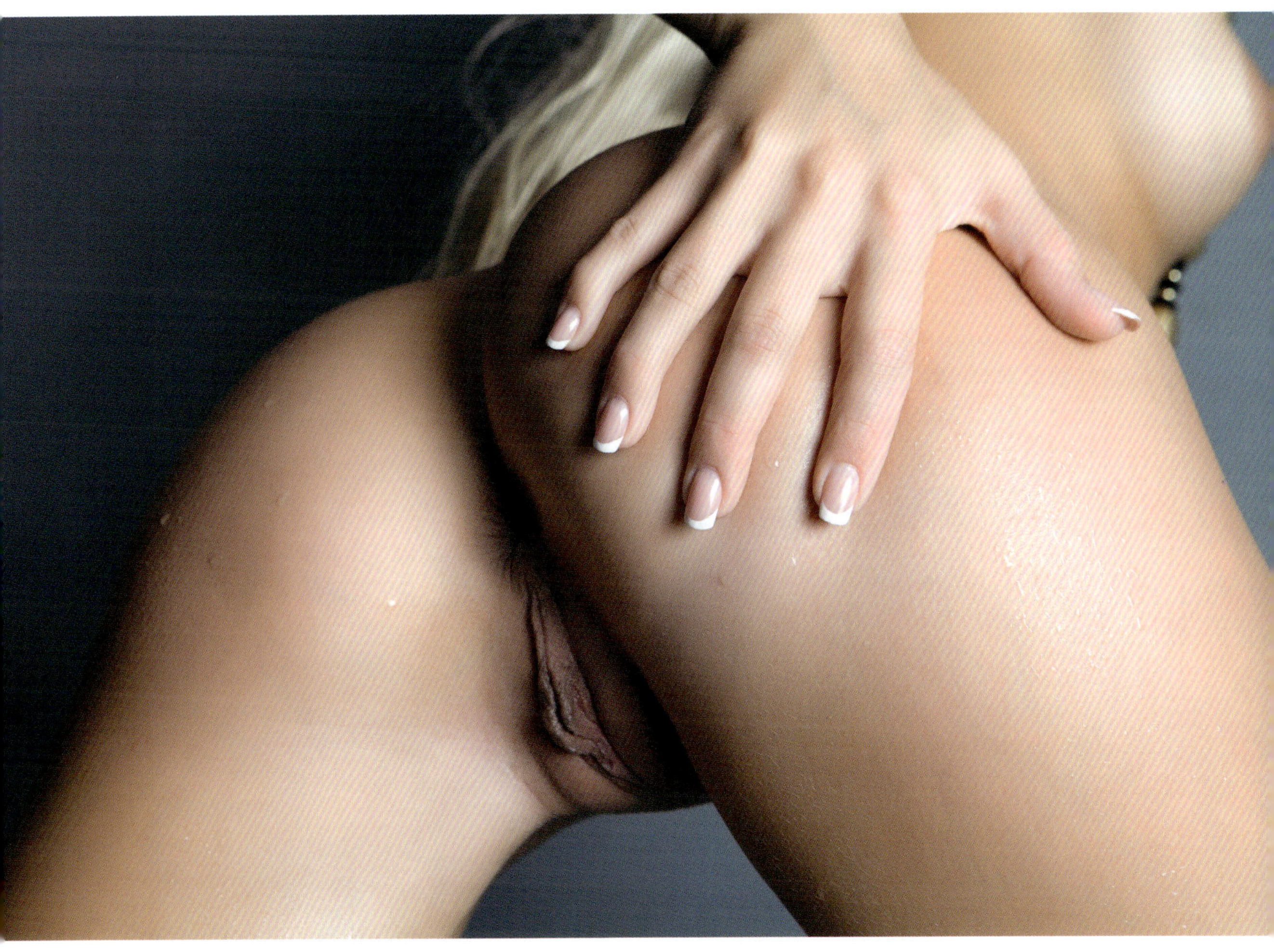

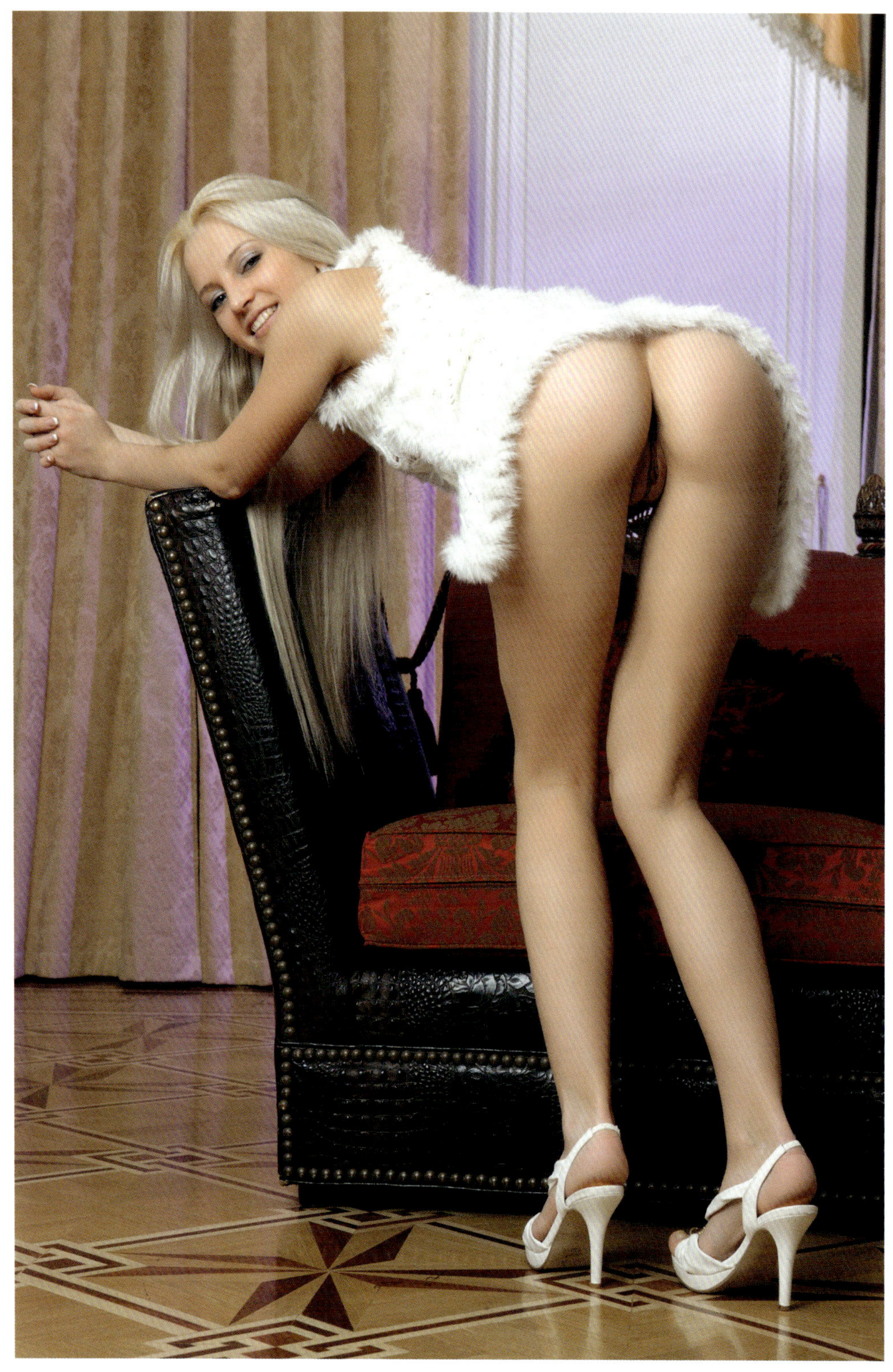

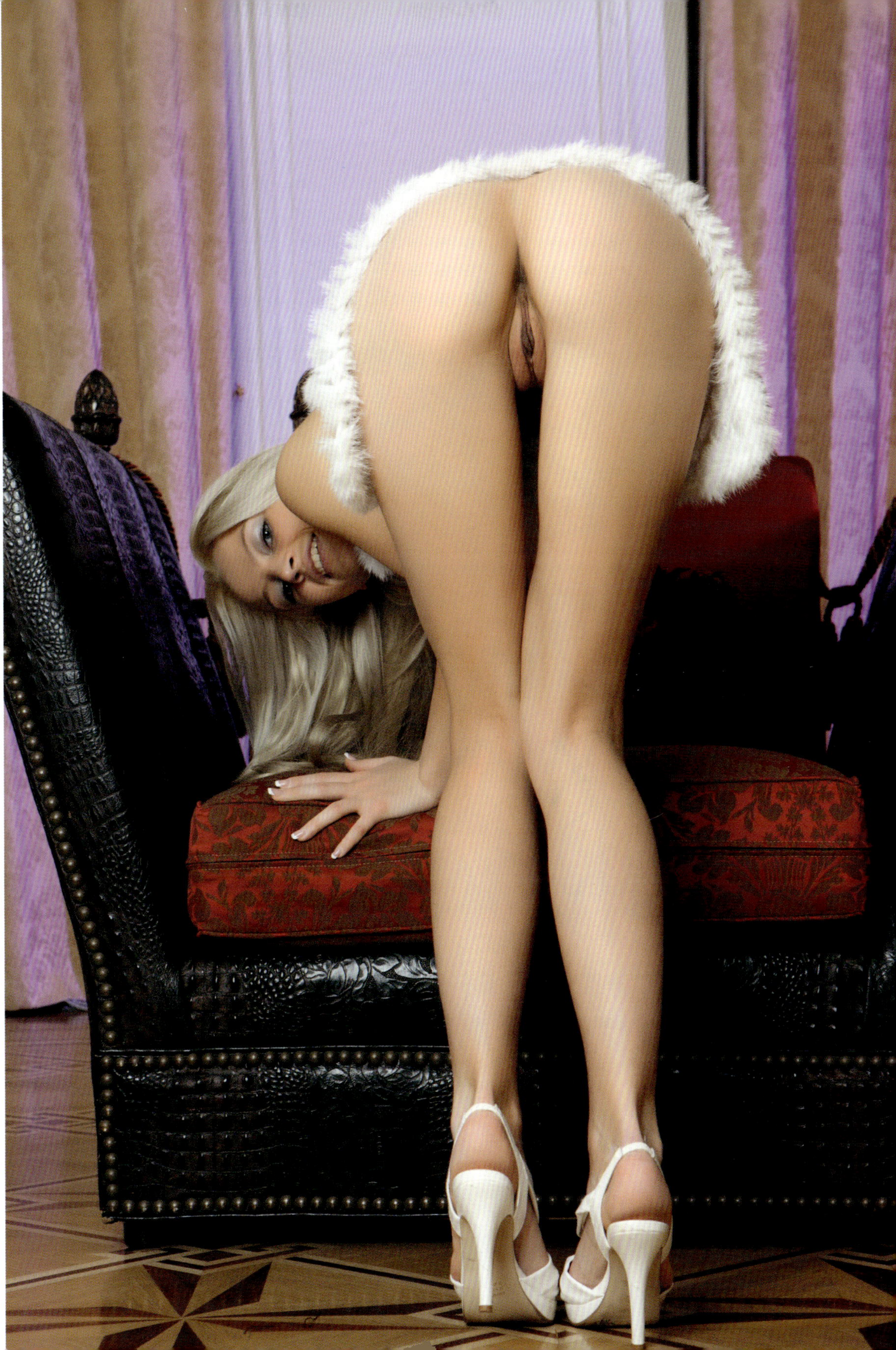

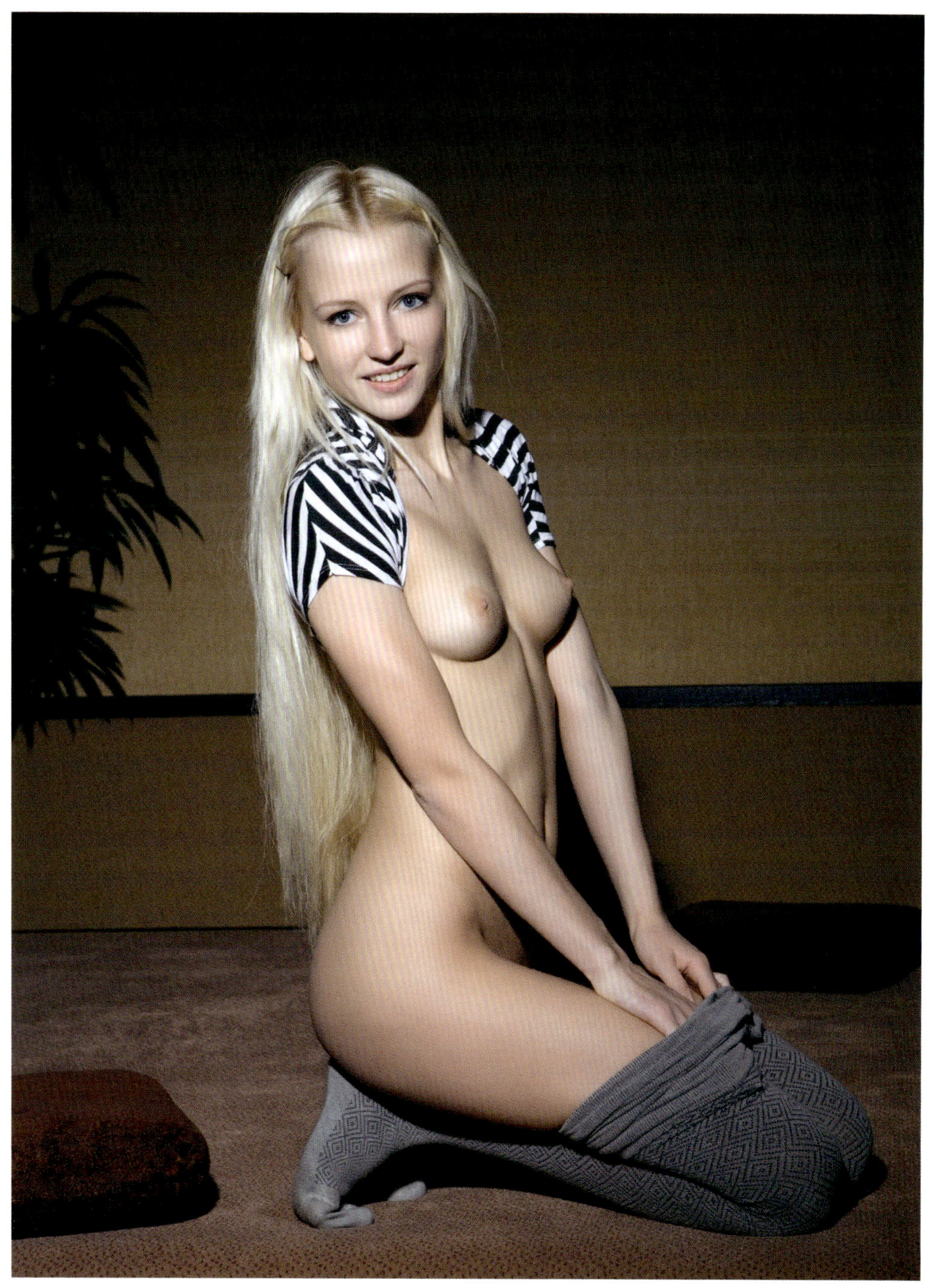

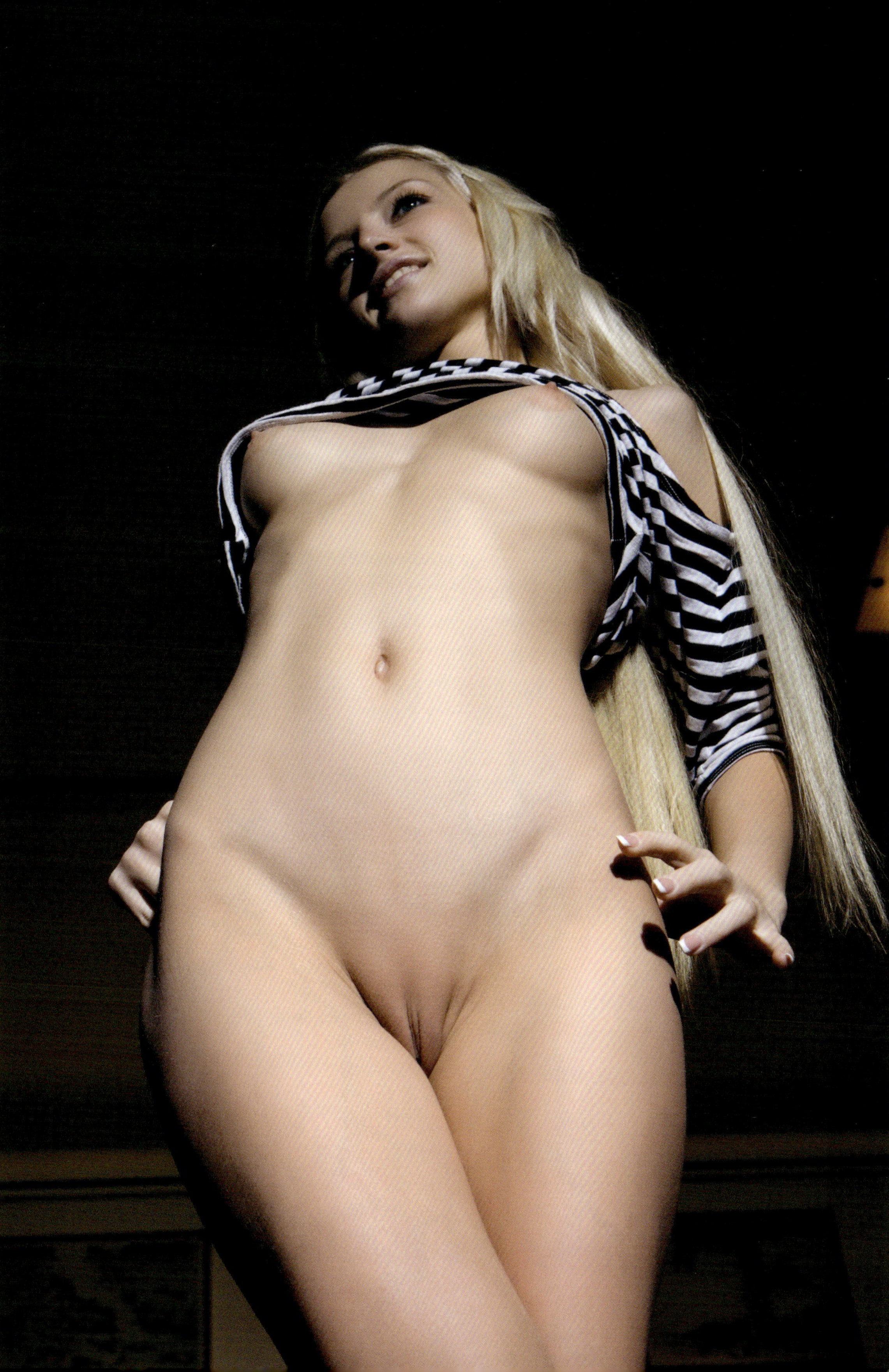

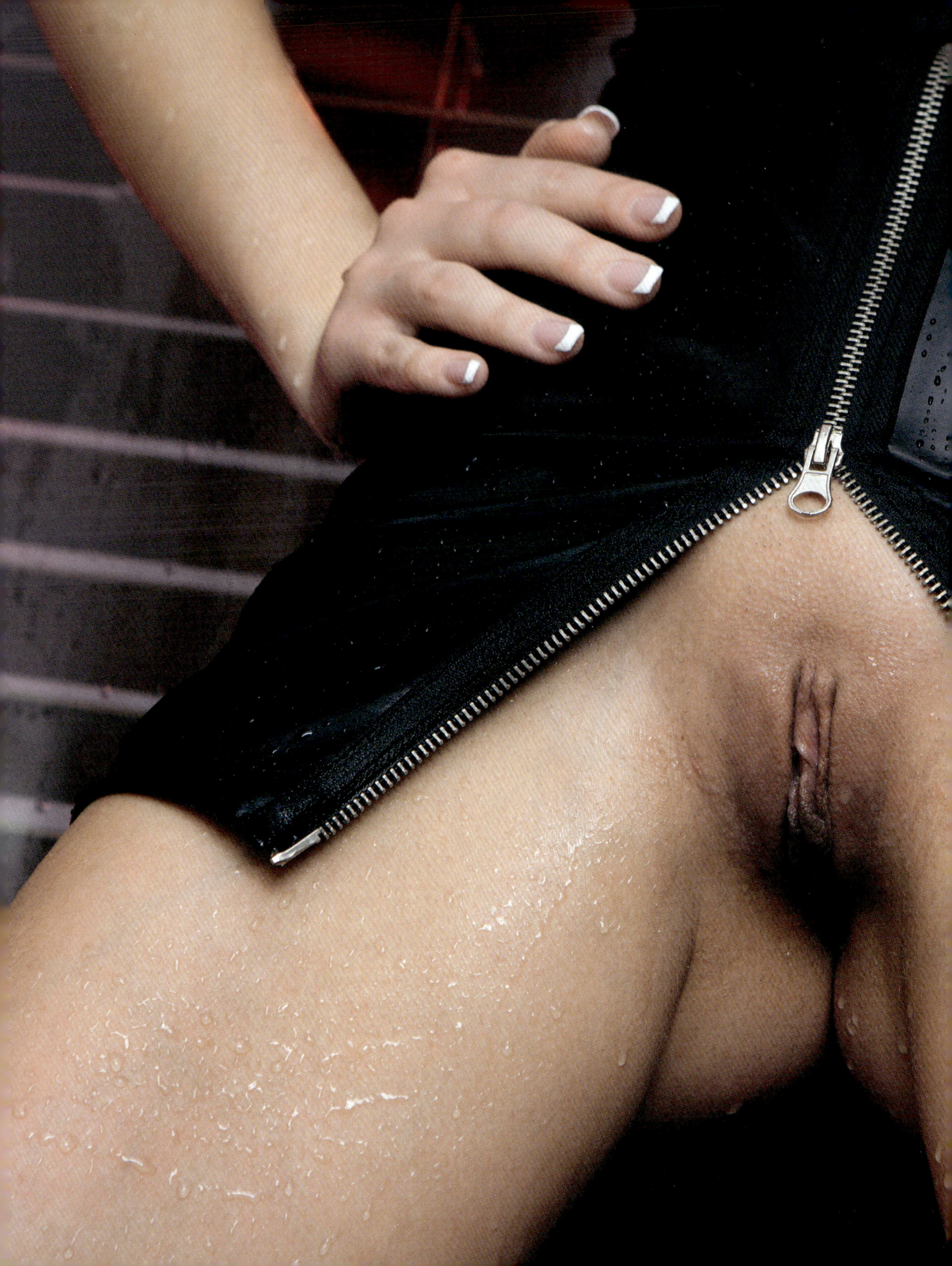

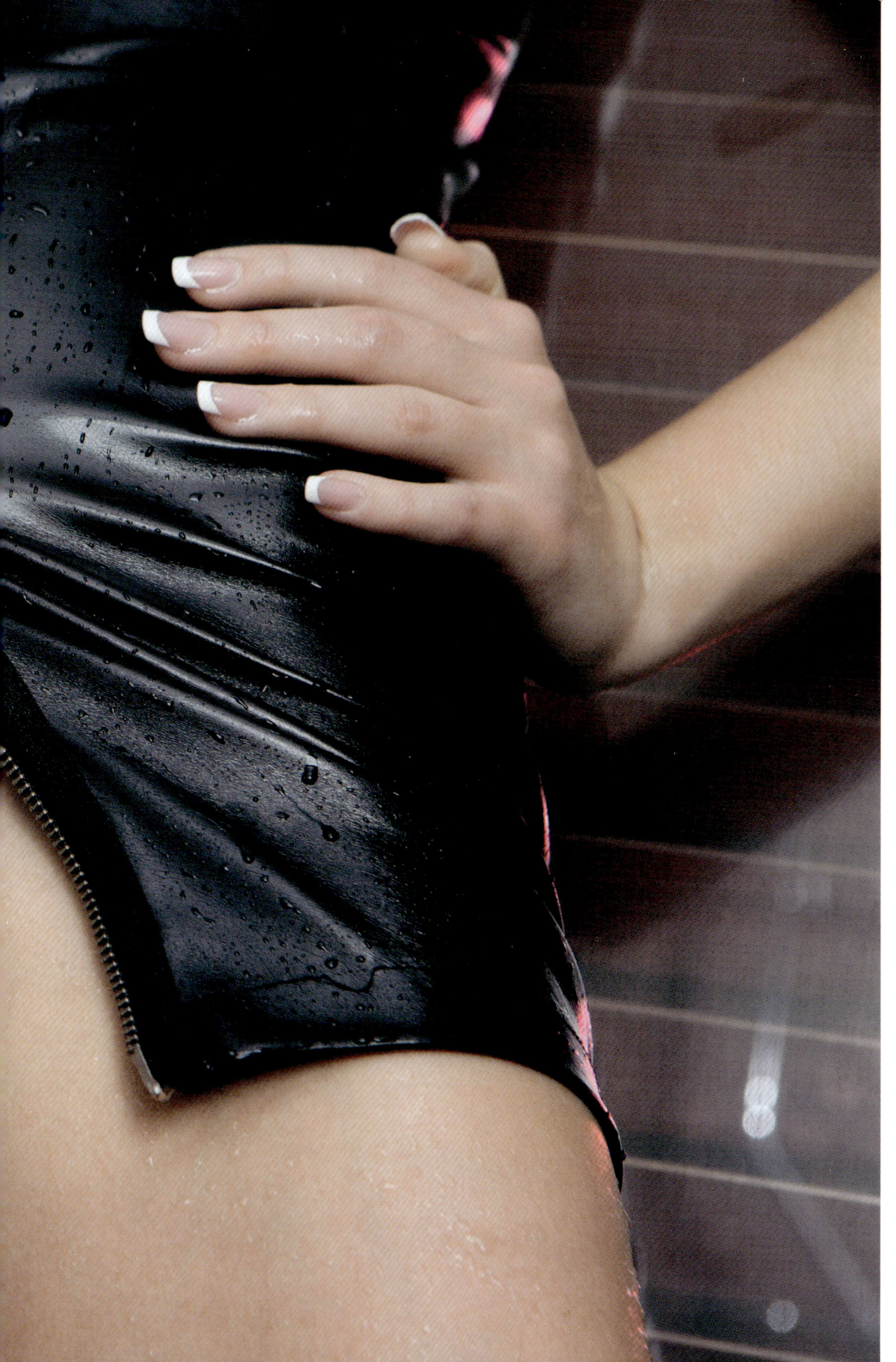

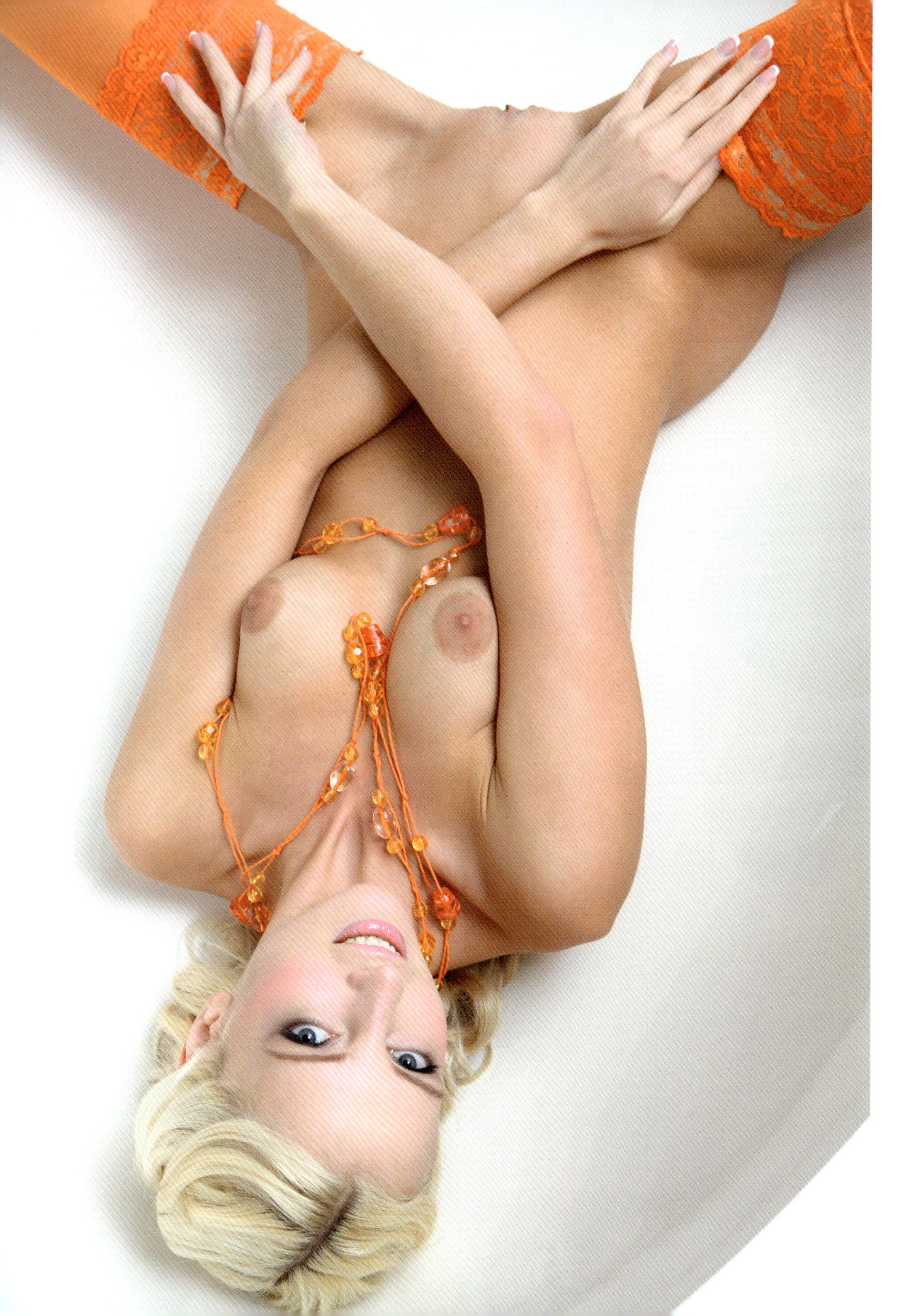

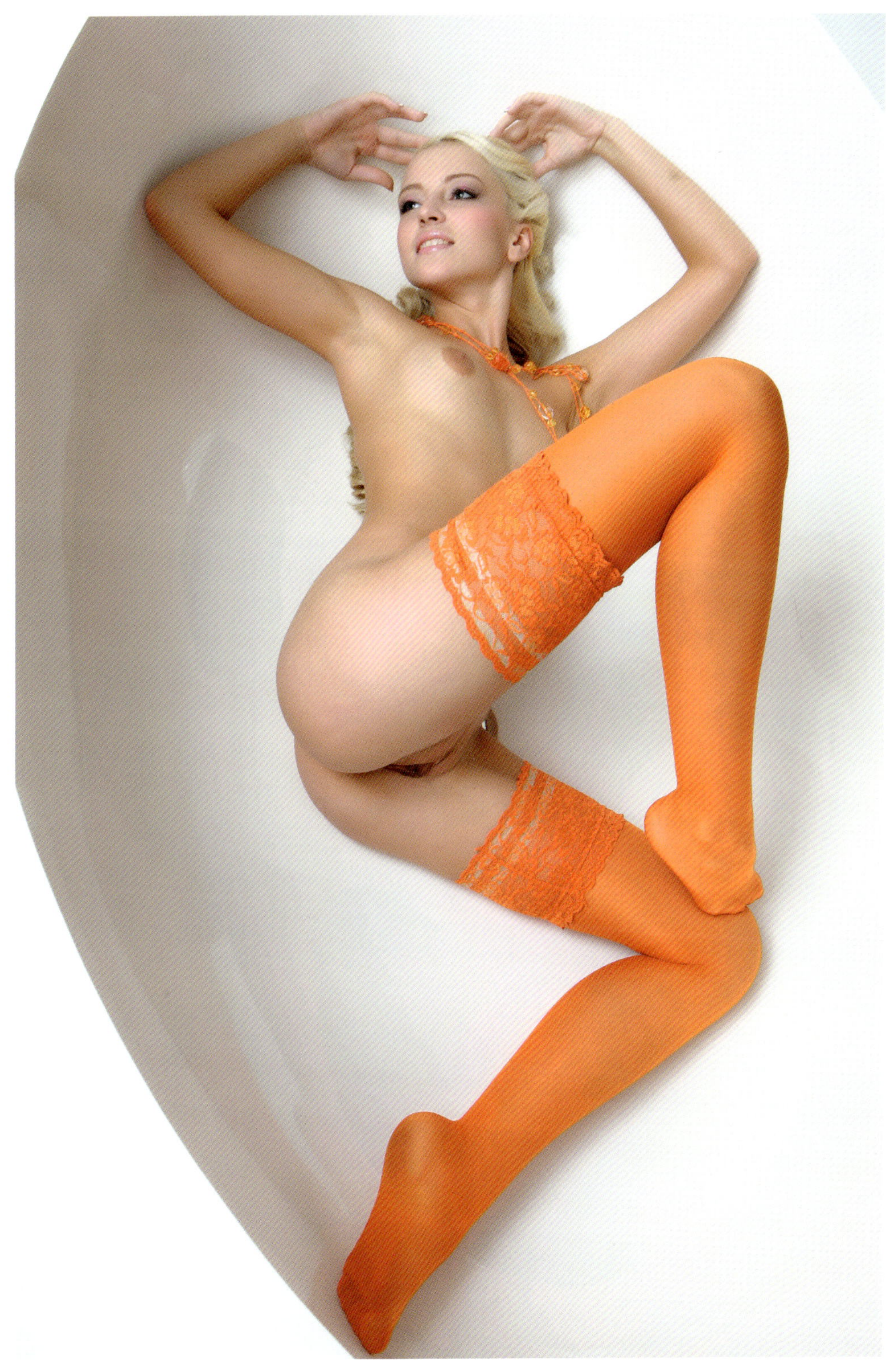

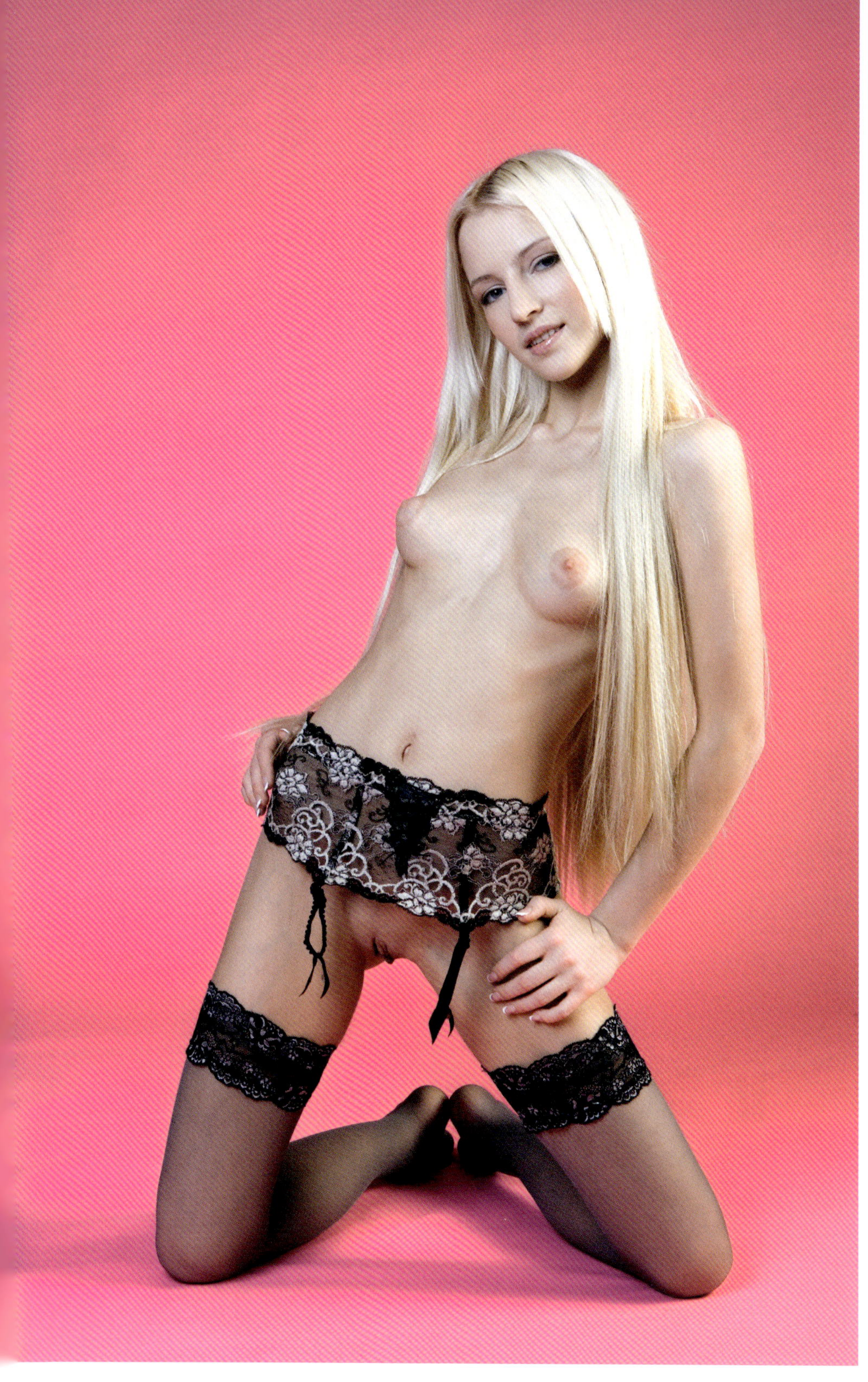

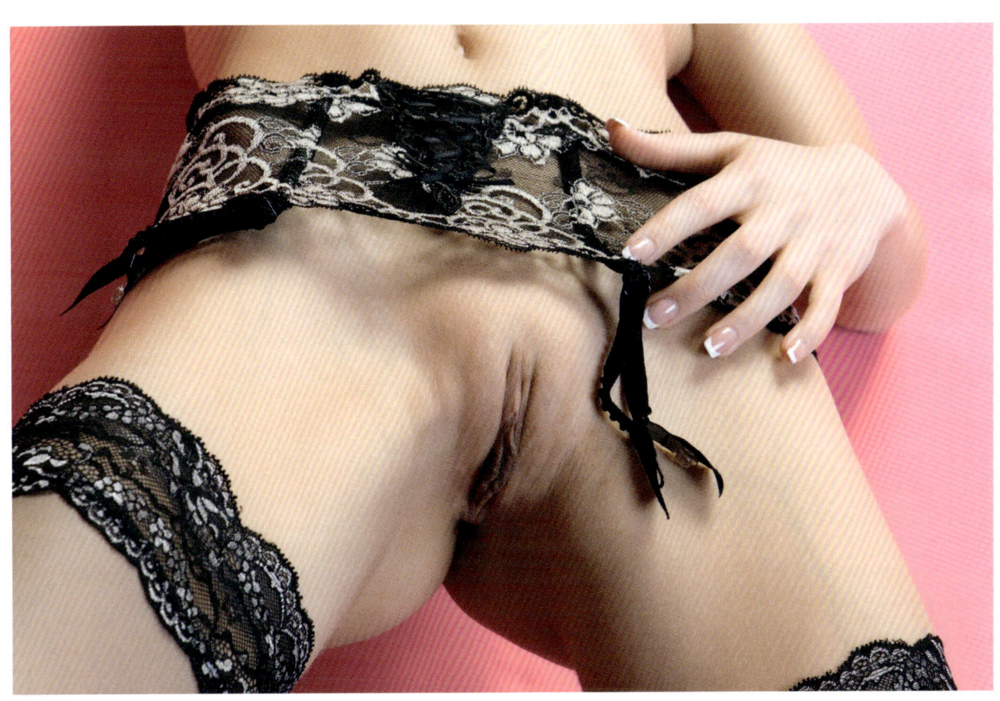

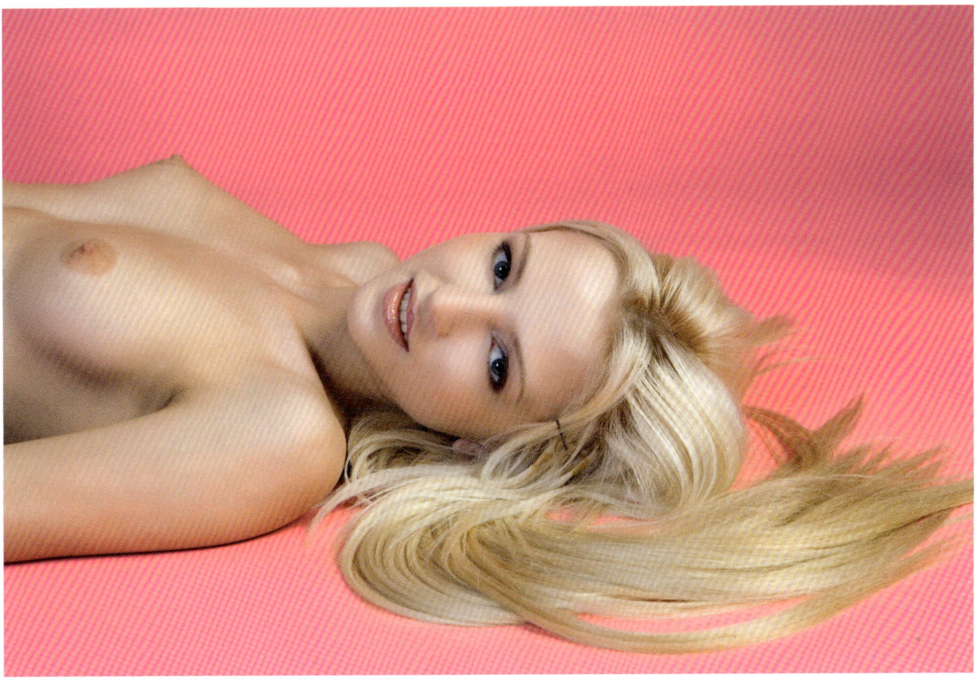

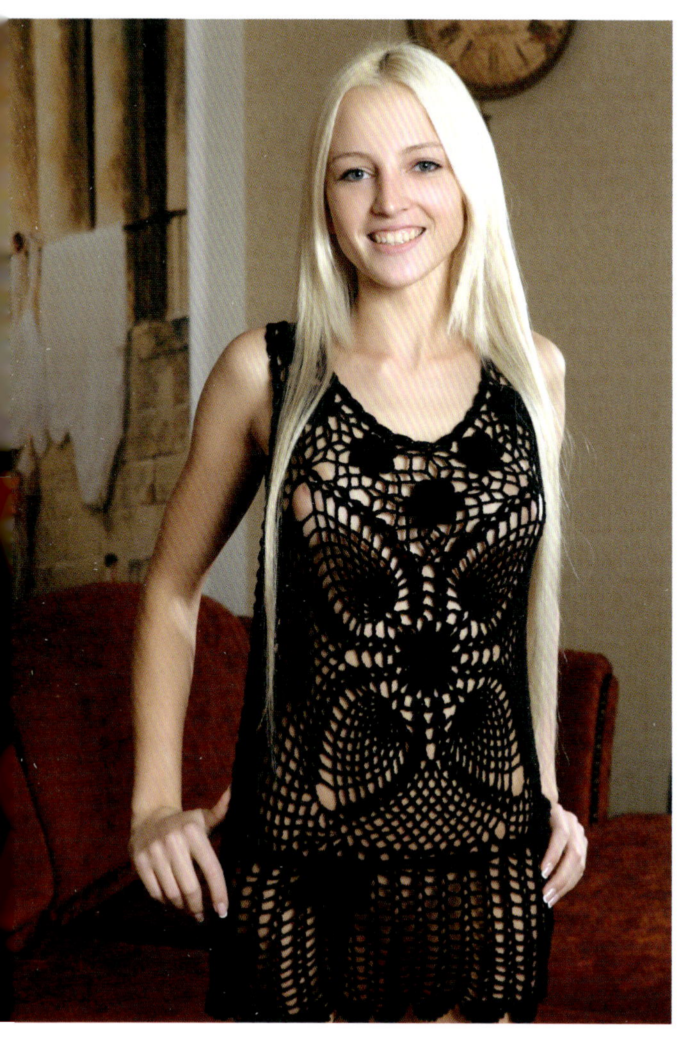
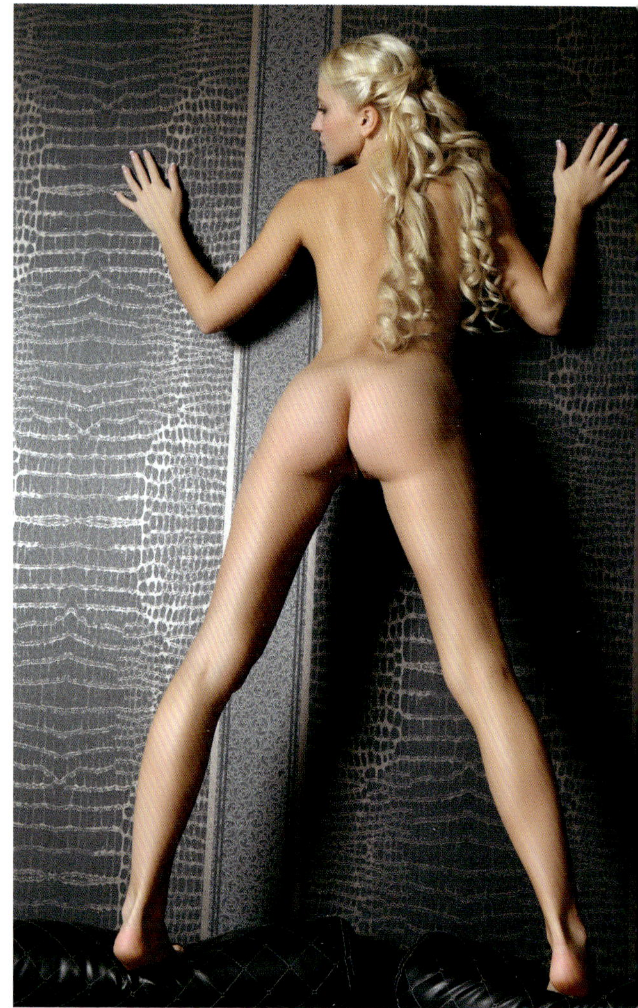

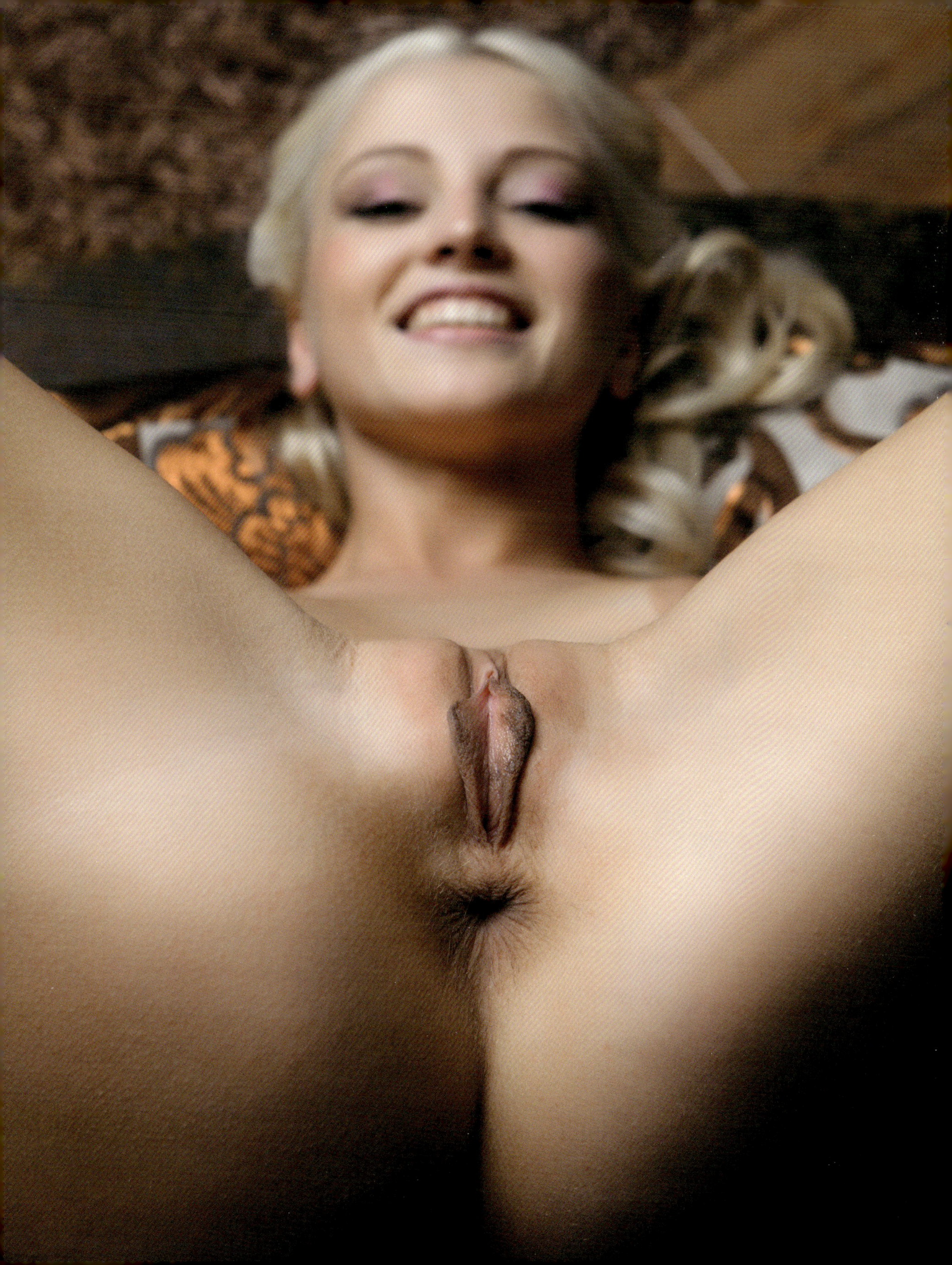

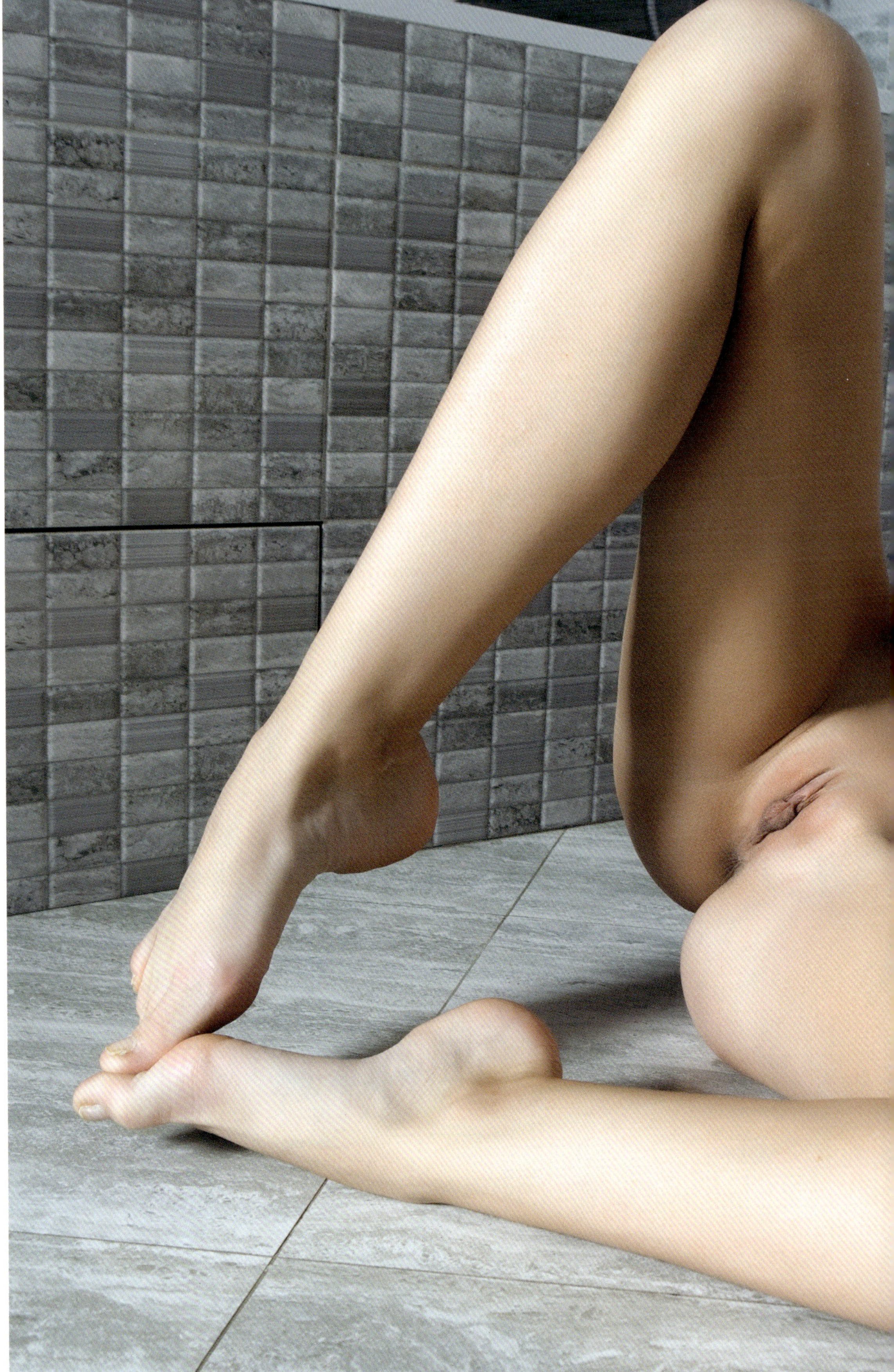

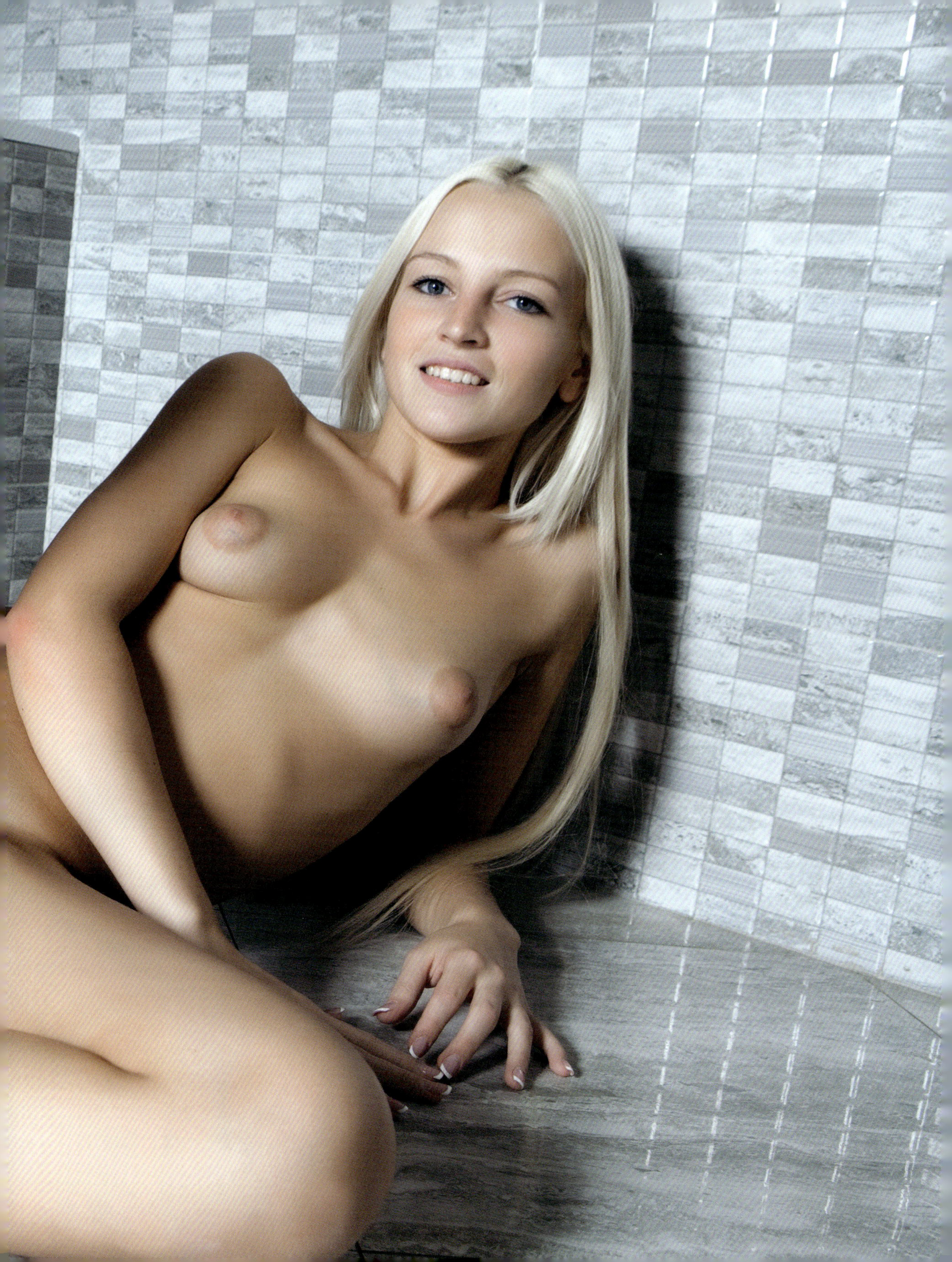

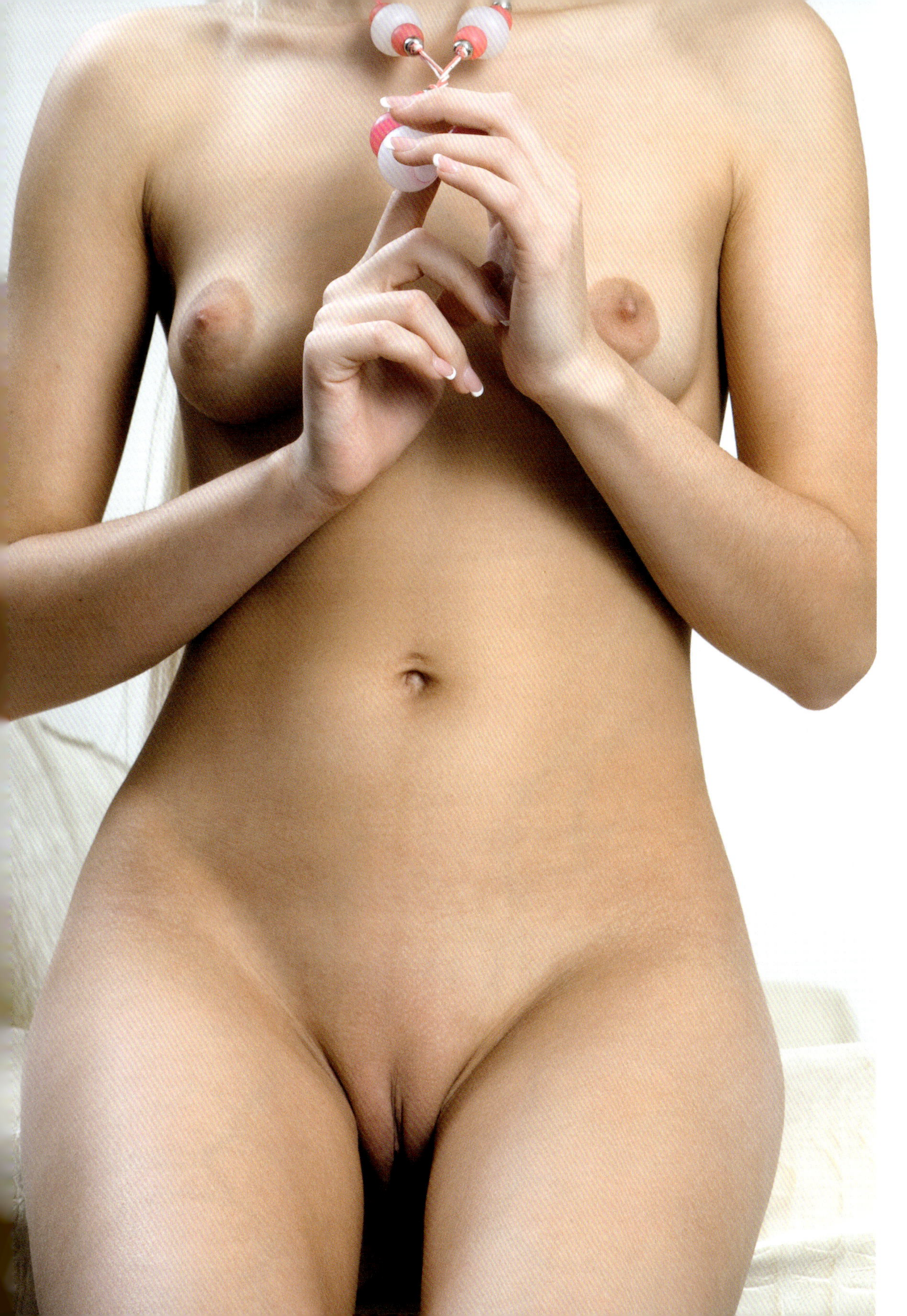

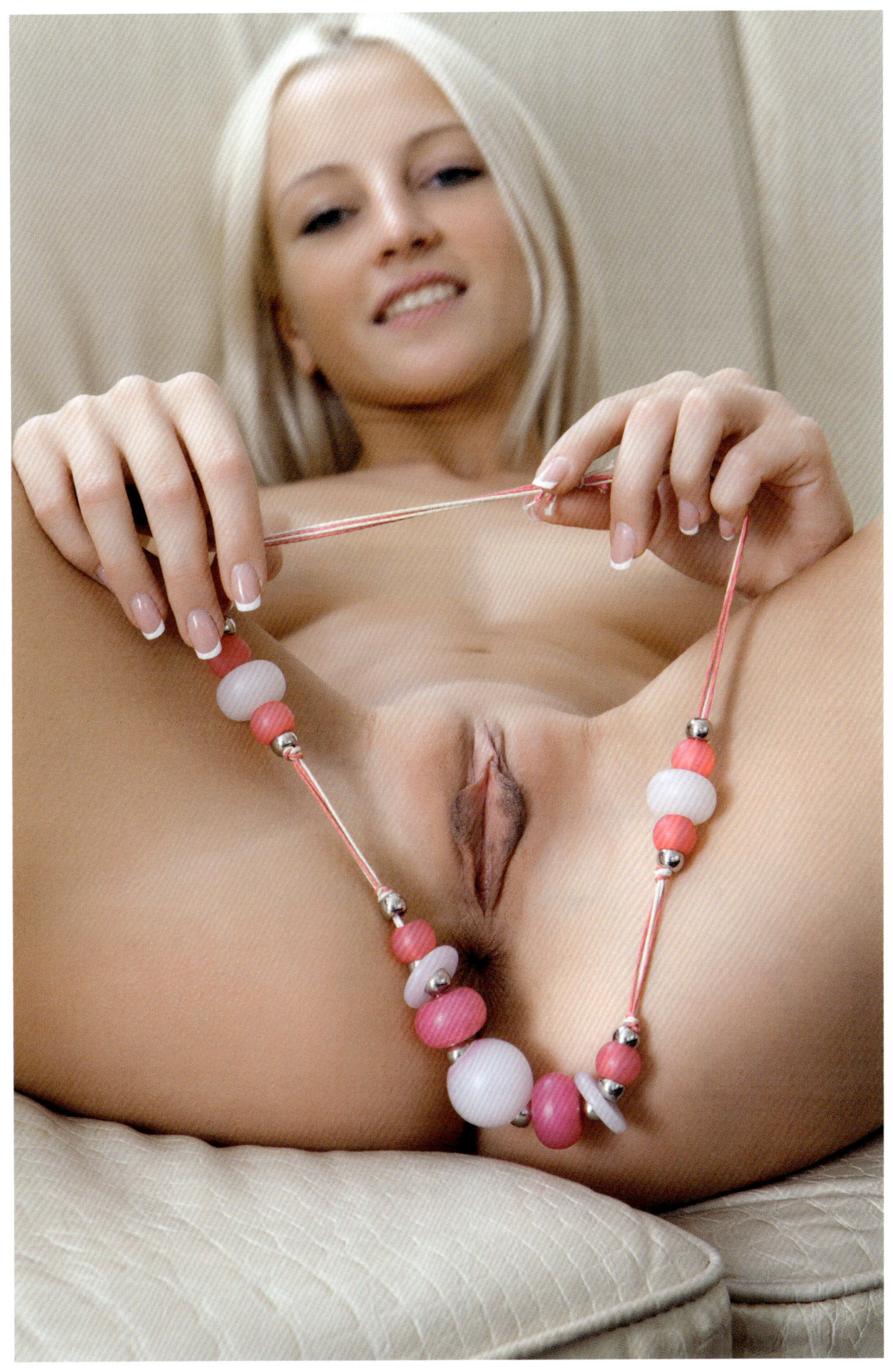

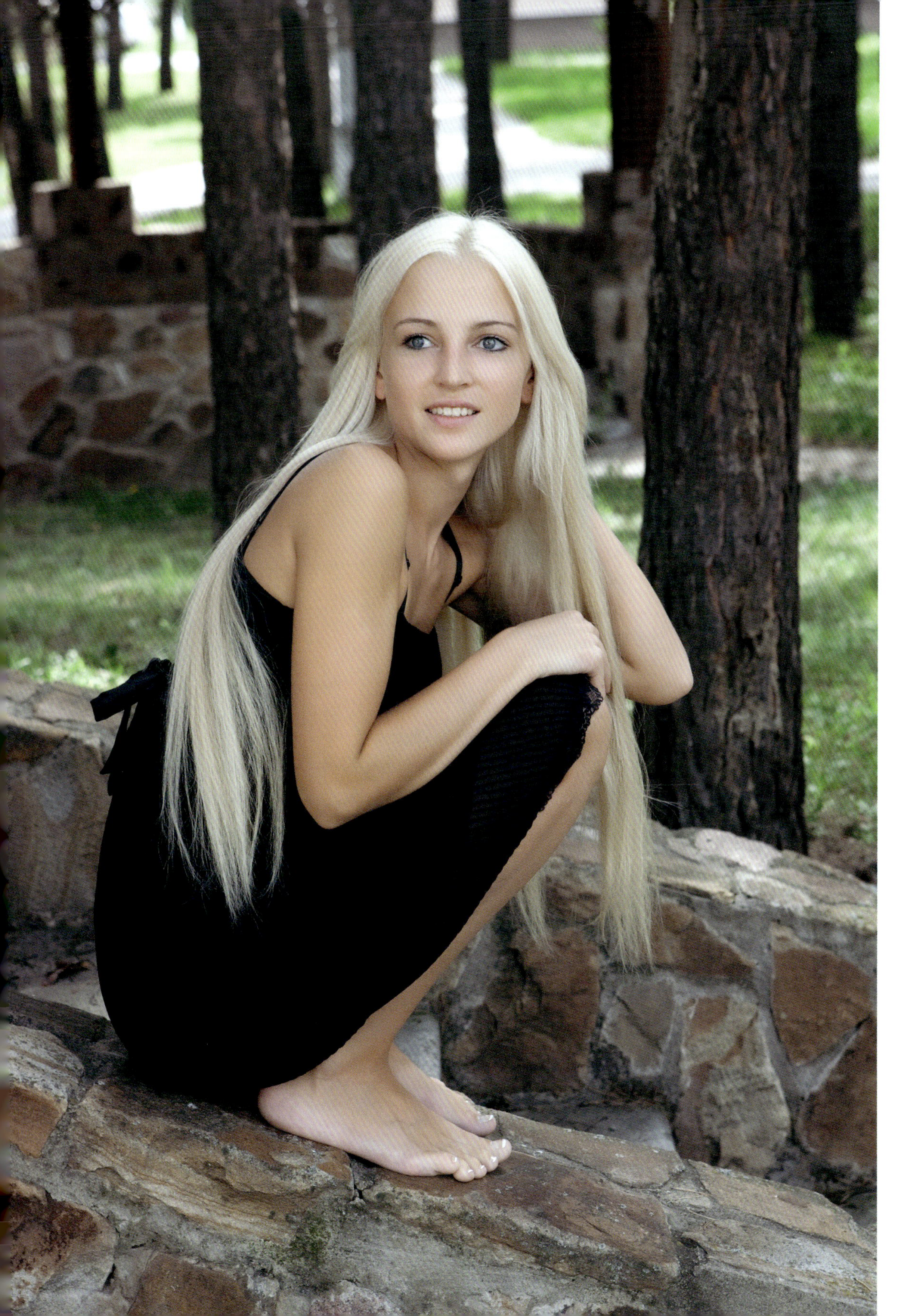

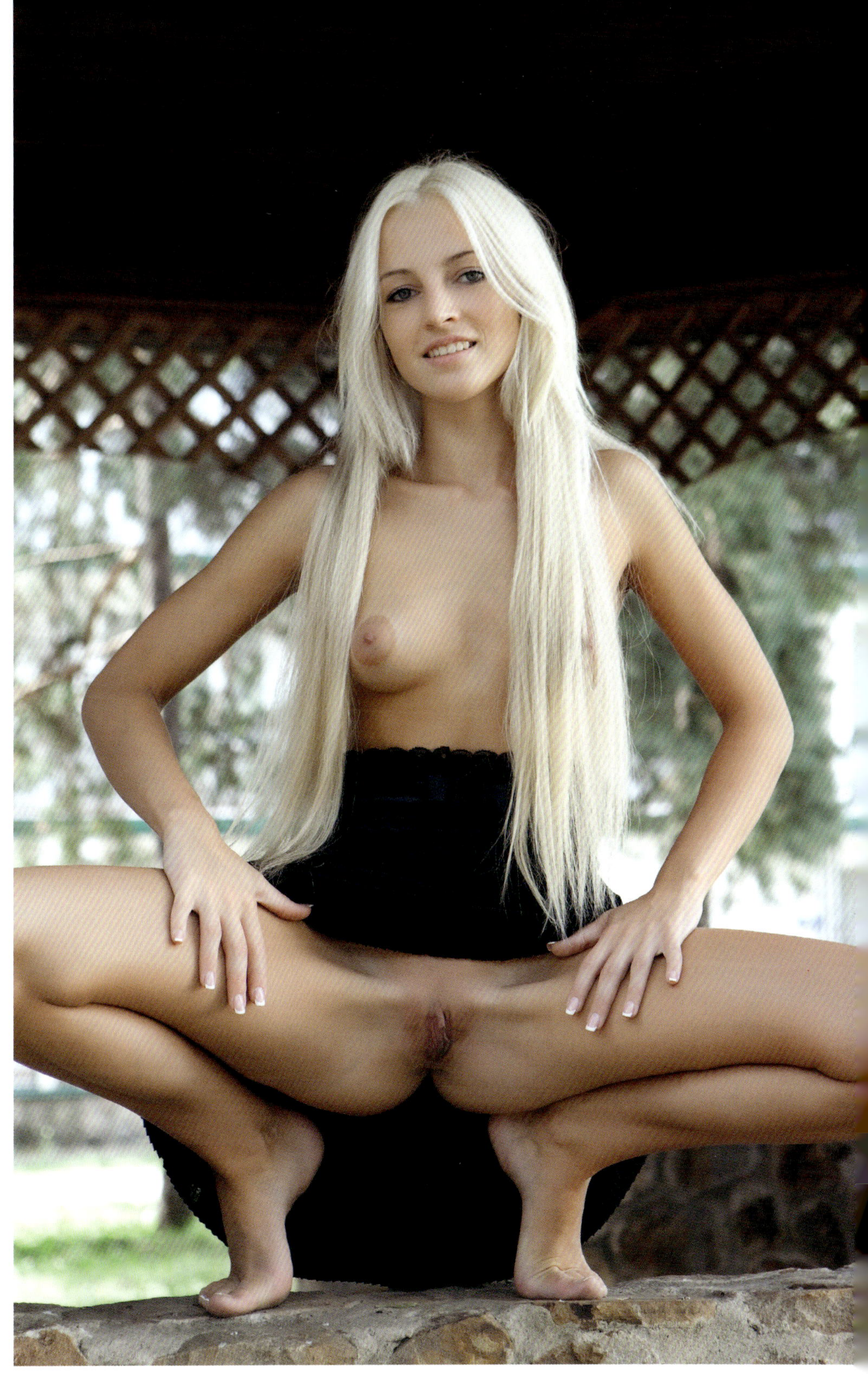

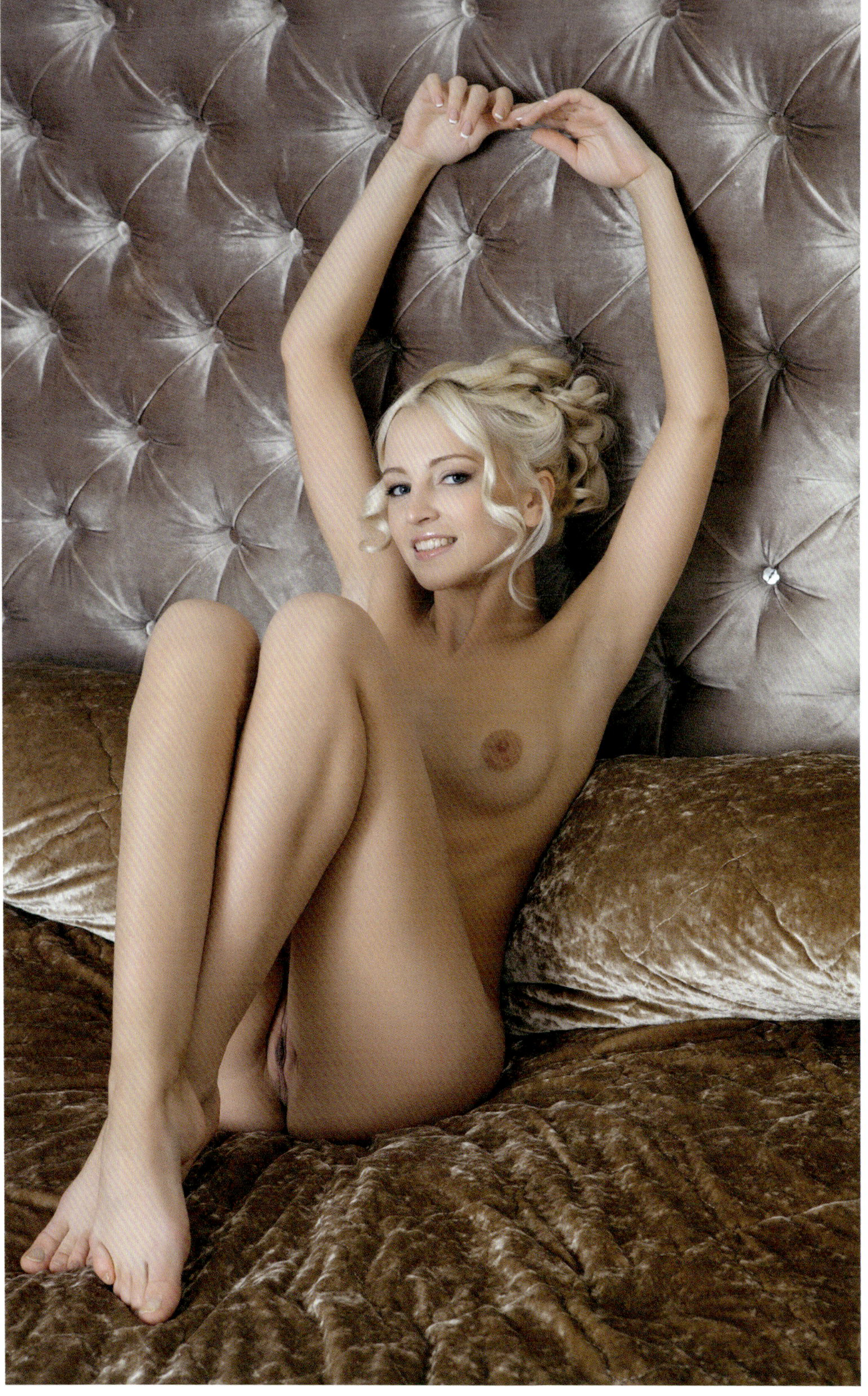

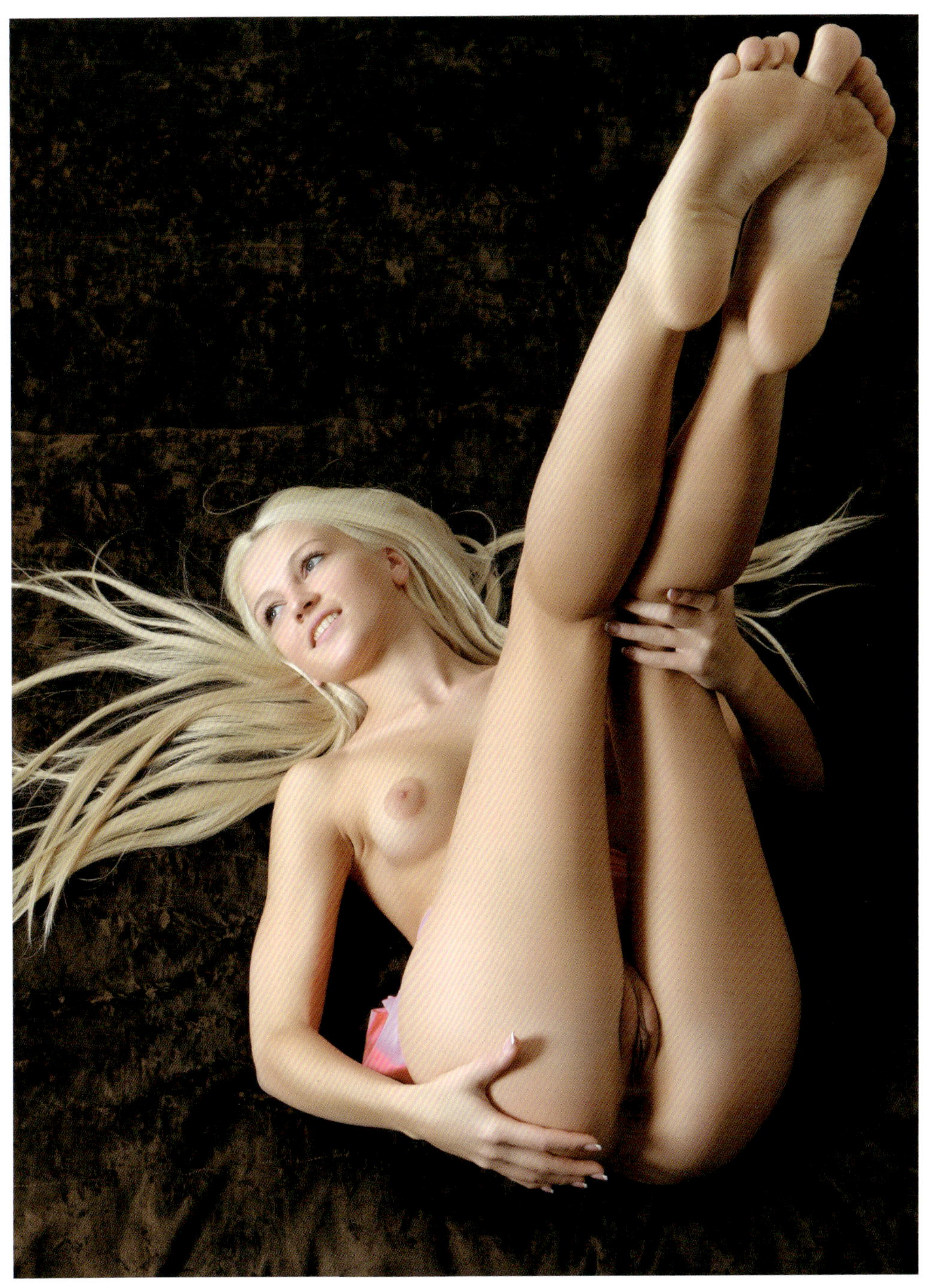

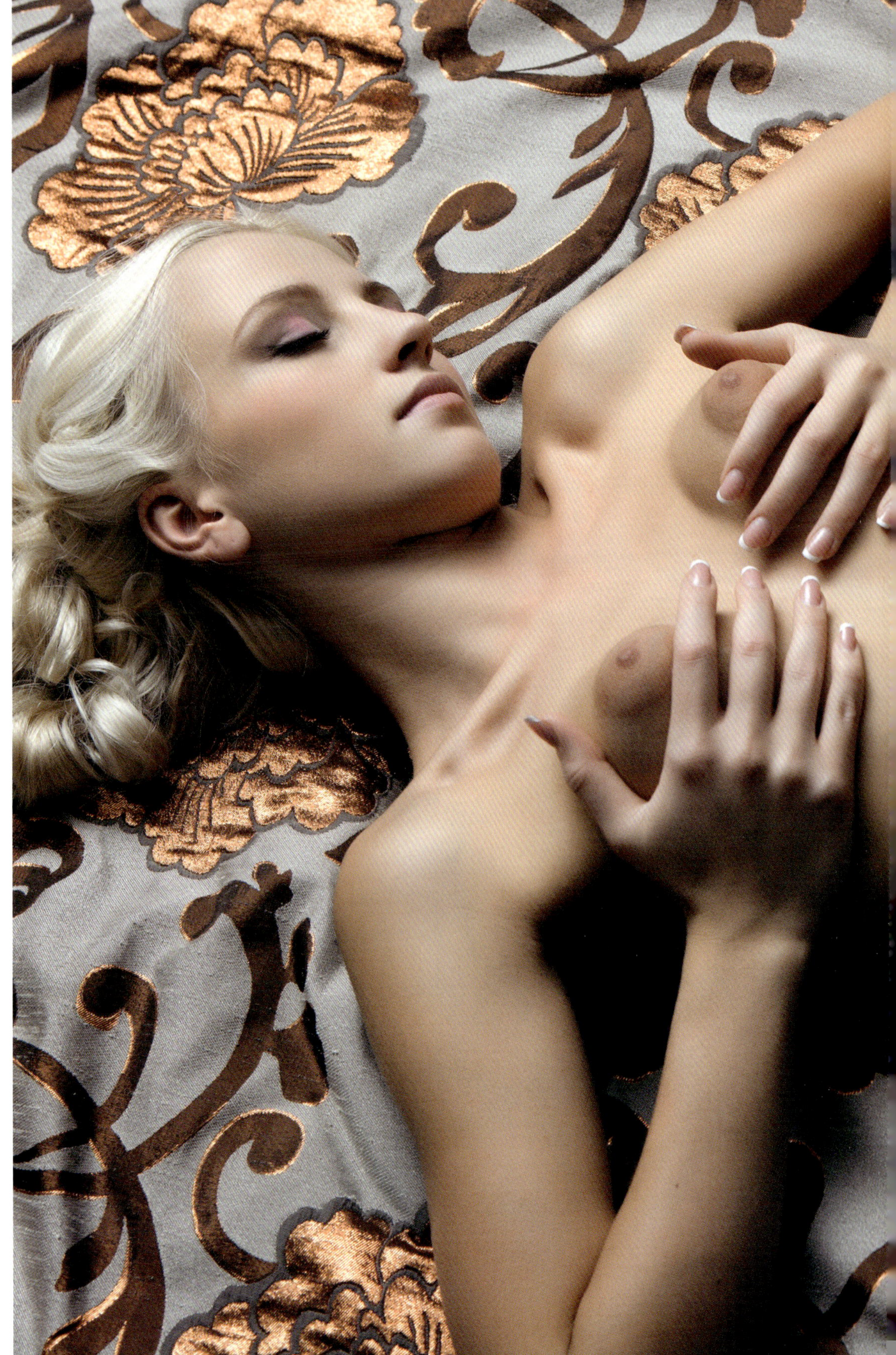

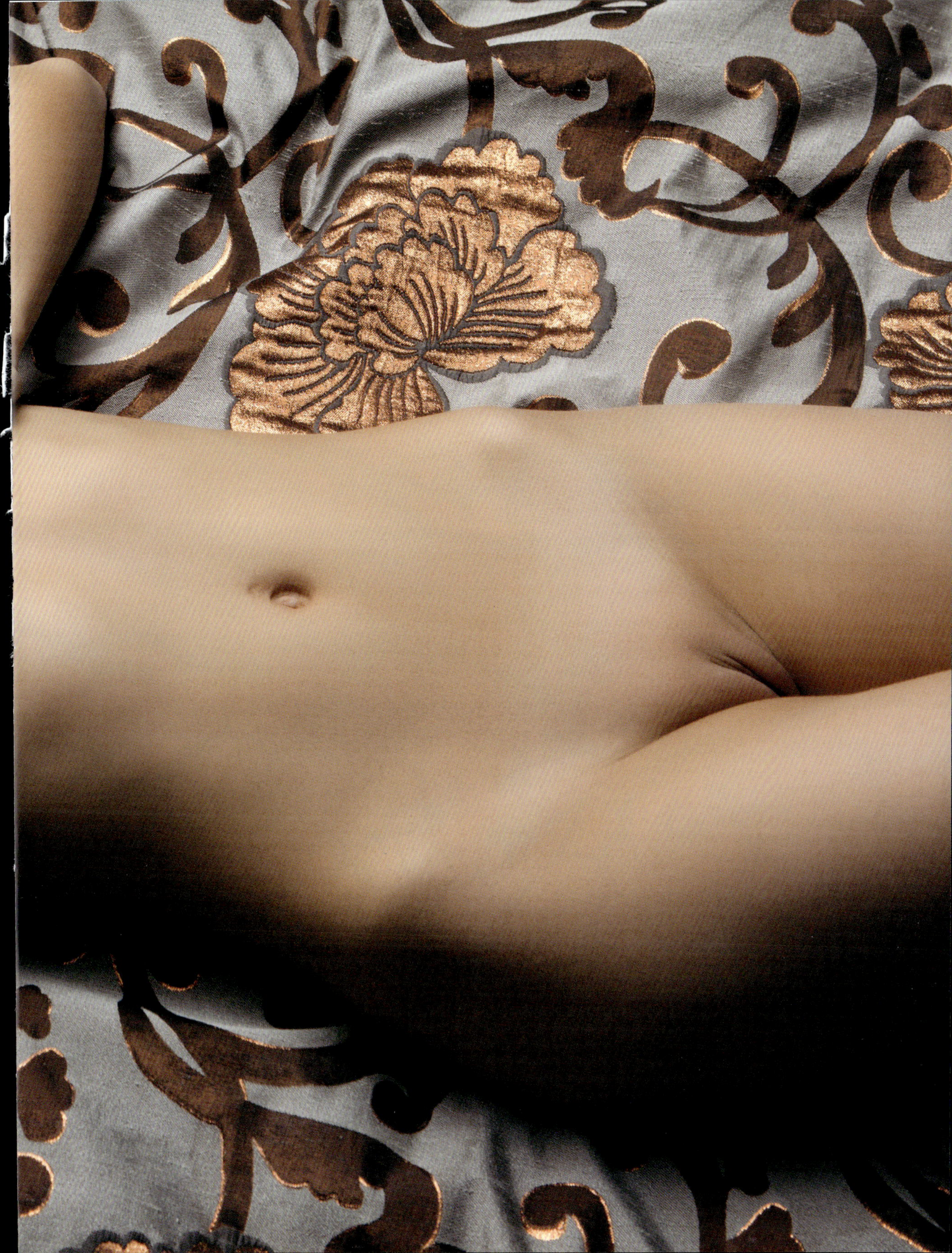

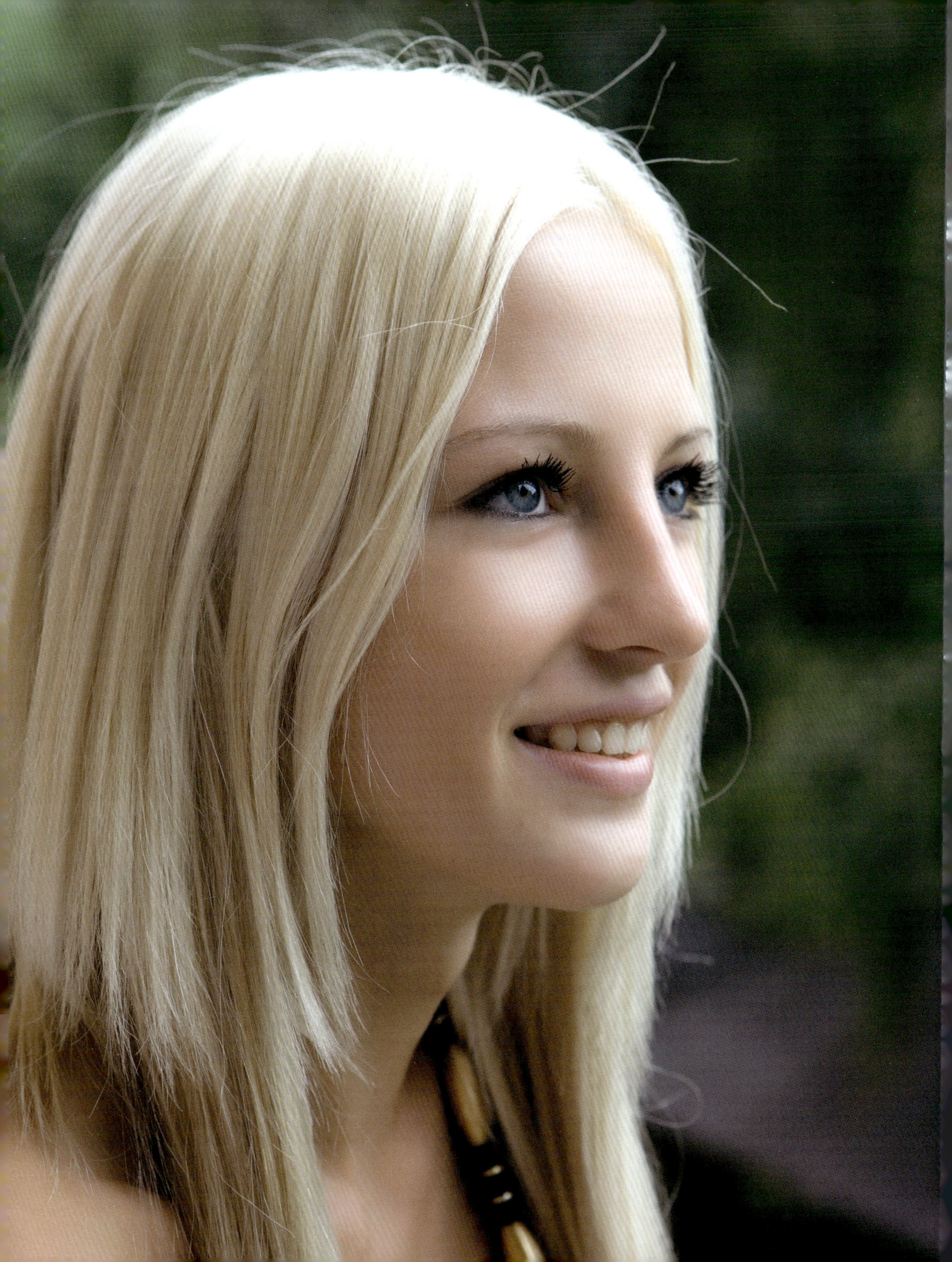

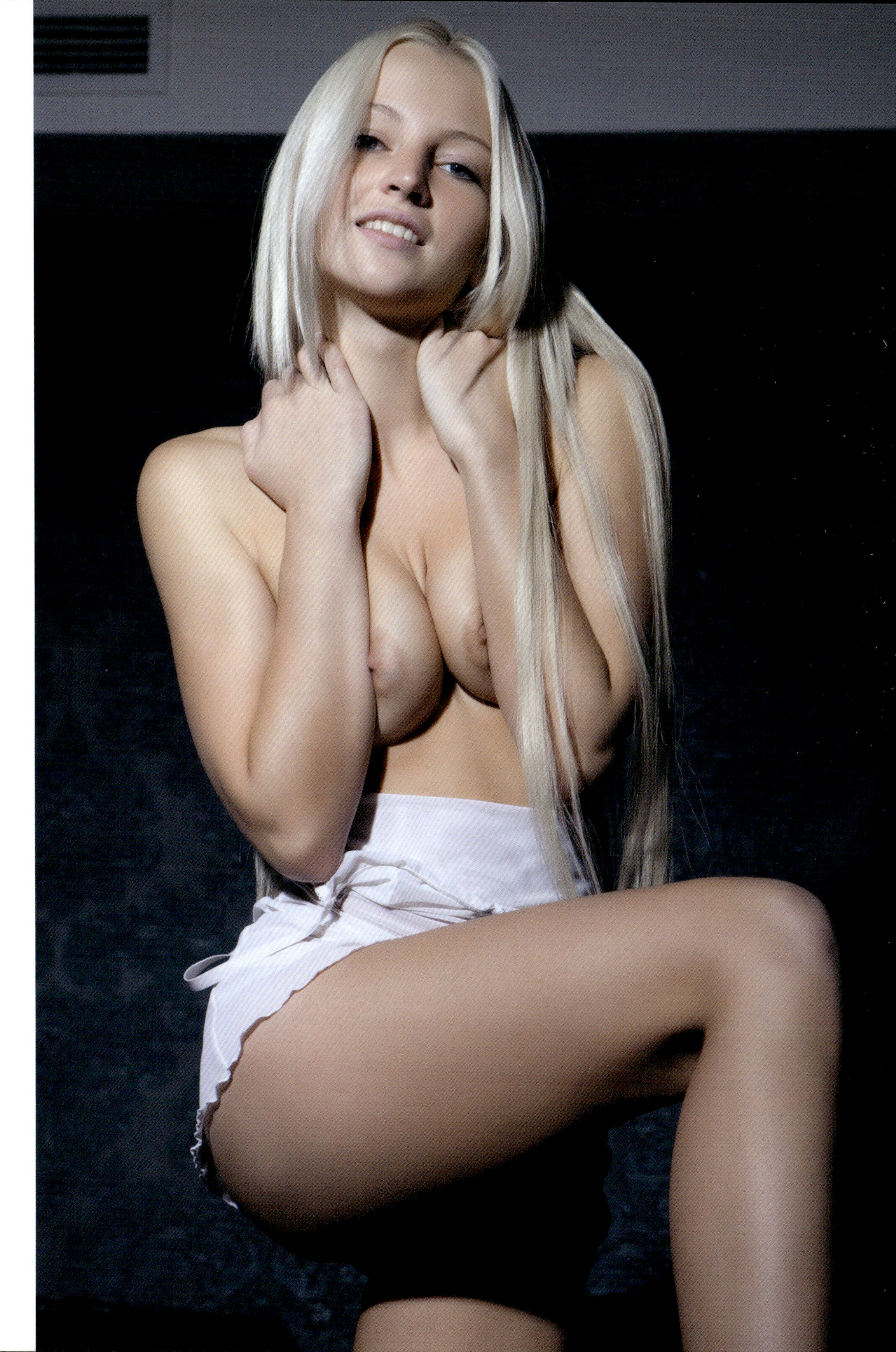

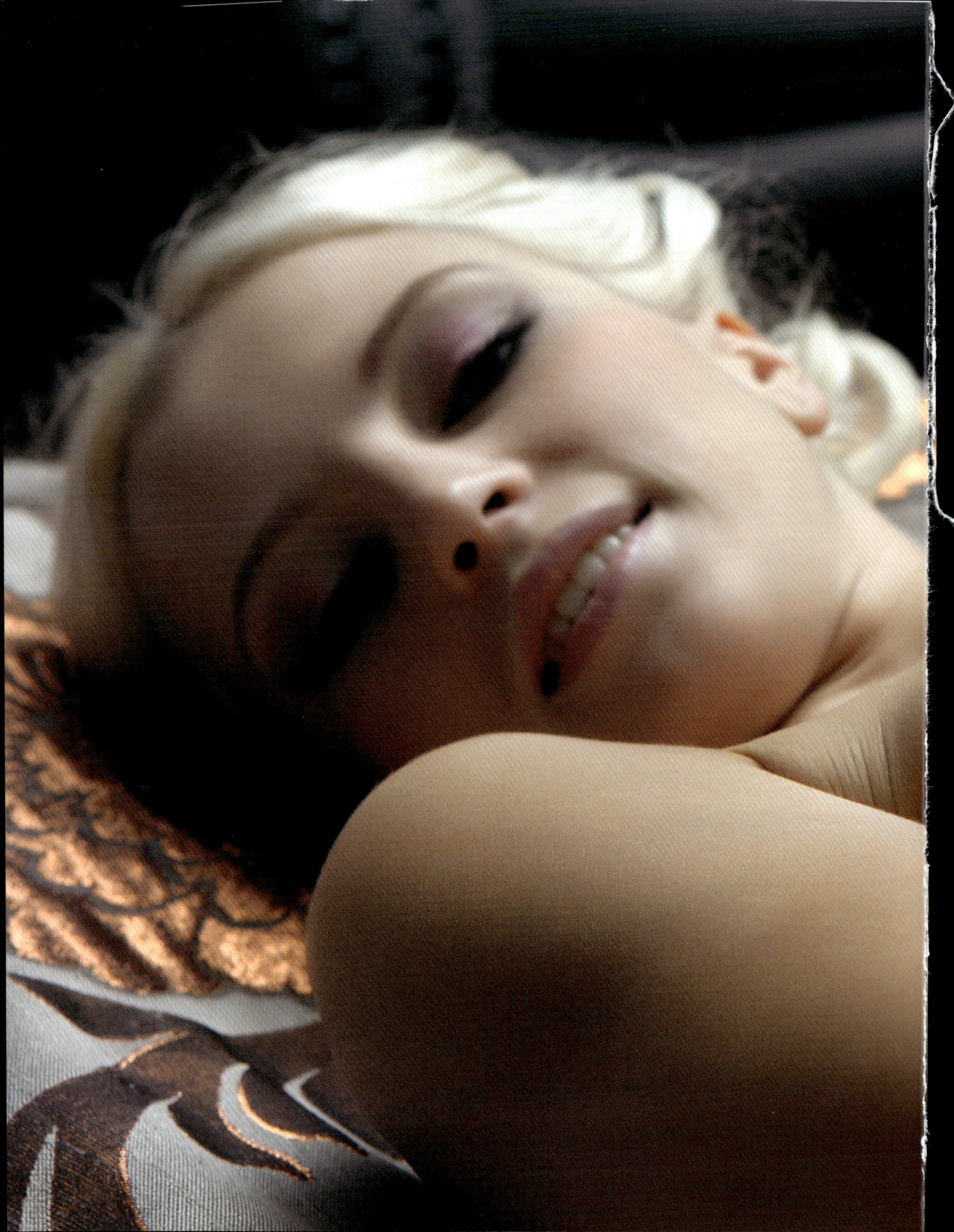

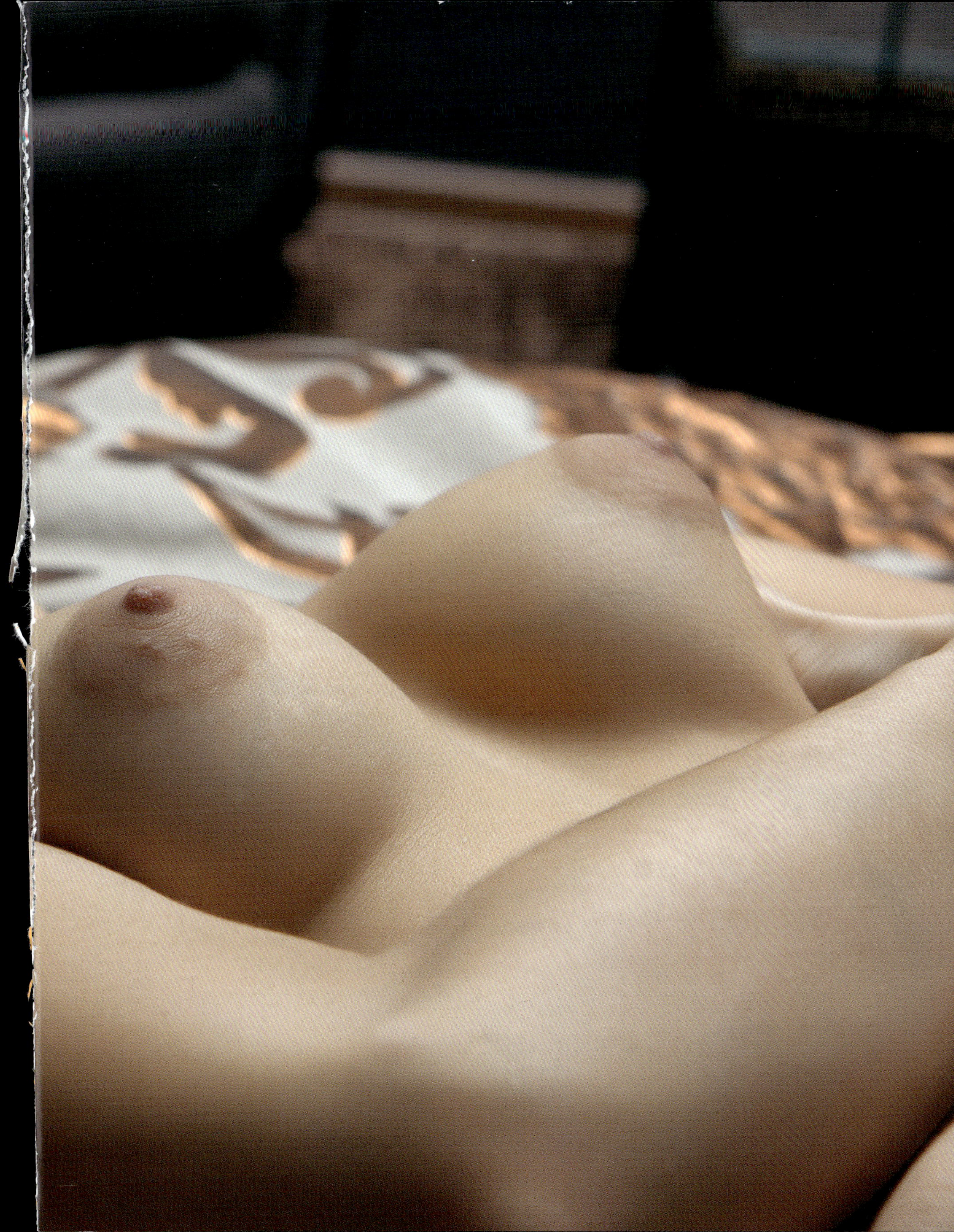

COLLECT THEM ALL: OUR MOST BEAUTIFUL

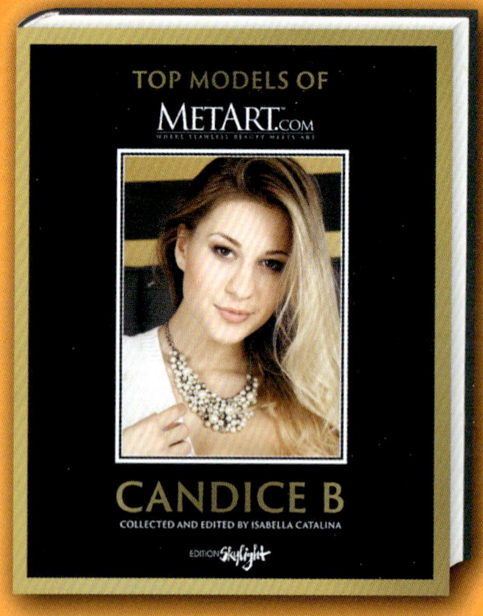

ISBN 978-3-03766-660-9

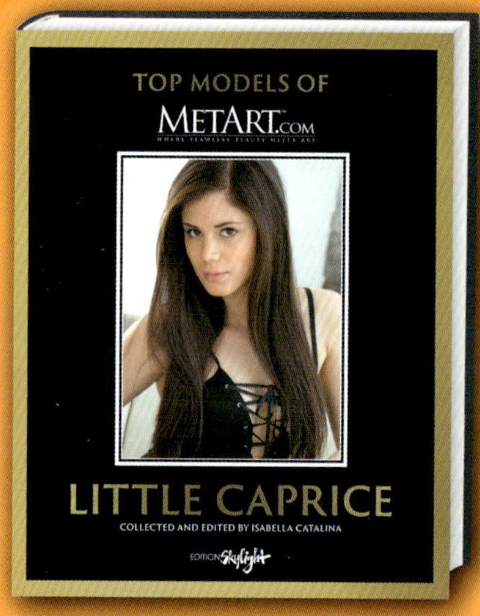

ISBN 978-3-03766-659-3

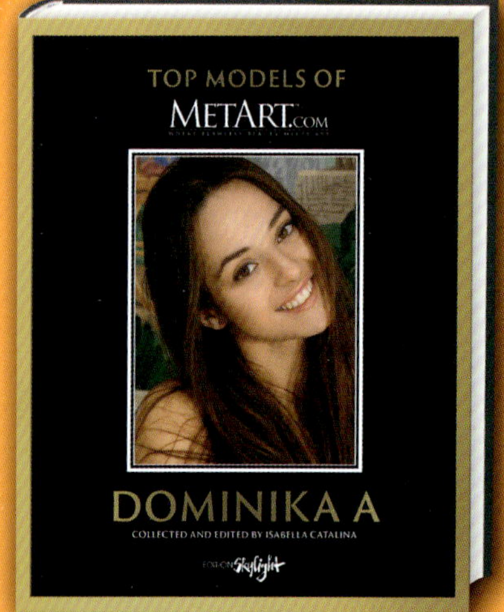

ISBN 978-3-03766-679-1

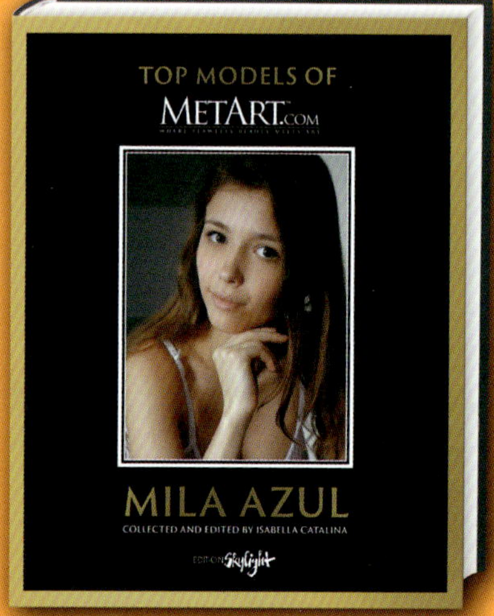

ISBN 978-3-03766-680-7

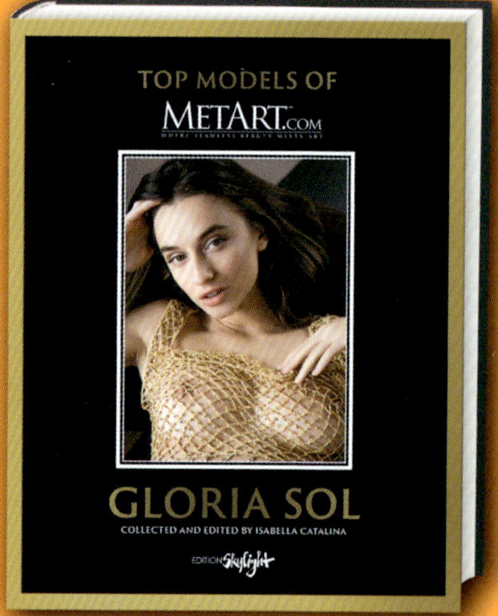

ISBN 978-3-03766-688-3

WWW.EDITION-SKYLIGHT.COM